40

1十

The End of Comedy

The End of Comedy

The Sit-Com and the Comedic Tradition

DAVID GROTE

Archon Books
1983

First published 1983 as an Archon Book,
an imprint of The Shoe String Press, Inc.
Hamden, Connecticut 06514

Printed in the United States of America

Library of Congress Cataloging in Publication Data

Grote, David.
The end of comedy.

Bibliography: p.
Includes index.
1. Comedy. 2. Comedy programs—United States—
History and criticism. I. Title.
PN1922.G76   1983   809'.917   82-18745
ISBN 0-208-01991-X

Contents

Acknowledgments

I would like to thank the following people whose help made the development of the material in this book possible: Dr. Hart Wegner, Sharon and Carolyn Cole, Andrew Rosenthal and his encyclopedic memory, and my wife, Susan, who knew when to read and comment and when not to, which is even more important.

1 • Introduction

During the fall 1981 network television season, thirty-one of the eighty-one series to appear were situation comedies. Some of those comedies were not particularly funny, and a goodly number were not particularly good. Few of the new ones even survived the fall ratings period. Even so, the quantity of the situation comedies was more than matched by their general popularity with the viewers. Six of the top ten shows in the composite ratings for the fall were sit-coms; if the two news/sports series are eliminated from consideration, eight of the ten most popular series in a dramatic form were comedies.[1]

At first glance, this seems only natural. Most of us like to laugh, and the sit-coms satisfy that desire. At second look, however, something seems to be missing. Where are the comedy/variety shows, for example? The last of these to rank in the top ten was *Sonny and Cher* in 1973. Where are the talk shows with comedian hosts? Where are the joke and sketch shows? For that matter, where are the comic movies? The largest money-making nonmusical comedy film in history was *Animal House*, which appeared on network TV in 1981, with a rating of 23.2 in its first showing. Not bad, until one considers that this was the same rating as the pilot for *Dynasty* and a full rating point below *The Brady Girls Get Married, Part III*, a position outside the fifty most popular special programs of the year and *far* outside the fifty most popular movies shown on television.

The situation comedy is not only extremely popular; it has in fact driven all other forms of comedy off the network television schedules, at least in prime time. Before 1962, the shows we call sit-coms were popular, but they shared prime time popularity with variety shows, quiz shows, melodramas of various stripes, and even a few anthology series. But beginning with the 1962 season, the sit-com took over the American imagination. In the twenty years since, only one season has seen fewer than four sit-coms in the top ten. (That was in a watershed year, 1970, when *The Mary Tyler Moore Show* and *All in the Family* were opening new fields, while shows like *Mayberry RFD* were beginning to look very tired and old-fashioned).

Even as the sit-com grew in popularity on television, it was matched by a major decline in the popularity of film comedies. Although 1981 was a very good year for funny films, most of the previous twenty years were not. If the Disney output is excluded, one would be hard pressed to name a dozen film comedies that met with any significant success between *Cat Ballou* and *Blazing Saddles,* and another dozen successful comedies except the parodies of Mel Brooks and the minority works of Woody Allen would be just as hard to find from *Blazing Saddles* until the *Saturday Night Live* gang started moving into films.

This was not always so. American films set world standards in comedy in both the silent and the early sound eras. And they were big box office as well. Although no reliable statistics are available for the silent era, there can be little doubt of both the popularity and the profits of such figures as Charlie Chaplin, Buster Keaton, Harold Lloyd, and many others now barely remembered. After sound was introduced, Paramount Studios was essentially built and sustained by the comedies of Ernst Lubitsch as was RKO by Fred Astaire and Ginger Rogers and later Universal by Abbott and Costello. Once public and reasonably accurate lists of top money-makers began to be kept, comedies consistently appeared on them until well into the sixties, when film comedies suddenly declined in popularity. Fewer comedies were hits and fewer were made until the very recent surge.

At least one obvious possible explanation is that people just chose to stay home, where the comedies were free, rather than to struggle with the costs and inconvenience of going to the theatre. But if this were the major factor, why didn't comedy films do better than they did when they were finally shown on television? In the sixteen years following the premier of *Saturday Night at the Movies* in 1961, during which the three networks had access to the entire sound film era, only five of the fifty most popular films on television were comedies, and those five included such marginal comedies as *The Ballad of Josie* and *The Sound of Music*, which started as a comedy and ended as a Nazi/World War II melodrama. Only three traditional comedies—*The Graduate*, *Cat Ballou*, and *Gidget Goes Hawaiian*—achieved any viewer response among the stay-at-homes who were watching for free.[2] Although this will probably change when *Grease* or whatever the network censors leave of *10* finally makes the networks, the general shape of the problem is clear. Even when people can get at home, for no cost and with no inconvenience, other kinds of comedy, which has been popular elsewhere, they still do not watch it with anywhere near the interest or intensity that they apply to the sit-com series.

The sit-com seems pervasive in contemporary American television, but it does not have to be. The sit-com is not a fact of life or a necessity forced upon us by the implacable requirements of the medium itself. Other nations have half-hour comedy shows, but they do not have the kind of situation comedies that the American audiences devour. For example, a jewel of a British sit-com, *Fawlty Towers*, has offered only twelve episodes within about five years, and the "series" *Butterflies* and *Man about the House*, which have the same look as many American series, went off after a fixed number of episodes, even though they were popular. Even in earlier television, the sit-com was not required viewing. *I Love Lucy* was actually the only sit-com to lead the ratings regularly in the fifties, the time most people associate with the sit-com world of scrubbed houses and wonderful families. The comedy series that dominated the era were shows like Milton Berle's variety series, *The Jack Benny Show*, and *You Bet Your Life*.

The sit-com was suggested by a number of radio series, but even those did not resemble the modern sit-com more than superficially. *Amos 'n' Andy*, the Fred Allen and Jack Benny shows, and many others used recurrent situations and places, but they ran very unpredictable stories and changing types of events. Some other series did take on the sit-com format, and many of these became TV sit-coms as well—*Ozzie and Harriet*, *Our Miss Brooks*, and *My Friend Irma*, for example. But these series did not dominate the form, even in prime time slots.

The sit-com on television is in fact something new. It is a powerful and popular form of entertainment. It has developed much by accident, growing from small ideas in radio series and encouraged by the unique economic conditions of American broadcasting. Most of us have watched

11

it all our lives, and for the most part we have simply taken it for granted as the most available and least demanding of the many forms of comedy.

Although the content of any series or episode may reflect the tastes of a given time, the sit-com is more than just a matter of taste. So many features are shared by all the sit-coms, no matter what the kind of humor or the tastes of their audiences, that the situation comedy must be seen for what it is, a new form, a new kind of comedy. In less than thirty years it has appeared, tested some variations, settled on its basic rules, and perfected its form. In the process, it has overturned more than two thousand years of comic traditions and established an entirely new and unique form of comedy.

This new comedy of television is, in its way, just as stunning and revolutionary as was the new comedy of Menander and Philemon when it replaced the Aristophanic Old Comedy with the forms, plots, and heroes that would serve all of Western culture down to the appearance of the American television sit-com. Those of us who were born after World War II have always known this television comedy, and it does not seem the least bit odd or unusual to us. But it is. It would have been incomprehensible to audiences of even fifty years past, not because they would not understand the references to everyday events but rather because they would not understand the part we take for granted, the form itself.

This American new comedy, available from a child's first conscious moment, has separated newer audiences from the traditions of both stage and screen comedy. It has done so, not by being cheaper or more accessible, but by refusing to accept or use the principles, formulas, characters, or social functions of Western comedy. The traditions that have served playwrights, performers, and audiences for two thousand years have failed to find a place on American television. Consequently, a person who views only the television screen may soon be unable to understand comedy as it has been known; the traditions and forms will become meaningless and incomprehensible to him.

Because this new comedy is so common, so comfortable, so much a part of our daily life, we will need to pay considerable attention to the old comedy. Only by understanding in some detail how comedy has worked since Menander can we begin to see how revolutionary the situation comedy is.

Comedy itself has taken many forms in our literature. The joke, the tall tale, the comic essay are all part of comedy. But comedy performed by actors in some kind of dramatic situation while an audience watches has remained remarkably constant. It has survived the fall of Rome and the rise and fall of both medieval and early industrial societies. It has served rich and poor alike in the Renaissance, the Restoration, the eras of sentiment, spectacle, and melodrama. Each time and place found its own variations, but all stage comedies shared a common culture and tradition, so common that as late as 1962, a major Broadway hit could be lifted almost directly from the two-thousand-year-old works of Plautus.

For a number of social and economic reasons, almost all the historical variations in comedy on the stage would be combined in American comedy films during the twenties and thirties. These films establish the continuity of the stage traditions in the new media of the twentieth century. The nearness of American film comedies dramatizes the difference between what we have always called comedy and what television now gives us as comedy. The long traditions of stage and film comedies from which the situation comedy has revolted must be clearly understood before the nature and the importance of that revolt can be fully understood.

Ultimately, the question that must be asked is "Why the sit-com?" Why, of all the kinds of comedy in our tradition, of all the forms that have served changing societies over the centuries in ways that tragedy, for example, never could, did we pick this one? What is its attraction for us as individuals and as a society? Since this is a new form, which we invented and made popular and which no one else has yet adopted, what does that suggest about us? The last chapter will look at these questions, after we have seen how revolutionary the sit-com really is. In the process, we will examine not only our present but also our possible futures as an audience and as a nation. Socially, comedy is very serious business and always has been. Tragedy, at least since the classical times, has dealt with our highest desires, but comedy has been our way of dealing with life as it happens. The kinds of comedy that we choose and enjoy tell us a great deal about the kinds of people we are.

Before we can begin this analysis, we need to define some terms. There is no single, generally accepted definition of comedy, and I will not presume to provide one here when everyone from Aristotle to Freud has already failed to do so. But for the purposes of this discussion, *comedy* will refer to a literary-performance *form*, rather than to the things that make us laugh, which we will call *humor*. The study of the causes of laughter has led into a mire of conjecture, half-truths, and wild rhetoric over the centuries and is not directly related to our subject. The TV sit-com does not have a different sense of humor—that is one of the reasons we have failed to recognize its new and radical form. Suzanne Langer has pointed out that "humor...is a by-product of comedy, not a structural element in it."[3] And it is those structural elements that concern us.

These structural elements are not always clearly understood, yet they are clearly sensed. Although most people use *comedy* and *humor* as interchangeable terms, they recognize, if only vaguely, that what is funny is not always comic. Few people have ever rolled in the aisles while watching *Measure for Measure* or *The Merchant of Venice*, yet no matter how many other terms critics try to attach to these plays, *comedy* is always one. There are far more laughs in a good production of Edward Albee's *Who's Afraid of Virginia Woolf?* or John Osborne's *Look Back in Anger* than in Neil Simon's *Chapter Two* or the Wheeler/Sondheim musical, *A Little Night Music*, yet there would be little argument among critics or audiences that the latter two are comedies while the former two are most certainly not.

Thus, although we may not be able to define comedy, we can certainly describe it. That description first identifies the elements shared in a reasonably continuous line from the work of Menander to that of Jerry Lewis, especially the elements of comic plot, comic heroes, comic actors, and the character's relationship with the world of the play and film. As television sit-com plots, characters, actors, and relationships are compared with this tradition, it will become obvious that the sit-com is much more than another variation. It is, in fact, a fundamental change in our cultural conception of comedy.

Throughout, it should be clear that references to television are to American television only, and American network television in particular, unless otherwise stated. Although it is difficult for an American to see much television from other nations, my observations and readings about foreign television comedy suggest that the changes described here are, at least for the moment, confined to the United States. A major factor in the development of this new comedy has been the peculiar form of network broadcasting that the United States maintains, unique in the modern world. Another factor is the peculiar socioeconomic history of the United States since World War II. Thus, the changes described are not necessarily inherent in the medium itself. Television comedy does not have to be this way; we have chosen to make it so. However, as more of the world absorbs the popular and economic culture of the United States, it becomes more likely that American forms of comedy will spread both as specific programs and as models for local programming.

2 · The Comedic Tradition

Sostratos is a young man who has fallen in love with a beautiful girl called Myrhinne. Unfortunately, Myrhinne's father, Knemon, is a tough old grouch who will not let anyone near his home, much less his daughter. Sostratos seeks the help of a friend, Gorgias, who agrees to help him get his love. Knemon is not only a grouch but also something of an old skinflint. When his servant drops down the well a bucket and then the hoe with which she is trying to pick up the bucket, Knemon chews her out and then goes down in the well to retrieve them himself. As might be expected of an old man, he cannot get back out of the well, and Gorgias seizes the opportunity to rescue him. Since Gorgias is already Knemon's stepson, the son of his wife by a previous marriage (the wife has left home because she could not stand Knemon's disposition), Knemon decides to reward Gorgias by adopting him as his official son. Gorgias remembers his promise and persuades Knemon also to allow Sostratos and Myrhinne to wed. Finally, Sostratos convinces his father to let his sister marry Gorgias, and everyone, even the old grouch Knemon, joins in the double wedding celebration.

The summary is a little skimpy and much of the original flavor is missing, but this is the plot of one of the most important literary finds of the twentieth century. It is the plot of *Dyskolos*, the only full play remaining from the work of the Athenian dramatist Menander. (The papyrus text was not found until 1957 during an Egyptian archaeological dig.) It is also the oldest extant New Comedy, first produced in 317

B.C. As such, it can be regarded as the foundation of the oldest form of dramatic literature still in use. Playwrights today still write works that can be called tragedies, but they have almost nothing to do with the Greek tragedies, differing in world view, organization, style, and staging practices. But the stage world of *Dyskolos* is still with us. Modern audiences might find the bald statement of the problems in the play a bit simple-minded and the play considerably shorter than they are used to in a modern theatre, but they would recognize and respond to the plot and characters immediately. It is a very small step from the grouchy father who frightens away the nice young man in Menander's work to the grouchy fathers who pretend to frighten away the lovers in Jones and Schmidt's *The Fantasticks*, which is *still* running in sophisticated New York City, as it has been continuously since May 1960. And it is a very small step indeed to all the other fathers, both literal and figurative, who separate the lovers until their will is circumvented or that have a change of heart that allows the young people to get together after all at the curtain of the play.

Most of Western comedy comes from the Roman Plautus and his somewhat less vulgar and more respectable compatriot Terence, because their Latin plays survived and were among the first classical works to be rediscovered and imitated in the Renaissance. But Plautus and Terence both freely admitted, sometimes even bragged, that they stole most of their material and plots from Menander. In that way, we are all a little bit Menandrine, even though we never actually had any of Menander's plays in front of us.

Menander's influence was not in his jokes, for jokes change with society. Although there are certain archetypal joke patterns, the joke needs the specific knowledge of daily life to work for humorous effect. Despite our fascination with Shakespeare's comedies, we get almost none of his jokes unless we are literary scholars, and the same holds for Menander, Plautus, and Terence. What Menander provided, through Plautus and Terence, was a frame, a basic arrangement of dramatic situation, character, and event that offered endless opportunities for variations while at the same time holding these variations together in a basic unifying plot. That plot would speak equally well to audiences throughout Europe for more than 2,000 years. Each generation of writers and audiences has used the ancient framework for its own purposes. Each new set of writers has tried to appear original and has found an endless number of twists and turns in which to disguise its comedies. But underneath the disguises, there has been really only one body.

Menandrine comedy used a very simple plot. Northrop Frye described it: "What normally happens is that a young man wants a young woman, that his desire is resisted by some opposition, usually paternal, and that near the end of the play, some twist in the plot enables the hero to have his will."[1] Menander and his compatriots established a comedy in which boy meets girl and somehow they overcome the obstacles that prevent their getting together, so that at the end, boy gets girl. It is a cliché, the "happy ending." It was and is not just a plot but The Plot of comedy.

Since Menander, all comedic works of noticeable length have used essentially the same plot. The variations on this single story are uncountable. The Plot survives, sometimes blatant, sometimes disguised, but always there. The only exceptions are the few successful parodies of other works, which use the plots of the original works, and some of the more vicious personalized satires, lost to us today because of their intense topicality. Even in fiction, the picaresque tradition has tended to use the theatrical comic plot to hold things together. Cervantes's *Don Quixote* has a second book, because the first has no real ending; in Henry Fielding's *Tom Jones* the hero, after all his adventures, ends up with Sophie Western, and there is an ending, and no sequel. But it is on the stage, and eventually in the film, where The Plot has triumphed for so long.

The comic Plot has been so pervasive, so common, that most scholars and critics have either missed its significance or chosen to ignore it, accepting it simply as a given. Many notice it only to comment that, although something or other is quite funny, it "panders to the masses" by a sticky romance along the way. But that romance, in whatever form, has been what held things together for the comic writer who tried to go beyond a few loosely connected jokes.

This Plot was not where comedy began. Aristophanes, who predates Menander, would have thought it an absurd way to put together a comedic play. But Aristophanic comedy was out of date and old-fashioned even before Aristophanes was dead. Changing social climates and audience responses, as well as increased political sensitivity, made the wild, fantastical, and satirical free-form works that Aristophanes had developed (and that remain unsurpassed classics of their kind) seem increasingly pointless and unsatisfying. Various playwrights, including

Aristophanes himself in his last few works, muddled around trying to find something better, but nothing seemed to be completely satisfactory until Menander and Philemon developed what scholars call the New Comedy. And the newest thing about the New Comedy was its plot, the introduction of boy-meets-girl as a reason for dramatic existence.

Ironically, this standardized Plot served to liberate writers of comedy in numerous ways. Since the basic Plot provided the beginning and the end, the writer could concentrate on the humor of his plot, inventing as many complications as he might wish, secure in the knowledge that the ending was at hand whenever he needed it. The *deus ex machina* could always be brought in when things got too complicated, and within the terms of the comedy, the audience would rarely object. For those who wished to do more than write inventive plots, the stable framework that The Plot provided allowed the writer to devote his full attention to those things that most interested him. There could be room for social commentary, subtle character development, political attacks, or even moral lessons, depending on the emphasis given to the various parts of the basic formula. But holding it all together was still The Plot.

The Plot has been blatant at times and heavily disguised or treated quite cavalierly at other times, depending on the interests of a particular author or audience. At one end of the continuum is romantic comedy, where the major interest of the play and playwright is in the lovers themselves. Such versions of The Plot tend to be explorations either of the meaning and nature of love, as in many of Shakespeare's works, or of the fashions and hypocrisies of a particular group, as in the Restoration comedies. This latter type of play begins to merge along the continuum into those works that are concerned more with the problems that separate the lovers than with the lovers themselves. These plays may involve characters and characteristics that disrupt society's health and the course of true love, as in many of the works of Molière, or they may involve the mores of society as a whole, as in the plays of Shaw. In these works, The Plot holds everything together and keeps it all moving toward some eventual happy ending, but it may be of minimal interest to the author and may occupy very little stage time, as in the extreme case of Plautus's *Aulularia*, in which the girl never gets on stage, or his *Casina*, in which boy and girl both stay off stage. In these plays, the pursuit of the lover is the framework on which everything else is built, but the subject matter and the humor are both in the problems that block the union rather than in the union itself.

19

That such a plot is common in comedy is obvious. That it is so pervasive as to be the basic plot of all comedy requires some additional explanation. A few examples will serve to illustrate not only the variety but also the underlying uniformity of the comedic tradition.

Among those writers who have devoted most of their attention to the lovers and for whom the pursuit of the male and female dominates the action of the play, Shakespeare is the most varied. He explored almost all the possible permutations of this plot emphasis, and all subsequent writers have merely updated and modified the variations he provided.

In the most basic version, the man meets the woman, falls in love with her, and woos her, but she resists until he has proven himself worthy. Petruchio proves his worth by taming his Kate in *The Taming of the Shrew*; Benedick almost has to kill Claudio but fortunately is saved from that responsibility and can rely on Beatrice's recognition of his other worthy qualities in *Much Ado about Nothing*; and Bassanio has to pick the right casket to win Portia in *The Merchant of Venice*. In most of these plays, the action starts long before the lovers realize that they are in love, and the woman usually loathes the man in the beginning.

In other plays, the action begins with the lovers already in love. The challenge comes when one of the lovers begins to stray, and the other has to find some way to win the wanderer back. In *Two Gentlemen of Verona*, Proteus loves Julia until he meets Silvia, but he returns to Julia when friendship and Julia's dedication persuade him of his errors.

A third major variation involves several lovers either in series or in direct competition, as in *Twelfth Night*, where Viola loves Orsino, who loves Olivia, who in turn loves Viola in her disguise. Similar problems beset the interchangeable Athenians in the woods during *A Midsummer Night's Dream*.

In Shakespeare's more problematical comedies, the emphasis remains on the lovers, but the plot variations reveal less pleasant aspects of love or of the audience's attitudes toward it. For example, although Shakespeare is almost contemporary in that his girls often pursue the boys more persistently than they are themselves pursued, when the basic plot is turned so that girl pursues boy completely, without the boy realizing he is actually in love with her all the time, *All's Well That Ends Well* becomes a "problem" play. In *Measure for Measure*, another variation appears, in which the boy (Angelo) pursues the girl (Isabella), thinks he gets her, and is then switched to a girl who is "better" (Mariana), at least for him, while Isabella, who has protected her virginity to the point of sacrificing her brother, suddenly gives in without resistance to the "right" lover, the Duke.

Finally, there is the most completely Menandrine version, in which the lovers share their love immediately but are separated by circumstances beyond the control of either. This separation often requires the intervention of the gods before the lovers can be joined and the *deus ex machina* will appear, often in beautiful verse and pageantry. Orlando and Rosalind fall in love at first sight in *As You Like It*, and neither wavers from that love. Separated and banished by Duke Frederick for crimes they have not committed, both wander in the woods until the usurper's miraculous reformation. In *The Tempest*, Ferdinand and Miranda also love as soon as they meet, but Ferdinand must endure a strange kind of imprisonment to satisfy Prospero. Only when Prospero's sudden restoration to his old life is finished can the lovers be completely united, which leads us toward the other major variation of the basic comedy plot, where the characters or events that separate the lovers are far more interesting than the lovers themselves can ever be.

Only one other variation that concentrates on the lovers seems to have appeared, the version perfected in nineteenth-century French farces. There, the lovers are often already married; the problem is that love is beginning to fade for some reason. Through a series of mistaken identities and false assumptions, the characters stray, pretend to stray, or prepare to stray until at the last moment order is restored and all the confusions are cleared up. There is no new marriage, since everyone is already married; however, the old marriage is renewed, made fresh and youthful again, as at the end of Georges Feydeau's *A Flea in Her Ear*, where the previously flagging husband prepares for an exciting and potentially fertile evening with the wife, who has been afraid he was straying.

Most later writers who have dealt with love in comedy have simply updated the Shakespearean guidelines. Mirabell and Millamant in Congreve's *Way of the World* are direct descendants of Benedick and Beatrice— only their clothes and their social habits have been changed—and the line is direct through such odd disguises as Annie and Bill in the musical *Annie Get Your Gun*, Elyot and Amanda in Noel Coward's *Private Lives*, and Cherie and Bo in William Inge's *Bus Stop*. The number of lovers who wander and return is beyond counting, and the

21

lovers in series variations provide some of the most complicated plots in every generation.

Most playwrights, however, have used the comic plot in the manner of Plautus, Terence, and Menander. In their extant plays, the lovers are almost ciphers, interchangeable young men and vapid young women whose only identifying marks are their physical attractiveness and a passionate desire to get married to each other. Their mutual pursuit is still the framework on which the play is hung, but the characters are only a plot device. The humor, the subject matter, and the real interest are all in the problem that blocks their union.

Most writers of comedy have chosen to follow this approach, primarily because it provides so many options. Anything may become an obstacle, so that anything may become a topic for the humor of the play. The most ancient of these obstacles are social class and proper birth. Plautine comedy abounds in slave girls who are revealed at the last moment to be the long-lost daughters of suitable social equals. The missing child with a mysterious birthmark thus becomes a cliché solution for any number of social class conflicts, from the Graustarkian operettas to the delicious baby in the handbag of Oscar Wilde's *The Importance of Being Earnest*. Probably the most imaginative variation on this theme occurs in Joseph Kesselring's *Arsenic and Old Lace*, in which Mortimer is convinced he is unworthy of the girl he loves because of the patent insanity in his family, only to find out, to his great joy, that he is a bastard and not really a part of the insane family after all.

Other social problems may be described in this approach. In *The Marriage of Figaro* it is the *droit du seigneur;* in Ben Jonson's *The Alchemist* it is the mania for the philosopher's stone and the general cult of personal greed. In Royall Tyler's *The Contrast* and Anna Mowatt's *Fashion,* two American examples, the problem is social pretension. In Shaw's plays, of course, almost any social problem may stand in the way of the final coupling, but lovers will be united when they both come around to Shaw's way of thinking. This leads to a number of interesting twists to the plot, as when Eliza marries the man we barely see in *Pygmalion,* or when Major Barbara marries Cusins only after she has surrendered her desire to do good through charity and he has surrendered his aversion to capitalistic profits in munitions work.

For the most part, however, writers have concentrated on particular traits expressed in the character of the individual who causes problems for the lovers, the central concern of *Dyskolos*. Shakespeare curiously enough tried this only rarely—in *The Tempest*, for example, making Prospero the man who both separates and unites the lovers. *The Winter's Tale* takes several acts to establish the nature of the two fathers, Leontes and Polixenes, before the potential lovers are even born. But in *The Merchant of Venice*, when Shakespeare devoted serious attention to Shylock's character, the character ceased to be humorous. As generations passed, Shylock became more real to audiences than did the lovers, and the play, in modern productions, often seems a tragedy that pointlessly continues after Shylock is sentenced.

It is with Molière, however, that we find the clearest examples of comic plays dominated by the character who blocks the young man from the young woman. *The Miser*, *Tartuffe*, and *The Hypochondriac* all reflect in their titles how the blocking characters overwhelm the rest of the comedy in audience interest. One hardly remembers Clèante and Marianne, Valère and Marianne, or Cléante and Angélique (even the names are interchangeable), but their romances provide the excuse for the story line and the union that concludes it. In *The Misanthrope*, the basic plot is almost completely buried because of the attention given to Alceste and his unrequited love for Célimène. But his misanthropy eventually forces him to try to destroy Philinte's love by offering to marry Éliante. When he leaves, he leaves behind a new couple, Philinte and Éliante, who are safely united now that Alceste is gone.

Some of the most popular and most respected comedies of the twentieth century almost hide their lovers, but the central characters eventually become important to plot structure as they begin to affect the course of true love. Grandpa Vanderhof only takes on Mr. Kirby because his grandchild wants to marry Kirby's son in Kaufman and Hart's *You Can't Take It with You*. Tevye's story in *Fiddler on the Roof* follows a succession of daughters who wish to marry, first over his opposition and then finally with his acceptance. But the most sophisticated variations have come consistently from the French playwrights, especially Jean Anouilh. *Waltz of the Toreadors* in particular is an inventive and deceptive modification of the tradition. Its principal character is General St. Pé, a retired soldier and reactionary, who desperately wants to be rid of his sickly wife and return to the one true love of his past, a girl he met at a ball years before. When Mlle. St.-Euverte arrives, also desperate after years of saving herself for him, it seems the General may at last find his love. She soon realizes, however, that he is not the dashing military man of whom she has dreamed. She turns to the young secretary Gaston, who fell in love with her the moment he saw her, when she literally fell from the skies into his arms. At that moment, the General is revealed as the old man he has always been, the father figure from the plays of Plautus who tries to take the lover who rightfully belongs to the young man. For the General, the end of the play is bitter and sad, but for the young lovers who have met and been united, it is a return to the way of all comedy. The bittersweet sympathy with which the General is drawn makes him the center of the play, but he is only the part of the plot that must be overcome for the ending to be reached.

If even such complex works as *Waltz of the Toreadors* are revealed to be little more than minor variations of an ancient plot, the power of this plot is worth some serious consideration. Where are the plays that do not use the basic plot at least as a framework for the comedy? In the Western tradition there are at best a handful of longer works that eschew boy-meets-girl as a central activity. There is, of course, Ben Jonson's *Volpone*, a long and unvarying attack on greed and cupidity; there is Samuel Beckett's *Waiting for Godot*, that extended vaudeville turn; there is Gogol's *Inspector General*; there are a number of parodies, now long forgotten and unperformed along with the originals from which they borrowed their form. There are also a number of shorter works, older afterpieces and curtain raisers and newer one-act plays, which are in general so short as to need no plot to hold themselves together. Yet even here the old Menandrine plot recurs regularly whenever the short work is clearly comic in intention. David Garrick's *Miss in Her Teens* is just a long comedy shorn of a lot of details, and it can stand for most of the afterpieces of the eighteenth and early nineteenth centuries. In a very real sense the one-act play as we know it grows from two plays, both by Susan Glaspell—the serious one, *Trifles*, established the form for events that have happened offstage and that are examined through characterization and implication onstage, usually after the fact; the comedic one, *Suppressed Desires*, gave us a couple who thought they were in love, who find their love challenged by psychiatry, and who are reunited in a better marriage after the psychiatrist is shown to be wrong. Although shorter works need less continuity, and thus permit their authors to use other plot formulas, most works longer than the revue sketch have moved back to the basic plot, as with Peter Shaffer's *Black Comedy* and *The Public Eye* and Terence Rattigan's *Harlequinade*.

The dominance of this plot is remarkable not only because it is so ancient but also because it is confined largely to dramatic literature. Comedy in other forms of literature has for the most part not relied on this comic plot. In the shorter forms, of course, there is little need for plot; the simple narration of a single incident or an observation or two expressed with wit and style is sufficient unto the poem, the essay, the short story, the tall tale, and folk tale. Most of these forms involve only a single incident or a set of loosely associated comments on a single topic, which are often quite humorous in the telling, but they have little need of real plot. From Aesop's fables to the reminiscences of James Thurber or Jean Shepherd, the writers have wandered far in search of forms as well as topics for their comic works.

In the longer works, beginning with such poetic materials as Juvenal's *Satires* or Apuleius's *The Golden Ass*, writers have chosen a rather random progression through life as the primary structure of comedic narrative. This progression may follow a character through his life or simply through a particular journey, but the events of the comedy tend to be randomly associated, often to no particular purpose. Things happen because they happen, and many things are reported simply because the hero chances onto them in his wanderings. For the most part, the events of the story could happen in a completely different order. When prose fiction came along and gradually shaped itself into the novel, the journey through life continued to be the major organizing form for the comedies. Rabelais's *Gargantua*, Cervantes's *Don Quixote*, Fielding's *Tom Jones*, Dickens's *Martin Chuzzlewit* and *The Pickwick Papers*, and Byron's *Don Juan* (still in verse) are the same story, with different heroes and societies. Some of these borrowed parts of the stage comic plot— Chuzzlewit gets his Mary, and Tom Jones his Sophie—but usually just to end the story; Pickwick and Don Juan keep going forever, while those works with heroes who get married at the end seem not to have sequels.

In the twentieth century, this is almost the only strain of comic novel. John Barth's *Sot-Weed Factor*, Thomas Berger's *Little Big Man*, Saul Bellow's *Adventures of Augie March*, Joseph Heller's *Catch-22*, R. M. Koster's Tinieblan trilogy, John Nichols's *The Magic Journey*—the American works are like the picaresque journeys of the past, simply transferred for comic effect to new places and times. These novels join the European strain and match in form such varied works as Jaroslav Hašek's *The Good Soldier Schweik*, Vladimir Voinovich's *Ivan Chonkin*, Evelyn Waugh's *Scoop* and *A Handful of Dust*, and the grotesquely horrible comedy of Günter Grass's *The Tin Drum*. For the most part, the comedy of literature, which is read rather than seen and heard, has followed the form of the journey, whether on the road or through life or, ideally, both.

Only one seriously regarded comic novelist, Jane Austen, has consistently used the basic comic plot of the stage. A few others, such as P. G. Wodehouse and Peter DeVries, also deal with variations of the old plot, but they are generally regarded as minor authors even by those who admire them. A few other comic authors occasionally deal with some variation of the Menandrine plot, but for the most part that plot is taken very seriously in the novel form. Since the love story was introduced into the late medieval romances, there have been thousands, perhaps millions, of retellings of the old plot of comedy, but they have rarely been seen as comedies by their readers or their authors. Although critics might find many of these novels ludicrous, no one would think of including Emily Brontë's *Wuthering Heights*, or Charlotte Brontë's *Jane Eyre*, Victor Hugo's *Notre Dame de Paris*, Thomas Hardy's *The Return of the Native*, or, at a less critically admired level, the collected works of Barbara Cartland and Emilie Loring among any list of successful comic novels.

This begins to suggest some important aspects of the traditional comedy plot that are not immediately obvious in a bald statement of the plot framework. Comedy performed is different from comedy read, and while one plot on stage may be seen as a source of humor and comedy, on the printed page the identical plot usually becomes intense, emotional, stimulating, or even erotic, and rarely if ever humorous.

Dramatic comedy is a public art. When many of its frameworks are shifted to the private world of the individual reader, they speak differently to a different part of the person. In a public situation we require a form that not only lets us leave after a fixed period of time (which the picaresque plots of the common comic novels can never allow), but also speaks socially rather than personally. We deal with all dramatic literature in public, and nothing in dramatic literature is so public as the comedy, with its dependence on the immediate public response of laughter for the detail of each performance. Consequently, it is in the social rather than the personal realm that comedy in its dramatic form must be examined, and it is in the social realm that the dominance of the basic comic plot can be understood.

The key to the social nature of the comic plot lies in the nature of the problem that keeps the young lovers apart. In its purest form, the block that stands in the path of true love is one person: Father. Father is the authority in the ancient family unit. He is lawgiver, judge, and policeman as well as support and protector; above all, he is obeyed if one wishes to stay in the family. From that simple family view of the role of Father, we extend Father's characteristics to almost any authority figure, from God the Father to the Father of our country, and to the Fatherland and all its power and authority figures. The comedy plot is a threat to all of this power and authority and stability, because in the comedy, Father never knows best. Pop is never right, and Junior not only rises in revolt but always wins. By implication, every social code, ever piece of social authority, can fall to the young lovers. Comedy, ultimately, is anarchy, even if only a most temporary form of anarchy. When Father can safely be challenged, temporarily anything goes.

Anything has gone in comedies, from the very beginning of comedy as we have known it. As Erich Segal has pointed out in his book *Roman Laughter*, the works of Plautus are a systematic rejection of almost everything in the official Roman culture. Rome honored parents; Plautine fathers are buffoons. Rome blessed thrift and good business; Plautine comedies are riots of spendthrifts and wastrels, all of whom succeed. Roman wives honored and obeyed; Plautine wives are shrews who boss and sometimes even beat up their husbands. Slaves of Rome were supposed to honor and fear their masters; Plautine slaves are so much smarter than their masters that they can trick them into anything. Near the time of Plautus's death a Roman senator was barred from the senate for kissing his wife in public; Plautus's plays pause in their public lust only long enough for a little public gluttony, or so it seems. Rome's pride, power, and worldwide authority depended on its unsurpassable military power; Plautine soldiers are braggarts and cowards. For the time of the plays, at least, the Roman audience was participating in total anarchy in the world as they publicly knew it.

Such persistent glorification of anarchy is rarely so clearly visible again, at least until the American comedy film, but the anarchic spirit of social upheaval continues in almost every period of comedy. The forces of authority are subjected to cruel ridicule throughout the history of the *commedia dell'arte*: Pantalone, il Dottore, and il Capitano are regular objects of derision and failure. Shakespeare's lovers often run away to the forest, where normal laws no longer apply, as in *As You Like It* or *A Midsummer Night's Dream*, or to foreign kingdoms, where they go in disguise and do not follow the normal rules, as in *Twelfth*

Night or *The Comedy of Errors*. In Molière's *Les Fourberies de Scapin*, Scapin steals from one father and beats up another. Beaumarchais's Figaro humiliates his Count. Shaw and Wilde stand the most cherished attitudes of their society on their ears and revel in the mess they make. In Kaufman and Hart's *You Can't Take It with You*, the Sycamores hold no jobs, pay no taxes, observe no formal laws, and have no social organization, except to have dinner. And so on, ad infinitum.

It is this specter of anarchy that has so consistently aroused the opposition of the authorities and the protectors of society. In Western culture, opposition to the theatre has been almost completely opposition to the comedy, and most of the great diatribes against, and the legal or quasi-legal suppressions of, theatrical performances have resulted from the habits of the comedians, not the tragedians or dancers or musicians or even the lowly melodramatists. The virulence of the opposition to comedy can be seen by the attack of one "I.G." in 1615. In a widely circulated and considered pamphlet, he claimed:

A comedy is. . .wholly composed of fables and vanities; and fables and vanities are lies and deceits. . .the fruit of vintage and drunkenness, consisting of sundry impieties, comprehending evil and damnable things, wherein is taught how in our lives and manners we may follow all kind of vice with art. For they are full of filthy words and gestures, such as would not become very lackeys and courtesans; and have sundry inventions which infect the spirit. . .with unchaste, whorish, cozening, deceitful, wanton, and mischievous passions. . . . To please the vulgar people [stage players] set before them lies, and teach much deceitfulness and dissolution, by this means turning upside down all discipline and good manners. . . . Of comedies, the matter is love, lust, lechery, bawdry, scortation, adultery, uncleanness, pollution, wantonness, chambering, courting, jeating, mocking, flouting, foolery, venery, drabbery, knavery, cozenage, hypocrisy, flattery, and the like. And as complements and appendants. . .is swearing, cursing, oaths, blasphemies, etc. . . . The action in deed is. . .active demonstration of cozenage, whorish enticing,. . .with embracing, clipping, culling, dandling, kissing; all manner wanton gestures, and the like. . . .The parts they [the actors] play are. . .unjust judges, magistrates, officers, covetous citizens, spend-all gentlemen, gods, goddesses, fiends, furies, devils, hags, ghosts, . . . whores, bawds, courtesans, rogues, villains, vagabonds, thieves, rovers, pirates, cozeners, cheaters, brokers, bankrupts, hypocrites, sycophants, parasites, flatterers, talecarriers, makebates, lecherous old men, amorous young men, wanton maids, lascivious dames, unhonest wives; rebels, whoremasters, gluttons, drunkards, spend-thrifts, fools, madmen, jesters, jibers, flouters, mockers; and finally contemners of God, his laws, and the Kings, and blasphemers of his holy name; with such like of infinite variety.[2]

Although it might be difficult to come up with many more "such like," the description is plain and, for the most part, accurate. That is what the comedy of the time showed, and what the comedy of all time in the West has shown. And this was during a relatively good period—1615 is only four years after *The Winter's Tale* and *The Tempest.* The theatre he describes is the very golden age of the English-language theatre, and the period of the finest and most respected comedies available, the stage of Shakespeare, Ben Jonson, Thomas Dekker, Middleton and Rowley, and Beaumont and Fletcher. There have been many worse periods.

Seventy-eight years later, Jeremy Collier would say the same things about the Restoration theatre. Speaking for a large and powerful group of "respectable" persons, he declared the "liberties" of the stage to be "intolerable": "their smuttiness of expression; their swearing, their profaneness, and lewd application of the Scripture; their abuse of the clergy; their making their top characters libertines, and giving them success in their debauchery."[3] Like I. G., he singles out for attack the best, not the worst. His polemic is aimed at Congreve's *Love for Love, The Old Bachelor,* and *The Double Dealer,* Wycherly's *The Country Wife,* and John Vanbrugh's *The Relapse,* all the characters of which were no better than the "strumpets" of Terence and Plautus.

In the years since, the arguments have not changed. Respectable people have attacked the comedy in sermons, in print, in committee, and in letter campaigns, and always on the same grounds—its immorality and its bad example. That immorality and bad example grow first from the overthrow of authority implied in every comedy, where sons and daughters refuse to marry as their fathers say, upset the very fabric of society, and succeed. Such lessons can be learned all too easily by the impressionable young and the lower classes who have traditionally fre-

29

quented the theatres. As the Hays Code, developed in the thirties as a guide and self-censoring control for American movies, explained, "Many scenes cannot be presented without arousing dangerous emotions on the part of the immature, the young, or the criminal classes."[4]

The immorality and bad example also result from the weapons to which the young must resort in their attempts to overthrow the rule of the father figures. Ultimately, any weapon is usable; "all's fair in love and war," and comedy is in a very real sense both. Most of the time, however, a little deceit and trickery are all that is required, with a modicum of luck and a *deus ex machina*. But this deceit and trickery mean lying, cheating, sometimes stealing, disguises, pretense, and a even a bit of blackmail if situations allow.

The most common weapon, however, is ridicule. The authority figure is exposed for what he really is behind his public mask, and his hypocrisy or his social inadequacy is held up for all to see and to laugh at. Here is where humor normally plays its most important role in the comedy, as a social corrective. One of the most common comic techniques is to ascribe a particular social habit to a character, exaggerate the habit, and then make that character the block in the path of the lovers. Sooner or later the character will be forced into a situation where he must tell the children, "Do as I say, not as I do." But since he has been publicly exposed, he has no power behind that dictum, and the young people can finally do as they wish.

The idea of comedy as a social corrective, with laughter as its weapon, is an old one. Donatus, in the fourth century, tells us that "comedy is a fable . . . in which one learns what is useful in life and what on the contrary is to be avoided."[5] The Elizabethans thought that mankind was controlled by various humors, which could become dangerous to society when out of balance, and that the comic writer was to expose those humors as the follies and vices that they were. As Ben Jonson explained in the Induction to *Every Man Out of His Humour*:

> If any here chance to behold himself,
> Let him not dare to challenge me of wrong;
> For, if he shame to have his follies known,
> First he should shame to act 'em. My strict hand
> Was made to seize on vice, and with a gripe,
> Squeeze out the humour of such spongy natures
> As lick up every idle vanity.

Vice was to be brought to the surface, and through ridicule, driven out of the social fabric. Henri Bergson in his famous essay on laughter clearly propounded this theory that "laughter is, above all, a corrective."[6] The social requirement of the comic play is to correct the person who is becoming "mechanical" or nonhuman, leaving behind his fellow humans. When some person ceases to be human, we laugh at him, and thus we both lead him back to the natural path and remind ourselves not to stray from that path ourselves.

Although there are a number of difficulties with this theory in explaining why we actually laugh at some things and not at others, there is no doubt that, over the centuries, comedy has used humor as the bludgeon with which to assault the rigid, authoritarian, and hypocritical aspects of public society, as personified by the characters and events that block the lovers from each other. Plautus attacked the core of all Roman society, the authority and morality of the *paterfamilias*. The *commedia* took on all fathers, intellectuals, and old men, as well as soldiers and judges. Shakespeare ridiculed the money-mad Jew in Shylock (or at least so his own audiences seem to have thought), and the bogus Puritan morality in Malvolio. Jonson took rapier, broadsword, and sometimes even siege gun to the greed and hypocrisy of every layer of the society around him. Molière personified greed in the Miser, religious hypocrisy in Tartuffe, misanthropy in Alceste, social and intellectual pretensions in his learned ladies, and doctors' ignorance and pomposities at every chance. The Restoration wits took on the social foibles and pretensions of their day. Shaw, of course, took on everything and everyone. And the most persistent method was exposure, peeling away the public face and holding up to public laughter the reality behind.

Much of the libertinage and the sexual perversity, whoremongering, and lasciviousness of the comedies that I. G., Collier, and many similar critics have attacked has belonged to the authority figures, the respectable people who publicly mask their duplicity, lubricity, and salaciousness until the comedy brings it to light. Count Almaviva, not Figaro, is the libertine, and he is the one who is outrageously jealous of a slip of a boy with the Countess while plotting to steal Figaro's fiancée away; it is the sweet little old ladies, not the young lovers, who provide both the arsenic and the old lace along with the bodies in the cellar. The customers of Ben Jonson's Alchemist as well as Volpone's circle are all respectable, mature, and ostensibly honest folk, despite their willingness to sell their wives and sisters.

31

It is significant, however, that there are limits. Comedy's sons and daughters attack their authoritarian elders, but they do not kill them. They destroy their authority, but they do not destroy them. At the end of the comedy, when the lovers are united and everyone is happy except the father figures, something that happens in no other basic dramatic form occurs. When the blockers have been outflanked, the stuffy unstuffed, and the hypocrites exposed, there is a big party. But there can be no real pleasure in the party if the parents do not come. Thus, the lovers usually include as many of the people whom they have just held up to ridicule as possible, to accept them back into the world from which they have just been driven. At some point in the ancient comedy, Plautus's fathers do exactly what Tevye does in *Fiddler on the Roof*; he shrugs his shoulders and says, "Very well, children, you have my blessing and my permission. . . . What else could I do?"[7] In the most marvelous of all the comedic transformations, the authority figures change their minds. In *As You Like It*, Duke Frederick wanders into the Forest of Arden and is saved from the lion; born again as a new man, he relents his usurpation and is welcomed at Rosalind's wedding. Mr. Kirby, in *You Can't Take It with You*, sits down to dinner amid talk of getting out his old saxophone. Tartuffe and Alceste, Malvolio and Shylock, and others of their ilk refuse the offer to rejoin the rest and storm off the stage unchanged and often swearing vengeance, but most of the others take the opportunity to stay as somehow different people.

This is a stunning characteristic of comedy. Despite the persistence in academic and popular discussions of literary character change in the course of a story, it rarely in fact happens. In dramatic literature, outside of comedy, characters almost never change their minds. This is the very foundation of Constantin Stanislavski's concept of the superobjective, which has been the theoretical underpinning for almost all twentieth-century acting, which states that a character ultimately wants one thing consistently and persistently throughout the course of the play. Tragedy, in one sense, is the result of characters who refuse to change their minds coming into such persistent conflict that at least one of them must be destroyed. Sometimes, as in *Hamlet*, the principal characters may shilly-shally around for much of the play while they try to make a decision, but once it is made, Hamlet or Claudius must go; the form allows no reconciliation. In the melodrama, characters are revealed to be better or worse than they were thought to be at the beginning, but the process is most often merely a revelation, not a change—the unassuming little man turns out to be the murderer, the dashing young gent is really a seducer and a cad, the old rummy marshal turns out to have enough gumption left to stand up to the gunfighter.

A persistent strain in the melodrama deals with the reformation of a leading character, most common in what were once called "problem plays" and are now called "drama" or "TV movies." But there is a significant difference between the changes of mind the comedic fathers have and these reformations. In its most blatant form, as in *The Drunkard*, the character has somehow strayed from the path of respectable life, and the reformation, if it comes, restores him to a socially acceptable life; the alcoholic goes to Alcoholics Anonymous and recovers, the runaway realizes her parents still love her and goes home, the white bigot shakes hands with the black man. Society's beliefs change a great deal from place to place and year to year, but the prodigal somehow comes around to a way of thinking that matches that of the society he wishes to be a part of. The comic father figures are society—they are the businessmen, the doctors, and the lawyers, the stable, responsible people who are trying to uphold the official world of the audience. When they change, they are signifying that the social order itself is wrong in some way, and that the prodigal children are right.

The children are not right about everything. More than likely, they themselves will get married, have children, and go through the same problems with the next generation. But they are consistently right about one thing: sexual attraction. They know whom they should marry. For most of Western history, this has been an outrageous proposition. Law and custom have demanded that marriage be arranged in some way, at least in those parts of society that have money and property to protect. The nobility arranged marriages for political advantage; businessmen arranged marriages to secure or enlarge the family wealth; farmers arranged marriages to secure or enlarge their lands. As industrialized nations began to surrender the idea of the arranged marriage, the custom survived in the bride's dowry and the widely accepted practice of old, declining families rebuilding themselves with the money brought in by the daughters of the *nouveaux riches* whom their sons began to marry. Custom, even in supposedly classless and dowryless modern America, still demands that young people find suitable partners: the sons and daughters of lawyers do not marry the sons and daughters of truck drivers, unless the latter children have themselves become doctors and lawyers, and college graduates do not marry high school dropouts,

33

except at great social risk. Comedy throws all that out the window. Much of the time, a last-minute revelation will make the match suitable—the birthmark or the amulet will be found that proves the girl is the long-lost daughter of the neighbor or the prince, or the nurse tells a painful story of a mislaid handbag—but the lovers do not know that is going to happen. They pick each other, and they pick for no acceptable social reason except that they know somehow that they are "right for each other."

The "right" lovers are almost never the socially proper lovers. The marriages at the curtain are never the ones arranged by the authority figures. Even when the birthmark or the nurse's story comes to light, making the lover socially acceptable, the lover is still not the person the parents had in mind when the play began. This is an important distinction, because it makes the lovers the symbols of choice, of freedom, of love, rather than of social stability and manners. One of the many frustrations of *All's Well That Ends Well*, for example, is that the plot is a long struggle to trick one of the lovers into accepting the arranged match, which makes the ending as much a defeat as it is a victory for love. In Sheridan's *The Rivals*, Jack must impersonate someone else to win Lydia's love, for she would never love him under his own name, because he is the man she has been ordered to marry by her guardian. Deep into the twentieth century, one of America's most popular musicals, *The Fantasticks*, finds two fathers with the old problem of how to get their children to love each other. The only way to guarantee it is for the fathers to pretend to feud:

> Your daughter brings a young man in,
> Says, "Do you like him, Pa?"
> Just tell her he's a fool and then,
> You've got a son-in-law.[8]

However, since established society is not as subtle as Hucklebee and Bellamy, the lovers will almost never be socially acceptable under the rules of current authority.

In fact, the lovers seem to require nothing except purely animal attraction. It is always difficult to understand what other persons see in their loved ones in real life, but in the world of comedy, lovers are incomprehensible. The lovers of one generation are anathema to another and become objects of ridicule themselves, as Jeanette MacDonald and Nelson Eddy are to a generation that sees nothing strange about

Gene Wilder and Jill Clayburgh or Woody Allen and Diane Keaton. Why in the world Congreve's Mirabell should want to saddle himself with Millamant, or why Shakespeare's Petruchio should want Kate, even with her money, or even more why Kate should come to want Petruchio, are questions beyond rational discussion. They want each other because they do; it is a given that the audience understands because the performers cast in the roles have been chosen so as to make it subconsciously obvious they are made for each other. Otherwise the play will not succeed with the audience. The casting requirements will vary from generation to generation for a classic comedy, with the lovers revealing one set of personalities in the seventeenth century and another in the nineteenth.

Age is often a factor, but not always. In the plays of Plautus, where the competition for the girl's love often comes from the boy's father, the son is obviously better suited. But in other plays, the father has his own candidate. In Molière's *Le Malade imaginaire*, Argan picks a doctor's son for his daughter, but she refuses. The young man is also a nincompoop, but only minimally worse than the young man who eventually succeeds with the young woman. In a number of Victorian comedies, especially the works of Shaw, the young man is noticeably older than the young lady. Audiences expressed outright anger at *Pygmalion* because Eliza did not marry Higgins, who, as Shaw gleefully pointed out, was as unsuitable for her in age, personality, philosophy, experience, and romance as a man might be. Yet, fifty years later, Lerner and Loewe accepted the public demand and had her return to him rather than to Freddy at the end of *My Fair Lady*. In most other plays, however, Shaw matched clearly older men with his heroines, pairing Cusins and Barbara in *Major Barbara*, Bluntschli and Raina in *Arms and the Man* and Jack Tanner and Anne in *Man and Superman* without upsetting his audiences then or now. So, although age is a factor in the suitability of comic lovers, it is not important if that other attraction, however nebulous, is there.

It is significant not only that the pairing of the lovers is so simpleminded, so instinctual, but also that so frequently the lovers end up married, or at least engaged. Although comedy is consistently a celebration of sex, it is rarely a celebration of sex for its own sake. Aristophanic comedy and the satyr plays seem to have accepted sex as its own comic reward, but since the Menandrine New Comedy, playwrights have for the most part rejected that assumption. No characters in literature have a more naked sex drive than the fathers of Plautus, yet they never get the beautiful young girl. There is another level to comedy's structure. As the Stage Manager in Thornton Wilder's *Our Town* says at Emily's wedding, "The real hero of this scene isn't on the stage at all."[9]

Ultimately, the basic comic plot is a promise of the future, symbolized by the union of a couple leading to the birth of a child. In what Northrop Frye has called "the mythos of spring."[10] comedy has been a demonstration and a guarantee of change, of growth, of a new day. But it is always a new future, a new society, a new beginning that is different from the society present at the start of the play. If having babies were the only requirement, there would be no play—the son would marry the girl his father picks for him, and everything would go on as it always has. Yet the son refuses, the daughter refuses, the fathers is defied, the social order is upset, and a "better" couple is put together somehow. In its way, the Menandrine New Comedy was a mythical demonstration of the theory of evolution thousands of years before the theory was formulated. Somewhere, somehow, the male and the female meet, the spark is passed between them, and they *know*. Once that spark is passed from eye to eye, no Demipho, no Harpagon, no Duke Frederick or Mrs. Malaprop, no class or economic system, nothing, in fact, may be allowed to stand in the way of their union and the potential production of a better future.

Comedy did not have to be this way. Aristophanic comedy, which the Menandrine comedy replaced, did not follow this plot, nor did it place such persistent symbolic emphasis on the future. It was firmly rooted in the present, and if it dealt with change, it was against it. Aristophanes' Cloudcuckooland could result if society let certain changes get out of hand, and much of the attack of *The Clouds* was designed to make sure such changes never came about. In the modern comic novels that avoid the dramatic comedy plot, the comedy goes on as long as the journey holds out. The outrageous incidents continue and the hero just keeps moving on with no effect on society or its future. The hero who wants to change things can sometimes escape or disappear, as Yossarian did in his rubber dinghy at the end of Joseph Heller's *Catch-22*, but for the most part he just keeps on going. Huck Finn keeps moving as long as the river runs, and when it runs out, he spends weeks freeing a slave who is already free; after that he can only join up with the rest of the folks or light out for the territories, never to be seen again. The comic novel offers hope of change, but not the promise of it; its hero, like Saul

Bellow's Augie March, is a "Columbus of those near-at-hand,"[11] in search of something better but not really attempting to make it himself. In that wide body of popular literature that uses the basic plot of comedy but that no one thinks of as comic, the lovers and their romance have been personalized. The author and the reader are more concerned with the experience of the love than with the result of it. The pleasure, the passion, the pain, and the thrill of it all occupy the interest and supply the vicarious and very personalized pleasure of the reading experience. In the course of that experience, the emphasis of the plot is subtly changed. In the vast body of romances, the lovers are forced apart by circumstances, or the virginal woman resists the cad she secretly loves, until the obstacles are surmounted. The message, the myth if you will, becomes "True love is eternal." This is an important and obviously popular idea, but it is not the idea or the myth of comedy. In the comedy, love can move mountains; but in the romance, love holds on even when the mountains move. The lovers of comedy make things happen, while in general the lovers of romance have things happen to them. The ultimate expression of the romance plot is in the ghosts of Cathy and Heathcliff roaming Wuthering Heights together in death as they used to do in childhood but never did in adult life. Comedy can rarely wait so long. It has to have its change now, while at least one of the lovers is young. It has to make the future, not hope for it or wait for it to come.

This makes the heroes of the comedy aggressive and active in a way few other literary heroes can be. It is rare, at least until the rise of the sit-com, to find a passive hero in dramatic literature, but many are defensive rather than aggressive, entering on their action in order to protect the things they care about from outside attack, and most are reactive, rising up only under the goading of others. Speaking in very broad terms, tragedy is peopled with heroes who are reactive but extremely aggressive. Hamlet needs his father's ghost and a great deal more confirmation before he is ready to do anything, but once he gets started, he is very intense. Oedipus kills his father by trying to escape the prophecy and does not begin his search for the truth until the plague forces him into action, but once he has begun to seek answers, he will not turn back. By contrast, the melodrama heroes tend to be both reactive and defensive. They need the interference of the villain to force them to fight back, and their goal is generally to drive out the villain and make the family (or the town, or the nation) safe again. The comic novel heroes tend to be aggressive but reactive; they set out on their adventures eager to do, to find, to get something, but what they do and find and get are a matter of accident, completely dependent upon the people or events they run into along the way. The comedic heroes usually make the first move—they fall in love—and they tend to be single-minded in pursuit of their goal. Sometimes the lover is not smart enough, or imaginative enough, or even lucky enough, to get what he wants under his own steam, so he seeks help. That helper, however, often responds to his plea for no reason except a desire to be active, to do for the sake of doing as well as for personal gain; nothing makes him help except that he wants to do so.

The comedic hero is usually the lover, although he does not have to be. Often he is poor, either as a result of his own social station (slave, servant, gypsy girl stolen at birth, wandering scoundrel without visible means of support) or because his parents have cut off the money. Most often, but not always, the character is male. In many of the most memorable comedies females actively and aggressively pursue their men and are perfectly able to solve their own problems and get what they want. (Shakespeare was especially partial to such women, with Rosalind in *As You Like It*, Portia in *The Merchant of Venice*, and Helena in *All's Well That Ends Well* setting examples for many who would follow.) They solve the problem that separates them from the men of their choosing, just as the male heroes do in other plays, and their men are the lucky beneficiaries of their daring. The Restoration era saw a number of similar female heroes in the popular breeches plays, in which the heroines, in male disguise that allowed the actresses to show off their legs, pursued their men, but these plays are rarely seen or read today. Twentieth-century drama finds such striking examples as Anne in Shaw's *Man and Superman* and Cynthia in Langdon Mitchell's *New York Idea*. Male or female, the lover who pursues is always a potential hero.

Quite often, however, the lover is either not very bright or just too "nice" to find a way to solve the problem. This seems to occur much more often when the pursuing lover is male rather than female, probably because most Western societies would not expect a pursuing female. When a woman is allowed to be the pursuer in the first place, she can be expected to be resourceful enough to win her goal. Whenever the lover is not quite up to solving the problem himself, he seeks help. This helper may then become the comic hero, by removing or circumventing the obstacles between the lovers.

Whether as lover or as helper, the comic hero usually has one of three basic personalities, or personae. The first of these is the Innocent, who is somehow unaware of the true nature of the world. His innocence comes from lack of knowledge, but he is no fool—he can learn, if forced to do so. He is unacquainted with evil, but because he has not allowed evil to taint his inner spirit rather than because he has never met it. He may commit crimes, he may sin in the eyes of respectable society around him, but in his heart, they are not crimes and not sins, a view that is ultimately upheld by the conclusion of the comedy. He is often naive, often sentimental; in a perfect world, he would offend no one. He is childlike, sometimes childish, but has the appetites of an adult, at least the healthy physical appetites. His nature is often demonstrated by his dependence on his parents or guardians for support. When he is ingenious, he is also ingenuous, and he is usually unsophisticated in some important way. There is often an engaging guilelessness about his guile, an art about his artlessness, which makes him the obvious hero for the audience and for the play.

In many plays, this innocence is indicated by circumstance. In Plautus, for example, the lover is usually in desperate need of money because he has been cut off from funds by his parent, a practical demonstration of his childlike state. Even when the parents themselves are absent, the young hero is still a social child, dependent on the whims and strictures of others, such as Charles in Sheridan's *School for Scandal*—open, generous to a fault, and depending on the bequests of Uncle Oliver. Sometimes, the hero must start from a position of worldliness and then rediscover his innocence before he can be successful, as shown most completely in *As You Like It* and *A Midsummer Night's Dream*. He may be an innocent by profession as well, as is Cusins in *Major Barbara*; being a Greek scholar, he of course knows nothing of the real world, any more than Mortimer, being a drama critic, does in *Arsenic and Old Lace*. Sometimes, particularly in American plays, the hero may become an Innocent by sheer force of will. In William Saroyan's *The Time of Your Life*, Joe wills himself into an innocent world, hiding behind his alcohol and playing with children's toys in the saloon, just as Elwood P. Dowd does in Mary Chase's *Harvey*, and Grandpa does (without liquor) in Kaufman and Hart's *You Can't Take It with You*.

In later eras, especially in America, the hero is born innocent by geography. As early as Royall Tyler's *The Contrast* (1787) we are introduced to the country fellow who comes to the city and makes fools of the city slickers, wise in his innocence and ultimately the leader for the lovers. At other times and places the bumpkin is a fool and the object of ridicule rather than of ultimate respect, reflecting a different social history in relation to the peasantry, but he is a consistent hero in American theatre through Anna Mowatt's *Fashion* (1845) and Joseph Jefferson's *Rip Van Winkle* (1865), to Lerner and Loewe's *Brigadoon* (1947).

American silent film comedians responded particularly sympathetically to this version of the Innocent, beginning with the very first feature-length comedy film, *Tillie's Punctured Romance*, which featured Marie Dressler as that most Innocent of all American character types, the country girl who is led astray in the city until she finally triumphs over the city slickers. Harold Lloyd perfected the most characteristically American form of the male Innocent in his bespectacled character: the innocent from the small town, a little cocky, inventive under pressure, athletic, honest, and absolutely good-hearted. Buster Keaton added an inability to cope with machines, a theme that Charlie Chaplin picked up brilliantly in *Modern Times*, and that many other comics would use almost as a signature, a consistent proof of their essential innocence no matter how outrageously they might act, down to Woody Allen in *Sleeper*.

In sound films, the Innocent as hero, especially as lover, is a persistent feature. Frank Capra gives us Mr. Deeds and Mr. Smith, with small town virtues and Boy Ranger moralities, loosed in the big city and again showing up the slickers in the end. Preston Sturges returns to the character constantly: Henry Fonda, the snake-loving heir who has been living in the jungle and is suckered by Barbara Stanwyck in *The Lady Eve*, Dick Powell in *Christmas in July*, Eddie Bracken in *The Miracle of Morgan's Creek*, and Joel McCrae, with that open, pure American face, in *Palm Beach Story*. Danny Kaye plays an Innocent usually demonstrated by his profession, in most of his modern dress features. Scholars are consistent American Innocents: Cary Grant in *Bringing Up Baby* and *Monkey Business*, Gary Cooper in *Ball of Fire*, and Danny Kaye in *Wonder Man*.

Musicals, which require simpler plot lines in order to leave time for the songs, have been especially productive of Innocents. Dick Powell in all of his Warner Brothers' Busby Berkeley films oozes innocence at every pore, while Ruby Keeler positively drips it. In Gene Kelly, however, the purest American Innocent since Harold Lloyd makes his appearance, open-faced, open-hearted, always on the make but always controlled by his heart of gold. Despite his early success on stage as *Pal Joey*, playing the skunk underneath the wholesome image, in film Kelly is the same optimistic young man that Lloyd was, willing to try anything, able to think up schemes, but essentially naive and pure at heart. This is most clearly demonstrated in *On the Town* and *Singing in the Rain* and is quite traditionally shown in *An American in Paris*, but it underlies even the machinations he develops in *The Pirate*.

As the Innocent, our hero may be the lover, as in Plautus and the Shakespearean plays, or he may be the helper, as in *The Time of Your Life* and *Harvey*. In either role, he triumphs over adversity by using and maintaining his social innocence to bring about the proper conclusion to the comic plot.

Not far from the Innocent is the Fool, the second major persona for the comic hero. Unfortunately, the line between a Hermia and a Thisbe in *A Midsummer Night's Dream* is a fine one indeed, and it is not always clear now on just which side of that line a particular character was intended to reside in his own day. At the same time, twentieth-century critics and philosophers have frequently tried to convince us of the genius behind the fool and the tragedy masked by his foolishness. Thus, assigning specific characters to this particular category can be controversial. However, the fluctuation of personae for individual characters from generation to generation serves to illustrate the effectiveness of the Fool as hero: whether the audience saw Rip Van Winkle as an Innocent or as a blithering Fool, he and the play still worked.

The Fool is, in a sense, the Innocent gone wild. He is a natural, so natural that he has no conception of the world, much less of society. He is often gullible, but he always survives. He is absolutely unpredictable, which is what makes him always a potential hero for the comedy. His brains are in his body, not his head, and he is a figure of awe, mystery, and derision simultaneously. He is as far removed from the Shakespearean Fool as he can be, for if he speaks wisdom, he does so without his own awareness. Perhaps he is really insane, but even so, he is loved in his insanity by his audience.

The classic illustration of this persona is of course Harlequin, the prince of numskulls. Under various names, Harlequin lived and prospered throughout the *commedia* era in Europe for at least three centuries. Then he was adapted by playwrights such as Carlo Goldoni and Molière, transformed in France eventually into Pierrot, and became one of the most persistent symbols of twentieth-century art and litera-ture. But he takes many forms in theatrical literature both as lover, as in the sentimental *The Time of Your Life,* and as helper. As helper in the comedy, the Fool is usually a helper unaware; he solves problems by dumb luck, or by being tricked into some absurd situation, as is Silvestre in *Les Fourberies de Scapin,* or Goat, an American hillbilly version of the fool, in Alfred Uhry's musical comedy *The Robber Bridegroom.* Often, he provides the solution to the plot problem simply by existing, as Throttlebottom does in the musical *Of Thee I Sing;* for most of the play, he exists only for the laughs he provides, but at the end, he provides an alternative husband for the designing woman and frees the lovers.

The undiluted Fool is a problem, however. For the most part, when playwrights have turned him loose in a play, he has been provided only for humor. There is often considerable difficulty in finding a reasonably logical place for him in the plot.

There has been a great deal of literary and philosophical discussion on the nature of the Fool, most of it concerned with why we laugh. In general the fool is seen as a countering force to Bergson's ideas: the Fool makes us laugh because he represents release from forces limiting our human existence. Susanne Langer talks of the "buffoon" as "the indom-itable living creature, . . . the personified *élan vital,*"[12] an important mytho-logical, philosophical, and psychological character. Yet many of the funniest characters in our performing literature and in daily life lie completely outside the structures of plot. Unfortunately the Fool does not exist in most comic stage or film literature. When he does exist, he is often completely outside the dramatic situation, a humorous filler. Someone like Rafe in Beaumont and Fletcher's *The Knight of the Burning Pestle* is both indefinable and uncontrollable when he assumes a major plot position, which is at least one reason why many of the Fool's great roles are in burlesques and parodies of other genres rather than in comedies. Otherwise, he is generally limited to a secondary role in plot development, no matter how important his role in the eyes of the audience, or he is introduced as simply another funny person met along the way, as are Trinculo in *The Tempest* and Bottom in *A Midsummer Night's Dream.*

The difficulty involved in considering the Fool as a regular hero, as well as defining the Fool as a distinct character, can best be illustrated by the films of Jerry Lewis. While working with Dean Martin, he was the traditional Fool, guided, controlled, and sometimes protected by the smarter Martin, making a team very much like Abbott and Costello. But when he and Martin separated, Lewis began to play a character with a split personality. He has referred to these characters under various names, but most commonly as the "Kid" and the "Idiot."[13] In most of his films, he starts the picture as the Kid: an office boy, the messenger boy at a film studio, the handyman at a girls' boarding house, a male version of Cinderella, a bellboy in a major hotel. This character falls in love, often from afar and even more often unable even to begin to express that love, another long tradition for the Innocent. Then, without warning, he goes berserk. The Idiot character surfaces, sometimes as a release for tensions but more often simply because the opportunity presents itself. Then the Fool takes over without a buffer, without a straight man or more normal hero or lover to help establish a viewpoint on his actions or control his lunacy. Just as suddenly he slips back into the Kid personality, shifting back and forth several times in a single feature. It is, all things considered, an eerie public persona, as strange and incomprehensible as that of Harry Langdon, but developed at much greater length and much more popular. But it is also very disturbing, especially to the American tradition, where public mythology asserts the essential wisdom of the Innocent. Lewis reverses that mythology, revealing an essential idiocy within the Innocent. This in some degree accounts for the schizoid nature of his audience. He was loved and idolized by the young and the ignorant but detested by parents and the more sophisticated, except in France, where the long tradition of intellectualization of the Pierrot character helped make him more acceptable to the intelligentsia than he was in other nations. For the most part, the Fool has been a helper to the lovers, or even a helper to other helpers, but he has rarely been released as a central character who is lover, helper, and destroyer all in one, which makes Lewis's solo films a most difficult set to characterize or analyze.

The discomfort Lewis's work gives to many critics illustrates the problem of the audience as a whole in dealing with the Fool. We love him, but we also fear him; he makes us nervous. The comedy offers us a sense of anarchy, which we wish to share and to celebrate, but the Fool begins to offer that anarchy as a permanent way of life. That may be acceptable as theory; it may even be acceptable to an individual safely in his study alone with his book. But it is very disturbing to an individual sharing a public experience with a public audience. Consequently, the Fool has usually been controlled.

The *commedia* found the method that has been most commonly used, a method that leads us to the third and most prominent major persona of the comic hero, the Scoundrel. In the *commedia*, Harlequin was the *second* zany; the first was often his partner, Brighella, the servant scoundrel. Rogue, rascal, conman, thief, liar, cheat, lecher, scamp, imp, and smart aleck, the Scoundrel is the man who really makes things happen in the comedy. The Innocent may develop intrigues because he has to, the Fool because he does not understand what he is doing, but the Scoundrel tricks for the sake of tricking, enjoying the mess he makes of the daily life of the others around him. He has few scruples and little respect for the rules of everyday society, using them when they are to his advantage and bending them whenever he sees any value in doing so. His machinations complicate the plots, confuse the other characters, and in the process often expose the vanities and cupidities of others. The schemes he develops either clear the way for the lovers directly or they make life so complicated that things can be set straight only by the *deus ex machina*, which always comes to his rescue, uniting the lovers when all seems lost and protecting the Scoundrel from his just desserts.

The Scoundrel may be lover or helper, and he may make his strategems for his own sake as easily as for the sake of others. In general, the role the Scoundrel takes depends on how socially acceptable deviousness is and who the potential lover is. The Restoration rake, for example, was an ideal among the upper classes, who controlled the theatres, and the young man who lived by his wits and still lived in style was highly esteemed. There are therefore a number of Scoundrel lovers. Millamant in Congreve's *Way of the World* and Horner in Wycherly's *The Country Wife* are only the most prominent examples in a group that includes such hard-hearted characters as Doriman in George Etherege's *The Man of Mode*, and the more pleasant but just as devious Aimwell and Archer in George Farquhar's *The Beaux' Stratagem*. Other eras have accepted Scoundrel lovers, but none so completely as the English Restoration. Petruchio in *The Taming of the Shrew* and Richard Follywit in Thomas Middleton's *A Mad World, My Masters* show the Jacobean English versions; Beaumarchais's Figaro shows the eighteenth-century French version. He appears in nineteenth-century comedies in other guises, from the Charles Courtly of Dion Boucicault's *London Assur-*

ance to Jack and Algernon in Oscar Wilde's *The Importance of Being Earnest.*

Even more often, the Scoundrel is the helper, the one to whom the young lover must turn after he has exhausted all his own abilities. Plautus's wily slaves, such as Pseudolus, begin a long tradition that extends directly into Brighella in the *commedia* and from there to Sganarelle and Scapin for Molière and in Goldoni's *Servant of Two Masters,* and then to Figaro's first appearance in Beaumarchais's *The Barber of Seville.* Shakespeare uses the Scoundrel both as supernatural and as mortal, Ariel (*The Tempest*) and Puck (*A Midsummer Night's Dream*) as well as Feste (*Twelfth Night*) and Autolycus (*The Winter's Tale*), and Jonson seems almost to idolize him, in *The Alchemist* and *Volpone* making both servant and master equally rascally. The Scoundrel of course does not have to be a servant; he may be a friend as long as he has the necessary wit and tenacity. In the enduring *Charley's Aunt* by Brandon Thomas, Babbs is a good example of the more pleasant side of the character, as Undershaft is of the more intelligent side in Shaw's *Major Barbara,* and both illustrate some of the variety possible with this character.

In the twentieth century, this variety has caused some remarkable developments in the nature of the Scoundrel, making him more serious and more ambivalent. Aubrey Piper in *The Show-Off* by George Kelly is a congenital liar and braggart, who gets the girl and makes everything work out for the best by a magnificent bluff, yet he causes a lot of damage as he goes along to people who love him as well as to people who do not. Murray in Herb Gardner's *A Thousand Clowns* saves his nephew and gets the girl, but he has to pay a price he has tried to avoid for years. In Alan Ayckbourn's *Norman Conquests,* Norman gets not one but three girls, and yet it is all to no avail. At the same time, more traditional Scoundrels have maintained a position on the stages of the West, from El Gallo of *The Fantasticks,* the longest-running show in New York history, to Hugo in Anouilh's *Ring 'Round the Moon,* to the most scoundrelly of all heroes, Mack the Knife, in Brecht's *Threepenny Opera.*

As partner of the Fool, the Scoundrel is a common character and hero of American comic films. Bud Abbott, Oliver Hardy, Dean Martin, and Bing Crosby (in the Road pictures) are all schemers and plotters, the men with the ideas who need their Fool partners to carry them out while they sit by in relative safety. (Hardy's relative safety is only minimally greater than Laurel's, since Hardy's ideas are rarely any good.).

Outside of the teams, the Scoundrel appears in a surprising number of American comedy films as the lover hero, surprising given the American devotion to the Innocent as a culture hero. Certainly the most charming of these Scoundrels is Fred Astaire. Astaire is so dapper, so pleasant and ingratiating, one sometimes loses sight of the amount of inventive trickery, disguise, and deception he resorts to in order to get the girl. With the possible exception of the biographical film *The Story of Vernon and Irene Castle*, all the features with Ginger Rogers place him as a lover who cheats his way into her good graces, usually by pretending to be someone or something he is not. She of course is a perfect match for him, a sharp and sharp-tongued woman of the world who is at last won over to his charm. As he grew older, Astaire's character took on a new plot; he was still a lovable rogue, elegant and debonair, but he was eventually won over by the innocence and integrity of the girl, as in *Easter Parade*, *Funny Face*, and *Daddy Long Legs*. In his last musical, *Finian's Rainbow*, he was a charming Irish rascal hunting his pot of gold, now past his prime and shifted to the helper's position in the traditional plot.

Outside the musical, Cary Grant often played memorable comic Scoundrels, a remarkable achievement for a man whose comic Innocents are often classics as well. The most delicious of these scoundrels is certainly in *His Girl Friday* where, as Walter Burns, he would sell his soul for a story, if he had one left anyone would want to buy. Rosalind Russell is a perfect match for him, just as devious and just as sharp, so that, despite their bickering, they are, like Shakespeare's Beatrice and Benedick, obviously meant for each other. This lovable Scoundrel reappears in such films as *The Awful Truth*, *Philadelphia Story*, and later *Father Goose*.

Other film actors have also had their fling with the comic Scoundrel, usually as lover and often with a female who could be an equal Scoundrel. John Barrymore and Carole Lombard in *Twentieth Century* are probably the most spectacular of these pairings. Lombard and Frederic March in *Nothing Sacred*, Herbert Marshall and Miriam Hopkins in *Trouble in Paradise*, Claudette Colbert and Don Ameche in *Midnight*, all illustrate a long tradition of rogue lovers that continues in films through James Garner and Susan Clark in *Skin Game*. Individual male rogues abound, from Clark Gable in *It Happened One Night* and

Maurice Chevalier in most of his musicals with Jeanette MacDonald through Burt Reynolds in *Semi-Tough*. Especially in the thirties and early forties, American comedy introduced the unusual pairing of a female Scoundrel who falls in love with a male Innocent and is ultimately reformed. Jean Arthur in *Mr. Deeds Comes to Town* and *Mr. Smith Goes to Washington,* is the prototypical illustration, but she was followed by a number of similar ladies, the most notable being Barbara Stanwyck, who played this role in almost all of her comedy features.

In general, the team comics are helpers rather than lovers, although the Road pictures always end with Bing Crosby getting the girl and Bob Hope getting the bird, and Dean Martin usually plays on his good looks to get the girl as well. But, more vividly, the teams, as in the *commedia*, are there to find the way for the lovers to get together; they are only secondarily lovers themselves. The Marx Brothers in *A Night at the Opera, A Day at the Races,* and *The Big Store* illustrate this position most clearly.

A unique three-man team, the Marx Brothers combine all three comic heroes into a single unit. Groucho is the Scoundrel, continually pretending to be what he is not—a doctor, politician, professor, or explorer—always keeping one eye on the main chance and Margaret Dumont's money and the other eye out for the younger wild woman on the side. Con games, insults, and planned confusion are his stock in trade. Chico is the Innocent, who is in a new world he is not quite prepared to cope with. Unlike most American Innocents, he is not from the farm or small town but is an immigrant who barely speaks the language. His innocence is most often demonstrated by his inability to speak the language (the "why a duck?" sequence in *Cocoanuts*) or to understand the customs of society (the contract in *A Night at the Opera*) or even daily manners (the phone sequence in *Duck Soup*). Harpo is, of course, the Fool. Nothing makes any sense when he is near, and anything he touches may be destroyed. If he can misunderstand, he will; if it will fit in a pocket, he has it; if it wears a skirt, he will chase it; and yet, put him near a child or a harp, and he becomes almost angelic. As if to underscore this separation of their characters, Chico usually refuses to chase the girls—the wedding with three husbands in *Horse Feathers* being an exception—and he is consistently the one who promises to help the young man in love and who gradually draws the other two into the activity. The Marx Brothers are unique in the history of comedy not only because no one else has quite duplicated their sense of humor, but also because they are a spectacular culmination of comedic history, tying all the comic heroes into a single, balanced functional unit.

These three personae are of course not confined to the dramatic comedy. They appear in many plays of many different types, sometimes as minor characters, sometimes as principals. Outside the basic comic plot, however, they tend to take on slightly different characteristics. The Fools, for example, become wise, cynical, world-weary men, like Lear's Fool, who hide their knowledge under a mask of buffoonery, or they disguise their real motives for revenge in the melodramas for which Triboulet in Victor Hugo's *Le Roi s'amuse* provided the pattern. In the novel, they often become the voice of not just metaphorical but also practical sanity, like Sancho Panza in *Don Quixote*. In the melodrama the Scoundrel becomes the villain; in the romantic novel, the seducer; in the adventure romance, the dashing rogue come upon in the passing moments of our hero's need, like Alan Breck in Robert Louis Stevenson's *Kidnapped*. Odysseus is a rare Scoundrel hero outside the world of the comedy. The Innocent, of course, is everywhere, but outside the comedy he follows a far different plot. The serious American novel probably would not exist without the story of the innocent young man who at last comes in contact with the "real" world, whether it be the city, or sex, or making a living, or war; the result is the loss of innocence. This pattern carries over into all but the most simpleminded melodramas—once Grace Kelly pulls the trigger in *High Noon*, her innocence is gone, no matter how pure her motives. Only in the comedy do these heroes in these particular forms exist.

And they are the only heroes of the comedy. One of these three will somehow cause the lovers to come together. When the lovers do not get their way immediately, they do not seek professional guidance, as Ann Landers suggests today. They do not reason with the parent figures, or draw up a better contract, or even go off in search of the missing half of the locket—they concoct a scheme. And when, for whatever reason, the scheme fails, they do not see their minister or doctor, they see the most crooked or crazy person in the area. When Kate resists, Petruchio does not send her to a marriage counselor—he tricks her into loving him. When Kitty Carlisle threatens to leave Alan Jones at the dock in *A Night at the Opera*, he does not take off to the provinces to make his career and prove himself; he goes to the Marx Brothers. Comedy did not have to work this way, but it did. That it did so not just in a few places or a few eras but throughout Western culture

for more than two thousand years indicates that these particular characters in these particular variations of a basic story express some very deep
and important needs of the audience, an audience that participates as a
group, in public, as a sample of society.

As we have seen, this comic plot and its heroes speak most persistently of change, of the possibility of personal change as well as social
change. If personal change is not possible, society is forced into some
very hard situations: without it people who become temporarily unacceptable cannot be reformed—they can only be killed or driven out of
the community. No memorable comedies have come to us from the
great repressive regimes of history; a society that accepts and uses the
traditional comedy as a major part of its public expression does not
make concentration camps. But comedy is even more dedicated to the
expression of social change, through new pairings of couples and new
children and new ways of doing things. There are few, if any, instances
of comedy that changed the world, but each comedy is a repetition of
the mythical promise of change implicit in all human sexuality. In
comedy we may overcome the strictures of daily social life, deny the
laws and the parents, if only for a time. For a while, we suspend
everyday life not for adventure or even for the pleasure of sexual fulfill-
ment but rather for the sake of the biological powers within us all.

This leads to a number of striking paradoxes, which demonstrate
the complexity inherent in this comic movement. Not the least of these
is that comedy is at once the most and the least realistic of all dramatic
forms. Comedies are full of the minutiae of daily existence, the pots and
pans, the food, the clothes, the money, the business habits, the family
relationships of husband and wife and children. Most of the humor
comes from jokes made about things and events that are common and
topical for all the audience. In Molière's *Le Bourgeois gentilhomme*, a
strong vein of humor follows the path of the outsider who does not
understand the minutiae of his world but tries to act as if he did. If we
wish to know about daily life in Elizabethan England, we look not at
Shakespeare's *Othello* or Marlowe's *Doctor Faustus*, but at Thomas
Dekker's *The Shoemaker's Holiday*, Ben Jonson's *The Alchemist*, or
Thomas Middleton's *A Chaste Maid in Cheapside*, just as we look to
William Wycherly's *The Country Wife* rather than John Dryden's *All
for Love* for the Restoration world, or to Neil Simon's *The Odd Couple*
rather than Edward Albee's *Tiny Alice* for recent America. The characters of tragedy and the more "serious" dramas do not have time to worry

about the more mundane aspects of life because they are concerned with important things.

At the same time, the comic ending is the least "realistic" of all possible endings. We know that a young man who has been having an affair with a middle-aged woman does not tear the woman's daughter out of the hands of her bridegroom and run off with her on a bus; if he did, we would do everything in our power to see that the girl was returned safely, not cheer, as audiences did for Dustin Hoffman in *The Graduate*. Certainly there is no more widely maligned theatrical device than the *deus ex machina*. It is almost uniformly regarded as the desperate device of a bad writer who cannot find a way out of his own story line. Yet some of our finest writers depended on it for their finest work: the king's messenger who arrests Molière's Tartuffe; the twin brother, thought dead, who marries Olivia in Viola's place in Shakespeare's *Twelfth Night*; the nurse who misplaced her handbag in Wilde's *The Importance of Being Earnest*; Victoria's messenger who comes to save Macheath in Brecht's *Threepenny Opera*. In real life, it rarely turns out that way, as Brecht for one tells us, but first he makes sure that this time is the exception. The very irrationality of the device is its importance. It serves as a promise that things will turn out for the best, not sometime down the road or even tomorrow, for tomorrow never comes in most lifetimes. When the gods interfere to unite the lovers and straighten out the mess, it is an affirmation of the importance of their union today. This is reflected in Northrop Frye's remark that the "happy endings do not impress us as true but as desirable."[14] This is the way we would like things to be.

Another of the many comedic paradoxes is suggested by James Fiebleman: "Comedy leads to dissatisfaction and the overthrow of all reigning theories and practices in favor of those less limited. It thus works against current customs and institutions."[15] This seems wonderful at first glance but not so positive on consideration. Even biologically, change is rarely an improvement—most mutations die. In any society, the impulse of most persons, even the poor, is to resist any significant change. Everyone knows the present, but no one knows the future; any change might be for the better, but there is just as good a chance that it will be for the worse. The *bourgeois* may wish to be a *gentilhomme*, but ordinarily he will not risk the possible destruction of all the nobility to reach his goal; the slave may wish to be free, but it is often so that he himself may own slaves. Changes that do more than adjust the relationships between specific individuals in any society are rarely instituted, and almost never by the majority. Yet change is a fundamental natural imperative. Thus, comedy, through its basic plot, reflects the urge for change in a comprehensible and acceptable form.

It is a simplification, yet a useful one, to momentarily examine tragedy. Comedy and tragedy both concern heroes who demand a change. In comedy, change is possible; in tragedy, it is not. The tragic character tries to change the unchangeable forces of nature—call them fate or God's will or human nature, what you will—and fails. The comic character tries to change the apparently unchangeable forces of men in society and succeeds, at least temporarily. Hamlet dies; Petruchio gets married. Although the old joke may say death and marriage are the same thing, they most definitely are not. While the failure of the tragic heroes may say there are some forces that we cannot change, although it is noble to try, the success of the comic heroes answers that there are some forces for change that we cannot prevent, and the one who tries to stop them is a fool.

The comedic heroes are swept along on the tide of natural forces, which habits, custom, and social requirements resist. The lovers love because they love—they need no other reason. The helpers help because that is what one does or because it would be fun. It is the resisters who have decided that, whatever shape it might be in, this is the best of all possible worlds, and they form up ranks to defend the world and themselves from these uncontrolled upstarts.

This defensive move in turn forces an escalation of the comedic aggression. Like the officer in Vietnam, the hero may have to destroy the village to save it. Because the mating of the lovers is so imperative, so natural, the hero may use any weapon in the attack on whatever stands in their way, at least short of murder. Molière's Scapin suckers one of the fathers into hiding in a sack and then pretends to be the enemy and beats him. Most comedies try in one way or another to get the fathers into a sack, but when the sack becomes a shroud, as it does for the King of France in Shakespeare's *Love's Labour's Lost*, the party has to be postponed. But short of bringing about a death, anything is acceptable.

For most of theatrical comedy, this aggressive impulse confines itself to physical damage to the characters. Often it backfires, and the heroes have to take the pratfalls just as often as the characters who stand in their way. But stage work is usually confined to damage that can be done to the person—beatings, exposures, insults, water poured on the head, and so forth—for very practical reasons. The mechanics of stage presentation do not allow for the use of more than the simplest physical jokes, for the stage lacks the room and the flexibility to allow more. In a production of Oliver Goldsmith's *She Stoops to Conquer*, we cannot see Tony drive Mrs. Hardcastle across the countryside or see him dump the horses and carriage into the pond; there just is no practical way to do that. What we do see is the result of that action—Mrs. Hardcastle wet and bedraggled and totally confused. For most of history, actors have worked either on tour or in repertory companies whose shows changed regularly, which meant that only minimal scenery and properties were practical. Even when shows began to play in long, unified runs, practical requirements kept the destruction away from the physical world of the play. If you break Harold's Buddha every night in Peter Shaffer's *Black Comedy*, the theatre company has to be able to afford a new one for every show. A play in which the entire house is destroyed, such as Kaufman and Hart's *George Washington Slept Here*, is relatively rare. Film, however, provided a flexibility that the stage had never offered. We could see the carriage go into the water in the movies, and we did. Also, since the film was made once and shown to thousands of audiences long after the actors and scenery were gone, much more of the physical world could be destroyed. As a result, the anarchical, destructive impulses turned American film comedy into one long destruction derby, fully releasing the forces that practicality had kept at least partially submerged in the past.

The most persistent of the destroyers in silent film, though by no means the only one, was Buster Keaton. In his short subjects and his features appeared a wonderfully American character, the man who loves projects and machines but who cannot quite make them work right, from the do-it-yourself house in *One Week* through the sinking of the *Damfino* in *The Boat*, from the disasters in *Electric House* to the grand destruction of *The General*. Numerous comics followed this lead, especially the teams of Laurel and Hardy and the Three Stooges, but again the purest expression seems to come through the Marx Brothers. Unlike Laurel and Hardy and most of the other teams of destroyers, the Marx Brothers seemed to have no need for cause and effect. The early steps of *Big Business*, the short in which Laurel and Hardy destroy their store and the grocery next door, are logical and sequential, but when one meets the Marxes, there is no logic, no sequence. They can be

logical if they wish, as shown in Harpo's lemonade-roast nuts battle in
Duck Soup, but for the most part, a stranger can just as soon expect to
have his tie chopped up, his phone dismantled, his cigar stolen, and
his moustache shaved as he can expect to have his hand shaken. Their
contracts are objects to be shredded. Their classroom exercises are
peashooter fights. In their assignations the blonde is dunked in the
pond or papered into the wall as often as she appears in someone's
arms. They destroy a hotel, a coming-out ball, the horse races, col-
leges, and football games, and not just the performance but also the
scenery of the opera. At their peak, in *Duck Soup*, they destroy an
entire nation.

The destruction derby continues in so many other hands that it
would be possible to call it a signature of the American film comedy
itself. The famous comics all participated at some time, from the Three
Stooges through Olsen and Johnson. Jerry Lewis, especially in the
features on his own, is a baby bull in a china shop, wiping out boarding
houses, department stores, and an entire movie studio. Even the comedies without comics glory in this anarchic urge. Katherine Hepburn
collapses the dinosaur in *Bringing Up Baby*; even in Washington, Mr.
Smith knocks over lamps; and Ray Milland starts the great automat riot
in *Easy Living*. In the films of Preston Sturges, such destruction is
prominent, from the pandemonium of the crowd rushing to take back
their goods in *Christmas in July*, to Henry Fonda's tripping over the
furniture in *Lady Eve*, to the Ale and Quail Club on the train in *Palm
Beach Story*. Even the most dapper of all Hollywood leading men, Fred
Astaire, first meets Ginger Rogers in *The Gay Divorcée* by catching her
skirt in a trunk and ripping it.

For the most part, in the shorts, the destruction is its own reward.
But in the features, the destruction is aimed at particular aspects of the
stable and restrictive society, particularly at rigid authority, the pompos-
ity of middle age, and wealth and property. The "haves" pose a threat to
all of society in the traditional comedy, because they are so concerned
with protecting what they have, or getting more, that they lose sight of
the importance of change in the future. Sex without property, as in the
traditional plot where the young woman has no dowry or the young
man has no future, is anathema to them, so they try to block the lovers.
But the natural impulse to produce the most flexible future must triumph
after property has faded or broken, just as it must triumph over passing
definitions of morality or class. Real life may be dominated by those

who have property and power, but at least for a moment, in comedy, the myth of change is renewed.

It is renewed by a reconciliation, however, rather than an exclusion. Authority in some way relents, rigidity becomes more flexible. At the same time, the lovers and their helpers, who have been as disrespectable and disrespectful as possible, become respectable by agreeing to enter the most stable and respectable state of social life—marriage. The happy ending is possible because, ultimately, everybody has been after the same thing. As Jacob Bronowski summarized our civilization's history, he noted:

> [The cultural factor in natural selection] is still expressed in the care that kindred and community take in all cultures, and only in human cultures, to arrange what is revealingly called a good match. . . . The preoccupation with the choice of a mate both by male and female I regard as a continuing echo of the major selective force by which we have evolved. . . . Most of the world's literature, most of the world's art, is preoccupied with the theme of boy meets girl. We tend to think of this as a sexual preoccupation which needs no explanation. But I think that is a mistake. On the contrary, it expresses the deeper fact that we are uncommonly careful in the choice, not of whom we take to bed, but by whom we beget children. Sex was invented as a biological instrument by the green algae. But as an instrument in the ascent of man which is basic to his cultural evolution, it was invented by man himself.[16]

What we call culture has been developed and passed along through our marriages. Where families have consistently made the "right" matches, they have prospered, and not only in physical wealth. The culture and tradition of a society are passed through its families, and built upon when a society is growing and progressing. The interference of social authority in the sexual process is an attempt to do better. The very institution of marriage is an attempt to guarantee the stability and care that the next generation needs and might not find if uncontrolled intercourse were allowed. Thus when parents overtly arrange marriages by drawing up contracts among themselves or covertly arrange them by sending the children off to the "right" school, where they will meet the "right kind of people," they are expressing a form of the same evolutionary urge that the young lovers are expressing. The disagreement concerns the definition of the perfect couple.

Comedy reminds us that the people in that couple have to be considered. There are things beyond wealth, property, social position, education, and political philosophy to be entered into the equations. The external, measurable, identifying marks tend to dominate the requirements of the social forces, and they remove the personal element from the marriage, making it possible for a medieval princess to be married off before her teens or for a modern family to assume that the daughter will want to marry the boy next door. Comedy says that there is more to be considered. It does not say that love is all, although we often wish that it did. That is the message of the romance, which is essentially a private reading experience. In the public world of the comedy, love attracts the lovers, but it is not always enough. The Graustarkian operetta's birthmark is a silly solution, but its persistence indicates its importance. After the lovers have established their personal preferences, it is revealed that they did pick the right kind of person after all. The butler turns out to be the son of one of the oldest families on the East Coast, the slave is really the long-lost daughter of a neighboring businessman; if love were all, we would not need these final revelations. Comedy puts biology back into the cultural selection process: it demands consideration for youth, beauty, strength, animal spirit, aggression, ambition, and intelligence, which can get left by the road when custom becomes too strict and too stable. Because custom can be so intensely defensive and so powerful when it is attacked, comedy is aggressive, anarchical when necessary, and destructive of both the public image and the property that symbolizes the public image of the upholders of custom, the defenders and guardians of the present against the forces of the uncontrolled and different future that the comedic heroes represent. The ancient saturnalia may have expressed the temporary overthrow of all society, but comedy has come to express the improvement of society, symbolized in the child that will eventually come from the perfect couple.

The simpleminded little plot of traditional Western comedy is somewhat less than simple. Implicit in its simplest statements is a dedication to change and progress, in people, in society, and in the species. Because this change is so important, because the union of the right lovers is so critical, anything may be called in as a weapon to aid them. The most cherished persons and institutions of the society may be attacked, ridiculed, and even physically destroyed, especially those centered around property and bourgeois respectability, which must be altered, ever so slightly sometimes yet nonetheless altered, to be readmitted into a new and, one hopes, better society of the future. Film and stage together, for more than two thousand years, have shared this dedication through the plot and heroes of the comedy. American television, as we shall see, has suddenly and completely rejected it.

3 • The New Comedy of American Television

Two young women decide to rent an apartment together. Even though they are not paid much and would like a third roommate to help with the expenses, this is such a wonderful apartment they want to move in immediately, whether they find the roommate or not. In fact, they move in so quickly that they find one man left over from the previous tenant's moving-out party still passed out in the bathtub. When he comes around, they find that he has just lost his apartment, too. Since he is such a nice guy, and a marvelous cook, and since these are after all modern times, they decide to let him be the third roomate. Everything will be strictly platonic, of course, and besides, the arrangement will not be forever—just until they get a little more money or find a better roommate or something like that.

What a terrific idea! You can almost see the producers and writers drooling over the opportunities in the situation; the joke possibilities are practically endless. You can use all the marriage jokes, from her nylons in his shower to his beer cans in her flowerpots. You also can use all the young single jokes, from each trying to hide a lover from the others to the dope and wild parties. And then there are the sex jokes—nothing has to happen on camera, as long as people can think it might be happening off. Is he or isn't he, and with whom? Or all three together? Or maybe someone will think he is homosexual? And what can he see and hear by accident while living with two women? Of course, you can also crank out the sex stereotype jokes: let one of the women be tough and businesslike, and let him be neat and a good housekeeper. And what about the parents, friends, bosses, and people they date—how do they react to this odd situation? The mind boggles at the wealth of potential material.

Of course, the really good part comes after they have gotten to know each other and he falls for one of the women. He can be jealous of her boyfriends and start acting really weird. Even better, he can fall for one while the other one falls for him (it does not matter which one); the humorous fights, the tricks, the mistaken implications could provide great comic situations. Eventually, everyone will be so confused that no one will understand what is going on. But everything will work out somehow; you might be a bit kinky and daring and let them set up a real *ménage à trois*, but probably they will sort it all out and he will get the right girl for him and everyone will be happy.

If you have been anywhere near a television set in the last five years, you will of course immediately have recognized the premise of *Three's Company*, one of the most consistently popular sit-coms of recent years. All of the above has occurred except for the last part about the young man falling in love with one of the young women—that part has not happened yet, and is not likely to happen, either. It did happen in Noel Coward's *Design for Living*, both on stage and screen, although it was two men and one woman there and the *ménage* was Coward's chic solution. It also happened in much more innocent circumstances in the movie *The More the Merrier*, although there it was also two men. More important for this study, it also happened in *Man about the House*, the British sit-com on which *Three's Company* was based. After all the entanglements were sorted out, the series ended; when the characters "returned" later, they were in a completely new series in which the young couple, still with considerable parental opposition, opened their own restaurant.

While *Three's Company* is certainly not the best sit-com ever produced, it is also hardly the worst. As a rather typical example of the form, it is an excellent paradigm that immediately demonstrates the most important characteristic of the situation comedy. Its initial premise is pregnant with humorous possibilities, which is why it was produced in the first place. But all those possibilities must ultimately lead to the one thing the sit-com form can not allow, the moment when the situation ends, when one of those people must move out of the apartment. There are innumerable ways for the ending to develop, depending on the tone with which the initial premise is developed, but because the characters have an artificial grouping, absolutely nothing holds them together except convenience. At some point, someone has to get a raise, get a new job, fall in love, get married, have an accident, get angry, or otherwise change the situation. But they never do in the sit-com. It is especially revealing with this show, because of the famous Suzanne Somers controversy. After she made contract demands that the producers considered outrageous, Somers was written out of the show and her place was taken by a new actress. The new actress did not play the same character that Somers had played; she just moved in, and everything continued as if Chrissy had never been there. They even got a new landlord, and not only did he fail immediately to raise their rent or convert the place into a condominium, he also did not alter the living arrangements or the attitude toward the trio. Even when external circumstances forced changes upon the series, the producers made every effort to act as if no change had happened. The essential point was that there must be two women and one man in that apartment, no matter what happened; nothing could be allowed to upset that situation. This is the situation of Jean-Paul Sartre's *No Exit*, not of a comedy, and it is a situation shared in public and private literature only by the bitterly ironic domestic tragedies in the mold of Edith Wharton's *Ethan Frome*.

The most important point of any sit-com is not what happens; it is, rather, what does *not* happen. No one could rationally expect to see complete versions of the traditional comedy plot every half-hour. If every show progressed to the traditional happy ending in every episode, not only would the audience soon become bored, but the shows would soon have no place to go with their stories and would have to be canceled. In most sit-coms, the question does not even arise—the couples are already married, or love and romance are not particularly important to the basic situation, usually a workplace. But *Three's Company* makes the missing points obvious, because its format not only offers the opportunity but demands its development. And yet it resists. The situation remains inviolate and undisturbed, no matter what transitory events may occur. The sit-com resists the change of the traditional comedy plot, but in the process it also resists all change of any kind.

Situation comedy earns its name in at least two different ways. First, individual episodes are built around situations rather than plots. A known set of characters is thrust into circumstances out of the ordinary, with humorous results. This technique was fairly common among the persona comics of silent and sound shorts. Writers and comics asked, what would happen if Charlie Chaplin were a policeman? Or if Laurel and Hardy tried to build a house? And so on. In television, it shows up in *I Love Lucy*, when Lucy thinks Ricky has been drafted; in *Alice*, when Flo finds a sack of money in Mel's diner; in *The Odd Couple*, when Felix Ungar stages an opera; in *Laverne & Shirley*, when the roommates have a fire in the bedroom; and in hundreds of other similar situations. Humor is derived both from the situation itself—certain things may happen that would be funny to anyone—and from the conflict of the character's personality with this situation, which might be normal for someone else but is very unusual for this person. The main thrust of the episode is to show how the characters cope with this particular situation. A significant amount of the humor depends on exactly how well the audience knows the characters. For example, staging an opera is not automatically funny, but when Felix and Oscar do so, it will be, because we know Felix cannot take the strain and Oscar cannot stand the music.

Sometimes, of course, the situation may be absolutely normal, or at least not out of the ordinary. The numerous family comedies develop their situations out of the normal problems of children growing up. What happens when a teenager wants to be a rock star? What happens when girls start to notice boys, and vice versa? What happens if the kids get in a fight, or stop believing in Santa Claus, or bring home a pet cat? Norman Lear's *All in the Family* and *Maude* opened up a lot of new territory by introducing normal situations previously avoided for political or social reasons, such as abortion and minority neighbors, but the procedure stayed the same. The characters were thrust into a situation and emerged from it with some solution at the end of the episode, with varying amounts of humor along the way. For these kinds of episodes, it helps if we know the characters, but what is important is not their eccentricity but their familiarity and normality. We share the humor because we have shared (or expect to share) the experience and, in some of the Norman Lear productions at least, we look to learn the socially proper way to respond to the situation.

Second, and much more important, the series as a whole is built around situation rather than events, actions, or even particular characters for the most part. People in the business usually refer to this as the "format" for a series. Well-known performers may not be successful in a series unless they also find the proper format, and the proper format may make stars of unknowns overnight. It is this situation that is essential to all understanding of the series as a whole, because the situation is what holds the series together. Characters may come and go, up to a point, but the situation must stay the same. Series that have survived cast changes are rare, but series that have survived changes in their basic situations and have sustained their ratings can be counted on one finger—*All in the Family*. For reasons of economics rather than philosophy or aesthetics, the basic situation of a successful series must be eternal.

If we are to understand the revolutionary nature of the form of the situation comedy, we must examine the form as it uses both kinds of situation, the situation of the individual episode and the situation of the series as a whole. When both are considered, it becomes obvious that the sit-com is like no other form of literature and shares almost nothing with what we have always known as comedy.

The situation comedy of American television is a most peculiar animal. It is both short and long: a normal episode may run between twenty-two and twenty-six minutes, depending on commercial limitations set by the Federal Communications Commission and titles, credits, promotional announcements, and other assorted factors. The series itself may run for years (the current sit-com record is *The Adventures of Ozzie and Harriet*, with fourteen years and well over three hundred episodes). It is very much like a collection of short subjects, each independent and complete in itself, and yet the episodes are not shorts and are not complete. It is like a serial, and yet it can be, and often is, shown, understood, and enjoyed completely out of sequence; many times, there is no sequence. It is like a picaresque novel, with a number of discrete adventures for the hero, and yet the adventures always come to the hero rather than the hero going to the adventure. It is the only form of performance or entertainment that is begun by writers and producers precisely in the hope that it will have no end, that it will, with luck, be a new *Ozzie and Harriet*, *All in the Family*, or *I Love Lucy*, that it will not only run forever (which is the hope of every Broadway producer), but will do so with new material every week. It is, in fact, something new under the Klieg lights.

This mixture of elements from so many different sources has served to disguise the important changes in the situation comedy as a form. Anyone looking at an individual series or individual episodes may find examples of almost anything, especially the various types of humor and

humorous characters. The something-for-everybody aspect of television
programming is most pronounced in the situation comedies, and a
viewer or a critic may find almost any kind of humor, from the local
yokel jokes of *The Beverly Hillbillies*, to the knockabout farce of *Laverne
& Shirley*, to the social consciousness of *Maude*, to something approaching wit and sophistication in *The Mary Tyler Moore Show*. At the same
time, this variety has disguised some extremely important similarities
among all of the successful comedy series.

Despite the similarities of episode length and subject matter, a
regular series episode is not the same as a film short subject or a weekly
one-act comedy play or sketch. Laurel and Hardy's *Hog Wild*, for
example, provides a situation that is similar to many an episode in a
man-about-the-house television comedy of the fifties. The principal
character has some job that has to be done and during which all kinds of
things go wrong. In this case Hardy is trying to put up an antenna with
the help of his friend Laurel. For Laurel and Hardy, this situation leads
to an orgy of destructive sight gags, which most series, for reasons to be
discussed later, would not develop. However, this short also includes a
tremendous amount of other material that the television episode would
not include. Most important, it includes exposition. It tells us Hardy is
married and Laurel is not. This is important, because the last time they
were seen, in *The Laurel and Hardy Murder Case*, neither was married,
and in the next short, *Another Fine Mess*, neither will be married.
Hardy's wife here is different from his wife in other shorts. His home is
different from his home in other shorts. The only things that tie *Hog
Wild* to any other short subject are the personalities of Laurel and Hardy
themselves. As traditional persona comics, they warn the audience to
expect a particular type of humor. But anyone in the audience may
enjoy and understand *everything* in the episode without ever seeing
another of their shorts.

The episode of the television situation comedy does not have the
same kind of exposition, because it does not need it. The audience is
expected to know not only who the characters are, but also where they
are and why they are there. There will be exposition to present this
week's situation, but not exposition of the relationships and background
of the principal characters. One of the problems with a show like *Three's
Company* is that if you did not see the early episodes, you spend all your
time asking, "Why is that boy still there? Why hasn't he moved out?
Why does the landlord *still* think he is a homosexual?" This may or may

not be important to a particular episode, but it makes each episode incomplete. No matter how slight, how brief, or how simple the material in the sketch, the afterpiece, or the short subject, each of them was intended to stand alone, to be complete within itself, even when it lacked developed plots of any moment. No matter how brilliant the material in an episode of a television situation comedy, it cannot stand alone. Thus, when we look for the structure of the form, we must look beyond the weekly episode to something larger and longer, to the series as a whole.

At the same time, the sit-com cannot really be considered a variation on the most open-ended form, the serial. The serial, whether in newspaper, magazine, or film, consists of a number of episodes, each episode usually short, part of a larger whole, but each intended to be seen or read separately. These episodes may be discrete or they may depend on the cliff-hanger ending to draw the customer back for the next installment. The television series is different, however, in one important respect. Although the viewer needs to see several episodes to fully understand the individual unit, he does not need to see all of the previous or the following episodes to understand. No television comedy series begins each episode with "in our last episode..." because it does not matter what happened in the last one. In fact, it may hinder the success of the series if the audience knows and remembers what happened last week.

The classic case in point is *Rhoda.* In the 1974-75 season, Rhoda was freshly ensconced with a new husband in a new town in a show of her own, after years with Mary Tyler Moore. Following the wedding episode, which was one of the highest rated single episodes since the three networks began competing, *Rhoda* was the number 6 show. In 1975, it was number 8, no appreciable difference (actually number 7, since *Rich Man, Poor Man*, an extremely limited series, was ahead of it). Then, in 1976, for perhaps the best artistic motives but some of the dumbest business motives in the history of television, Rhoda and Joe separated and eventually divorced. The ratings collapsed, the show dropped out of the top 25, and the next season saw a major overhaul of the format—new friends, new job, new apartment, the works—to no avail. Although the network kept holding on, hoping the new format would catch on and draw back the audience, it never did, and the show was eventually canceled in the 1978 season.[1] The situation in the situation comedy changed, and the audience could not cope with that

63

change. For at least a few episodes, the producers tried to treat the form like a serial, and its initial success was completely destroyed in a way that made it impossible for the series to recover.

Before continuing with this point, some terms should be defined. For the purposes of this study, the measures of success and survival for television comedy are those used by the industry itself. Survival means the show stays on the air. Success means it stays on the air long enough to become syndicated, which usually means a show must have more than three seasons on the networks, to provide enough episodes for syndicating stations to broadcast them in the same time period five or more times a week without repeating them too obviously close together. Three years is the accepted minimum for this, although now that the networks are down to fewer than twenty-two episodes a year, successful stripping, as this programming is called, requires about five years of *Laverne & Shirley* to equal three years of *I Love Lucy*. This further means that the ratings are the most important way of evaluating the success of a particular series. Despite the arguments about the validity of the Neilsens, there is no doubt that, in the business of television, they determine what stays on the air and what leaves. Using them is no different from using the box office take as the ultimate arbiter of films and stage productions. Sometimes good programs are taken off, but most often the shows that are canceled are bad by any standards, just as most plays that flop are pretty bad. Among the successful shows, time, luck, and critical opinion determine which are classics and which are only popular, but all eventually have to establish their popularity with a significant proportion of the potential audience, or they are not seen often enough to reach classic status. (For a list of shows that meet these criteria for success, see the appendix.)

It is tempting to see the sit-com as a video version of the modern comic novel, with a series of sequential but not necessarily causally related episodes. Much of film and television is, after all, based on the traditions and the structural vocabulary of the novel rather than of the drama. Many of the comic novels simply follow a principal character through his life and report the interesting and funny things that happen to him. In a similar fashion, many of the sit-coms ostensibly follow characters, or more often a family, through their lives. Many of the earliest practitioners of the form, such as the Nelson family, used their real families and based their fictional material at least in part on their real life experiences. Yet even here the sit-com resists some essential

64

connections. Despite the appearance of movement through life, few events from "real" life ever occur. How many of the numerous couples who have peopled the successful sit-coms, for example, have ever had a baby? Lucy did on *I Love Lucy*, as did Samantha on *Bewitched* (in both cases because the actress got pregnant during the shooting schedule and either had to have a baby or had to leave a successful series rather than because the producers thought it would be a good idea). Barbara Feldon's twins on *Get Smart* were a ratings ploy that failed to save the show's last year. That is all in thirty-five years. All the other families came with fully grown children, at least old enough to read their cue cards, and if they ever needed a new child, they just adopted one of the requisite size and shape. Adding a baby to a couple that became successful without one would upset the situation. Thus, series principals actually experience few normal lifetime activities—few ever change jobs, get married or divorced, or even change their apartments.

More important for this particular tradition, the sit-com characters never *go* anywhere. The comic novel heroes are active; they go places and do things. The sit-com people sit at home or around the job and wait for things to happen to them. In 1955 Lucy went to Hollywood and in 1956 she went to Europe. Since then, only the Partridge Family in the early seventies has gone on the road for anything, and then the family took home with them in the form of a tour bus. *Alice* was based on a film about a woman who traveled the roads to escape a bad marriage until she accidentally wandered into Mr. Right while in a temporary waitress job. When it got to the sit-com, however, Alice was permanently stuck in her coffee shop and perfectly happy at the situation. Few waitresses stay at the same job for six years, especially in a coffee shop, yet Alice does, although she has supposedly already gone through several jobs and towns to get there and is on her way to Hollywood to seek a singing career.

M*A*S*H is even more curious. Despite the fact that the Korean War had the most fluid front lines of any war ever fought by American troops, the *Mobile* Army Surgical Hospital is never moved. Some strange magic keeps it in the same place all the time yet always within reach of the front lines, whether before or after the Chinese joined the war, or after Inchon, or after the peace talks began, all of which have been mentioned on various shows. In regular viewing, I have found only three episodes in which the hospital has moved at all (the bug-out show, the trip to the caves where Hawkeye got claustrophobia, and once when

65

Frank moved them across the road just to prove he could do it), and in all three cases, it was moved back to where it began by the end of the episode. Many sit-com premises encourage stability, particularly those built around middle-class home life, but even when the series is based on a premise that demands movement and action, it resists. Thus, it rejects comparison with even the most generalized forms of literary comedy.

The sit-com, however, is a dramatic form of the comedy. We watch it as audience. We do not read it, and we do not listen to someone tell it to us. The audience may be very small in our living room, but the broader audience includes simultaneously the entire nation (or at least the eastern two-thirds—the West Coast showing is delayed because of time zone changes). The makers of the sit-coms encourage us to believe we are part of a larger audience with "live" tapings and laugh tracks. So, ultimately it is to the comedy in the dramatic tradition that the sit-com must be compared.

Every television series requires a certain amount of repetition. Some characters appear on a regular basis, doing the same kinds of things. But the sit-com carries this repetition to an extreme unmatched by any other genre of regular television programming. In the process of rejecting the basic comic plot, it has all but rejected the concept of plot. William Gibson has provided a valuable perspective on the question:

> A play begins when a world in some state of equipoise, always
> uneasy, is broken into by a happening. . . . A play is an energy
> system, and the business of the precipitating event is to intro-
> duce a disequilibrium, that is, to release energy. . . and once
> begun, the "play" is that of contradictory energies working to
> arrive at a new equilibrium, if it kills everybody.[2]

In the sit-com, the disequilibrium is broken into by a happening that establishes the equipoise—Jack moves into the *Three's Company* apartment, Mary Tyler Moore leaves home and gets a job, Andy is hired to shake up the programming of WKRP. Once that occurs, nothing else ever happens. Nothing changes. Individual episodes may begin with a threat to the equilibrium of the situation, but by the end of the episode equilibrium is restored. But unlike any other form, the sit-com does not reach a *new* equilibrium; it achieves the equilibrium with which the episode began.

The basic plot of the television situation comedy is a circle rather than a line. In the traditional basic comedy plot, some characters, usually a boy and a girl, start at point A and want to get somewhere else, usually in bed together, at point B. No matter how many twists and turns, no matter what the confusions, at the end of the play the characters have moved from A to B. In the usual situation comedy, however, the character is at point A and does not want to get to anywhere else, no matter how much he protests that he does not like where he is. When something or someone threatens to shove him over to point B, he somehow manages to avoid the move and gets back safely to point A. Anything that threatens the basic situation is repelled or expelled, and all live happily ever after only if they accept the present. Such plot as exists lies in the situation of the show rather than in the events of the show. At the episode level, the principal characters meet situations and deal with them and then go on, except that they never go on to anything. The audience needs to know the larger situation, the fundamental premises of the series, or the individual episodes make no sense, or at least make less sense than they should. But the viewers need not know what happened last week because what happened last week does not matter. In fact, as in the case of *Rhoda*, if the audience remembers what happened last week or last year, confusion or particular problems might make viewers feel uncomfortable with the series and quit watching. For the television comedy series, the situation is the story. Seen as a whole, each series has a plot in which the principal element is the suggestion that nothing important has ever happened.

If you come onto a series in reruns that you never watched before, some peculiar things occur to you. The most striking is that you have no idea where any particular episode belongs in the shape of the whole series. If you did not watch the series originally and did not pay much attention to its publicity, you cannot even guess what year the episode appeared, or whether it was near the beginning or the end of the series. The various episodes live in a kind of time-warp without any reference to the other episodes. I know of no other performance form with this feature. Anyone with experience can watch half an hour of an unfamiliar movie or play and at the very least tell whether that half hour comes near the beginning, the middle, or the end. The amount of exposition, the intensity of complexity and suspense, and the number of references to both past events and expected future occurrences all provide clues that place any particular segment in some imaginary sequence of events. The sit-com has no imaginary sequence of events. The things that happen to the principal characters can happen in any order, even in their original airings. The order of many episodes is switched before the initial showings on the networks. The sequence of many others is changed by the network even after early showings. In the 1979 rerun season, ABC chose to rerun episodes of *Mork & Mindy*, the format of which certainly required some explanation, not only out of sequence but actually in reverse order, ending the summer sequence with the first episode. Occasionally, some episodes have been in two parts, a process apparently begun by *All in the Family*, but for the most part the two-part episodes have now disappeared. When the material takes more than one half hour, the networks tend to use it in an hour-long "special edition," such as the bug-out episode of *M*A*S*H*, (the first episode in the year following Col. Potter's arrival), rather than try to establish a sequence that lasts through even two weeks

The basic sit-com plot formula can be illustrated by almost any episode of any successful series. Like so much of television comedy, the formula in its purest form can be found in many episodes of *I Love Lucy*. In several different episodes, Ricky plans something special or unusual in his nightclub act. Lucy, as always, wants to break into show business and tries to horn in, over Ricky's opposition. Somehow, she sneaks into the act, wrecks it, and makes a fool of herself. However, Ricky forgives her, and everyone is restored to happiness at the fadeout. The shape of this formula may be seen every week: there is a problem; after much consideration, the problem is solved. But the problem is solved in such a way that no change results. Everything goes back as it was at the beginning of the episode. Lucy never learns to stay out of the nightclub shows, and Ricky never relents and makes her a part of them. In a few weeks, she will do the same thing again, with exactly the same results. The solution rejects all changes, and nothing that might in any way affect the basic situation ever carries over to the next episode.

This formula, this new plot, is a constant in situation comedies, no matter what the outlook or style of their humor. *All in the Family's* Archie Bunker, bigoted and ignorant, never learns his lesson, nor does Meathead ever give in. In *The Andy Griffith Show*, Andy always finds a solution that returns Mayberry to the peace and quiet with which each episode begins. In *I Dream of Jeannie*, the spells are always erased and things put back so that the magic appears never to have existed. The situation is only a situation, never an event. At the end of the episode, the original order is restored, as if the middle never existed at all, almost as if all occurrences were a dream.

Even when there is the appearance of change, the change does not in fact exist. In the *I Love Lucy* episode in which Ricky is worried about going bald, Lucy concocts a perfectly disagreeable treatment, which he will have to continue for six months. In a humorous twist, instead of being shaken out of his obsession, Ricky agrees, thereby leaving Lucy with the comic discomfort. The treatment, however, appears in no later episodes, and no further mention is ever made of Ricky going bald or even thinking he might be.

The same process is at work on a more sophisticated level in the *Mary Tyler Moore Show* episode in which Mary meets Ted Bessell. After years of dating and losing the man at the end of each episode, Mary meets Mr. Right and is ready to tell him she loves him, only to discover another woman just getting out of his bed. After a painful scene, she forgives him and agrees to stay the night, because she still loves him. This is a major change, a cataclysmic development not only in the series and the image of Mary but in the life of any character.

As if in recognition of this importance, Bessell returned in another episode in which his relationship with Mary is threatened by the return of Mary's old love. After a difficult evening, and a serious dilemma, Mary rejects the old love, vows to stay with Bessell, and seriously professes her love in a very professional, intensely acted scene far above the level of work in almost any comedy series and even above the already high standards of that series. This was a realistic and serious event in the life of the Mary character, an event with major implications for the series as a whole.

Then, at the end of that episode, Bessell is seen leaving for a "couple of weeks," with no explanation. One assumes it is business of some kind. And he never returns. Much more important, however, is that *no one notices he is gone.* By the next week, he has simply ceased to exist. Murray never says, "Hey, whatever happened to . . . ?" Lou never reminds her, "Yeah, Mary, remember when you had this big thing for. . . ." (In fact, not long afterward there comes the famous episode in which Mary and Lou try to have a romance and fail.) The previous episodes had made Ted Baxter a nosy partner in the romance, and even Ted, the supreme clod, never says, "What happened to the hot romance?" or "Where's my old buddy. . . ?" If you missed those episodes, you never knew they existed; they vanished without a trace and for all practical purposes simply did not exist. It all looked as if something had changed, but it had not. It looked like an event, a genuine piece of plot development, but after the commercials cleared, everything was just as it was before Bessell ever appeared on the scene.

It is not easy to write material like this. The writer really has to work to find a way to suggest changes that are sufficient to maintain interest in an episode but that are not in fact changes after all. Sometimes there are no subtle solutions available. Ultimately, the series must lose all contact with the reality in which it is supposed to exist. Ricky Ricardo gets a film contract and he and Lucy take off for Hollywood in *I Love Lucy*. But what would the show be like without Fred and Ethel? So Fred and Ethel pack up and go with them, despite the fact that Fred makes his living as the resident manager of his apartment building and is outrageously tight-fisted as well. Gilligan wrecks every escape attempt from *Gilligan's Island*, yet the others continue to allow him to be the key element in each new attempt. In *All in the Family* Archie celebrates Meathead's college degree, until Meathead decides to go to graduate school and stay in Archie's house. On *My Three Sons*, one son eventually grows up, so Fred MacMurray simply adopts a new one to keep the family at three, and when William Frawley, the curmudgeon uncle, dies in real life, he is replaced by William Demarest as a new curmudgeon uncle. Eddie Albert lives on the farm at *Green Acres* for six years and still never gets the house finished. Even after the *Happy Days* kids are forced to graduate from high school because they look thirty years old, they still hang around with Fonzie.

The initial situation changes only when things are not working as well as the programmers and producers expect. A sure sign of ratings problems is that they begin tinkering with the format, and yet such tinkering is almost always doomed to failure. The show may be "better," as they thought *Rhoda* and *Mork & Mindy* would be, but the audience never accepts the change; except for *All in the Family*, any sit-com that has tried to alter an established format has died a quick ratings death. Old viewers are either confused or upset by the change, and new viewers are never attracted. As *Get Smart* began to wear down, Max and Agent 99 got married, but the ratings kept sliding. When *The New Dick Van Dyke Show*, set in Tucson, failed to live up to expectations, it packed up and moved to Hollywood, but still had to be canceled. The best case in point is *The Doris Day Show*. When the show premiered in 1968, it seemed to have everything going for it, especially its star, one of the most consistently bankable actresses in all of Hollywood, with proven drawing power across Middle America. Its initial situation seemed promising as well, with proven elements: an attractive widow and two cute sons moving to the country, providing not only family humor but also humor built from the conflict between city and country. This also provided a sophistication level bridging audiences that responded to country comedies such as *The Andy Griffith Show* and the Ross Hunter movies in which Day had made her name. Unfortunately, the show never quite caught on in that form and, rather than lose the ratings Day should have delivered, they began tinkering with the format.

In 1969 Day went back to work in the city as a commuter from the farm. This change delivered the success missing in the first year, probably because she got to wear nice clothes while continuing the normal family life. In the Neilsen averages for that season the show ranked number 10. But for some reason the producers and network were not satisfied, and in 1970 she and the boys left the farm and went back to the city. Doris Day was now a more regular working parent. The ratings dropped to number 20, still respectable but not nearly what they should have been. In 1971, without warning or much explanation, the family disappeared, and the show edged closer to *The Mary Tyler Moore Show* in format and tone, but the ratings continued to slide, down to number 24. In the next season, the show did not average in the top 25 and was duly canceled at the end of the season. [3]

Once a sit-com finds an audience, the situation is frozen in place; it simply cannot change and stay on the air. Any change is a sign of desperation, not a sign of plot development. Because the successful sit-com is built to resist change of any kind, it rejects not only the basic comic plot but also every impulse, attitude, and characteristic of the comedy.

Nowhere is this more pronounced than in the development of the sit-com hero. It is something of any anomaly even to use the term *hero* in relation to the situation comedy. Almost by definition, the hero as he is commonly understood can not occur there. In all other forms of Western dramatic material, the hero is committed to bringing about a change of some kind, usually to making the world a better place. The hero may succeed, fail, die, or become rich and famous. But from Oedipus to Dirty Harry, from Pseudolus to Cyrano, the dramatic hero has reflected the roles of the mythical hero by daring to challenge existing natural or social structures and, one hopes, producing something a little better. Though the heroes in comedy have most often expressed this effort through the symbol of male and female union, they have been involved in the same heroic pursuit of the future as the heroes in the crudest melodrama or the most intense tragedy.

Since the situation comedy is committed to the prevention of change and the protection of the present, the hero must be different, someone who keeps things the way they are rather than who dares to alter them. This inversion, in effect, makes the family the central unit, with a power it never had in the traditional comedy. In the process, it inverts and perverts all of the traditional roles and relationships within the family.

The family has always been the fundamental social unit of comedy. The boy and girl are usually in revolt against their own parents and at the end are headed toward their own new family in which they will become the parents. But where traditional comedy concerned itself with children trying to break away from their parents, the TV sit-com deals with children who almost desperately refuse to leave, even long after they are grown and ought to be acting as adults.

This feature did not appear in the earliest sit-coms, although there are signs of it in *The Adventures of Ozzie and Harriet*, when the Nelson boys stayed close enough to visit weekly even after they got married, and in *The George Burns and Gracie Allen Show*, with the college-boy son. Initially, the television comedy family was the basic middle-class family, so common in the fifties and early sixties that a popular joke claimed that if *Hamlet* were to be made into a series, he would probably marry Ophelia and have three kids and a pet bear. Mom, Dad, the kids, the house, and the pet were the formula. You distinguished one show from the next by counting the kids at the table or by the favorite animal. The Nelsons (*The Adventures of Ozzie and Harriet*), the Andersons (*Father Knows Best*), the Partridges (*The Partridge Family*), the Bradys (*The Brady Bunch*), the Cleavers (*Leave It to Beaver*), the Williamses (*The Danny Thomas Show*), and the Stones (*The Donna Reed Show*) were all the same family. But the problem with families with real kids is that real kids grow up, and every inch the kids grow brings the show that much closer to the end of its basic situation.

One solution is to keep the kids as close as possible after they get too long in the tooth to be believable children. This technique was used by the Nelsons and later revived by such shows as *All in the Family* and *Happy Days*. Another solution is to keep plugging new kids into slots when old ones grow up, whether by adoption, as on *My Three Sons*, by taking in an exchange student, as on *The Danny Thomas Show*, or just by a general accretion of bodies, as seems to have occurred on *One Day at a Time* after Mackenzie Phillips left the show.

But all of these solutions leave something to be desired; things are just not the same, no matter how close the approximation might be. At some point in the sixties, a much better solution was developed, the single-parent family. Most of these shows revolved around single fathers, although overwhelmingly single-parent families in the United States, because of divorce and alimony practices, are headed by females. Such a predilection may be partially explained by certain assumptions about humor. Since mothers are supposed to know how to raise kids, there are more humorous possibilities in forcing the single father to take up what has been traditionally the woman's role. For the most part, in Western societies the family unit has divided responsibility between mother and father for the different aspects of child-rearing. The mother has been, for most of the time, the representative of the child. Her job has been to nurture and develop the child to the best of his potential, at first physically, through control of food and general health, and then also emotionally, through love and encouragement. The father has represented society. He has provided the means of existence, but in return he has also been the ultimate control, the punisher, the court of last resort. His job has been to control the individualistic tendencies of the child, to train the child in the ways of the world, and to see that the child grows up to fit in with the rules and requirements of society at large. The mother has had certain functions in this area as well, primarily as a first line of defense; she has been supposed to establish those social rules so that the father did not have to worry about them. The mother has generally tried to establish the rules by love and example, while the father has done so by authority and punishment. There are thus far more humorous possibilities in situations where the traditional father has to act like the mother than in the reverse. Television programmers emphasized this tradition, almost without exception, until the success of *One Day at a Time* demonstrated that the audience as a whole would accept a female single parent.

At first glance, this seems to be an unlikely solution to the problem of children who outgrow the format and critics such as Rose Goldsen have claimed that these shows proved television was opposed to the family.[4] It was not really opposed—it was just looking for a "better" family.

One of the difficulties of a traditional family is that it is really two groups, parents and children. When there are two parents, they can at any moment become a separate unit that excludes the children. The spouse can provide emotional, psychological, and social support without the rest of the family. Removing one of those parents forces the remaining adult to depend more on the children for this support, thus paradoxically making the family unit tighter and more cohesive. For reasons of humor, the removed spouse was usually the wife, but the remaining father had to depend on the children as much as the children depended on him. Most of these fathers were ostensibly looking for new wives (*My Three Sons, Family Affair, The Courtship of Eddie's Father, The Andy Griffith Show*), but no women were ever found who could offer as much as the family the man already had. In *The Danny Thomas Show* the father remarried and carried on, but that was in 1957; after that, if the character decided to remarry, as did Andy Griffith, the series ended.

A curious result was the increasing sophistication of the children. American entertainment has always loved the precocious youngster, who reflected the purity of the innocent. But television youngsters soon became wise in the ways of the world, adults before their time. They knew the ways of the world long before their parents did. In more ostensibly lower-class situations, they showed this by being street wise in ways their parents were not, as on *Good Times*. In more typical middle-class situations, they simply provided the love and understanding that the missing wives would have provided and often fulfilled adult functions within the family, no matter how childlike their functions might be outside. Eventually, the powers that be in television allowed women to head those single-parent families, beginning tentatively with the widows of *The Lucy Show* and *The Ghost and Mrs. Muir* and culminating in the divorcée heroines of *Alice* and *One Day at a Time*. The latter show in particular continued the children's role as an emotional support for the mother, as she also was for them.

From there it is only a small step to children who are already adult. This step was first taken by *The Beverly Hillbillies*, with Jethro and Ellie Mae fully grown physically, whatever their mental ages might have been. It was not far from there to *All in the Family, Sanford and Son, Chico and the Man,* and the newly popular *Too Close for Comfort,* which provides the titillation possibilities of *Three's Company* while the girls' real father serves as their landlord.

At the same time, this is still an awkward situation to maintain. The real world on occasion does intrude, and viewers begin to wonder why those kids are still hanging around. This problem led to the artificial family, a new concept that maintained all the advantages of the family arrangement while providing a sense of permanence by using only adults. The quintessential example is *The Mary Tyler Moore Show*, which ushered in an entire generation of similar programs, most of which ostensibly revolved around people at work. Mary worked in a newsroom, but she was surrounded by what quickly became a new family for her, a sixties single-parent TV family, consisting of a father figure (Mr. Grant), three kids (Mary, Murray—they even sound like siblings—and baby Ted), and two crazy neighbors who might be aunts (Rhoda and Phyllis, later replaced by Georgette and Sue Ann). They all went to separate places to sleep, but the real life of the show revolved around these people as family members who supported each other in complex emotional ways that went far beyond the needs of friendship or the working place. This artificial family was developed in a number of popular variations: *The Bob Newhart Show*, *Alice*, *WKRP*, *House Calls*, and *Taxi* are only the most obvious and popular of dozens of examples.

Even *M*A*S*H* became a sit-com about a family. Because it has received such an enormous amount of praise for some very real achievements, it needs to be examined in detail to see how this successful sit-com completely overturned the traditional sources from which the series was developed. Adapted from a raucous, outrageous, and successful film, the series has been one of the most daring and sophisticated productions of the seventies, achieving a success in character development and structural innovations as well as topicality that makes most traditional sit-coms pale in comparison. It is the only sit-com in American television history to make not just one but several major cast changes and still retain its ratings. A military comedy, it even went so far as to kill one of its major characters (although this was carefully done off camera). It has also made some significant changes is characterization, the most remarkable of which is the growth and change of Major Houlihan. Beginning as a bigoted, hypocritical antagonist, she shifted to a put-upon mistress, then a desperate married woman, and after a divorce to a friend and colleague of the rest of the unit, a growth matched by no other series regular that I can recall. The show also manages to be clearly and consistently antiwar, thus giving it a surface "message" that can pass for controversy and daring in the world of prime time programming. At the same time, this sophistication also reinforces the messages of the other situation comedies, giving *M*A*S*H* essentially the same message as *Father Knows Best*.

M*A*S*H has been on for so long and has been so successful that it is something of a shock to see the film again or to see episodes from the first season in reruns. During its initial season, the series used much of the structure and relationships of the film, and *it was not particularly successful*. It did not average in the top 25 series that year; for whatever reasons, which are unknown at this time, CBS stuck with the series, and the next year it vaulted to an average ranking of number 4. It has been out of the top 10 only once since then, during the season when Trapper John and Henry Blake both left. But the series in 1973 that suddenly became popular was not at all the same series that had premiered in 1972. Not only were seven small regular roles gone, but also every major relationship between the principal characters was redefined. This redefinition of relationships shifted the show from a military comedy to a family comedy. It was only after this shift that the series achieved its signal popularity.

In the film and in the series during the first year, Colonel Blake is the traditional comedy Army officer, a bumbling idiot who is saved from disaster by clerk Radar, an enlisted man who always knows what Henry wants and needs before Henry does. His surgeons get away with outrageous behavior because they are crack doctors and there is a war on. Frank Burns and Margaret (Hot Lips) Houlihan are Old Army, and in the film Burns is a religious fanatic as well. Blake would be on their side if circumstances allowed it, and if he were competent enough to do anything. The men are surrounded by sexually attractive nurses, especially in 1972 Nurse Cutler, who, it is suggested, is sleeping with both Hawkeye and Trapper when they are not bouncing around among the other four regular nurses and numerous incidental ones.

By 1973, all of this is gone. Radar quits being a slick, almost city-tough enlisted man who resembles Joseph Heller's Ex-PFC Wintergreen of *Catch-22*. He becomes a lost little Iowa farm boy, with a rediscovered virginity and a teddy bear. Blake becomes Radar's surrogate father, and Radar's sensitivity to the colonel's needs becomes a sign of his respect and love for a still ineffectual but kind-hearted guy. Blake's incompetence as a commander is attributed to his civilian unfamiliarity with military ways mixed with his almost overwhelming desire not to hurt anyone's feelings by making a decision. No one asked how, if he was a draftee with no ambitions, he came to be a colonel. Although Larry Linville never tried to bring the intensity to the role of Frank Burns that Robert Duvall brought in the film—such power and fanaticism are still a bit strong for television—even Frank Burns still had to change. In the second year, Frank's ostentatious Bible reading tapers off and his surgical skills decline. Frank had been an incompetent surgeon, but the Army did not know that; somewhere during the second season, everyone but Hot Lips knows it, and Hawkeye even becomes chief surgeon after a couple of seasons. Even more important, it becomes clear that Frank is a draftee, too, just like everyone else. He wants to order people around and hold inspections and so on because he is a little kid playing at soldier, not because he is a career military man who lives (and drives himself crazy) by the book. This is an extremely important change, because it puts all the male regulars in the same boat: all are draftees, all want to be civilians again, and *none* of them is really military. The film, and much of the first season, had built its conflicts between the free, civilian impulses of the draftee doctors and enlisted men and the regulated, hypocritical, and destructive world of the military. By the second season, the conflicts are between individual personalities who are part of an ad hoc family or between that entire family and the military forces outside. It is significant that whenever Frank goes over Colonel Blake's or later Colonel Potter's head with complaints to headquarters, the Army always rejects Frank's complaints. He has ceased to be a representative of the organized ways of the world and become a part, although a clearly unhappy and unaccepted part, of the family.

In this new family, the commander has ceased to command and begins to mediate. He was the decision maker, but he becomes an increasingly wise mediator, who lets the "boys" work out their problems if they can and settles arguments when no one else can. Blake becomes a clear father for Radar, but he also becomes an admittedly unwilling father for the rest of the unit. The center of the series becomes the Swamp, the messy bedroom of the boys. There the three inhabitants live, fight, spy on each other, play practical jokes, and, when things get out of control, tattle on each other to the colonel. After Harry Morgan joined the series as Colonel Potter, this relationship became more obvious, because Potter was much older, wiser, and more competent than Blake (and also called everyone "son"), but it was underway long before that. When Frank loses both his attachment to the Army and his fanaticism, he becomes a petulant little boy. After he leaves, the new man, Major Winchester, is very competent; his only problem is his social pretension, which provides opportunities for humor and insult but no real threat to the basic situation. Winchester soon becomes just one of the boys as well. With Potter as the white-haired patriarch, the unit is a tight, sit-com family: a father, three teenage boys plus one baby, Aunt Hot Lips (who gradually comes to be just like one of the family), crazy Uncle Klinger, and eventually a minister who drops in regularly, just like back in the good old days.

The show had one real crisis and one significant drop in the ratings at the beginning of the 1975 season. But it recovered by making cast changes that strengthened the family in the show. The changes made when Henry and Trapper simultaneously left the series could have wrecked the show completely. That they did not has to do with the "improvements" made by the new characters. The one problem of the 1973 shift to a family arrangement was that Trapper really had no place in the family; as a comrade in arms, he was fine, but as a family member he was so much like Hawkeye—bright, talented, a little wild—that they sometimes seemed like twins. No series needs twins who are alike; twins are only fun if they are different. Trapper's replacement, B. J. Hunnicutt, was different. He was still on Hawkeye's side against the Frank Burnses of the world, but he was much more stable than Hawkeye. This gave a much better set of "boys": one who was bright but a little wild, one who was bright but very stable (the kind who always got good grades and cleaned up his room as a teenager), and one who was immature, spoiled, and jealous. Colonel Potter, as already noted, clarified and intensified the commander's role as father. Finally, the family was perfected when Burns left and was replaced by Winchester, a signal improvement because he was also bright and capable. His pretensions were just those of the smart kid who likes to show off for the family and show up his brothers when he can. Now it was a perfect family, because the father was both authoritative and understanding and all the boys were both smart and good at heart. Eventually the baby would grow up and "graduate," but his place could be taken by Uncle Max Klinger, and the family would continue unaffected in its fifties-dream perfection.

All problems, aside from the war itself, can be solved within the family. Whenever the Army intervenes, it always disrupts the existing routine. The unit establishes its routine, and outsiders—wounded soldiers with problems, Colonel Flagg from Army Intelligence, visiting generals, the war itself—disturb that routine. At the end of each episode, the outsiders are ejected and the family vindicated and preserved— the wounded are healed (or die) and are shipped out, Colonel Flagg is tricked and leaves, the generals decide that this is one great hospital and leave the staff to their own devices. The family stays and the family always wins. Those who can fill roles needed in the family, like Winchester, get to stay, and those who are not needed go away at the end of the episode.

In all of these situations, the emphasis on the family completely overpowers any attempt to present realistic or believable situations. The newer series are ostensibly about people at work or people mixing home life with working life, but each series carefully falsifies the situation so that it resembles the perfect family situation. Mary Tyler Moore works at a news department of a competitive television station in the fifteenth largest city in the United States and there are *no reporters*. After John Amos left the series, there was not even a weatherman, although in this part of the country the weather report is often the lead-in to all local news. Occasionally, vague bodies are visible at the desks in the back of the newsroom, but those people never have lines and are never even spoken to in most episodes. They are walking properties: because they are not part of the family, they are of no interest, even as continuing minor characters. The show operates on the assumption that Ted cannot possibly be fired, yet if any real show, especially a local news show, had such consistently low ratings as WJM was supposed to have had over such a long period, the first person to go would be the guy in front of the camera. It is his job to deliver ratings; these shows have newswriters so that he does not have to waste his time with anything else.

Similar problems may be seen in almost every series supposedly set in a work environment. On *WKRP* the station operates a full schedule with only two disc jockeys, who are often off the air at the same time. The staff of Mel's Diner on *Alice* work together all hours. On *Taxi*, Louie does not give instructions to any drivers outside the central group; they are, like the desk jockeys on Moore's show, walking set decorations. *M*A*S*H* has no regular nurses, except Major Houlihan. The four surgeons all work at the same time, and although there is the Officers' Club and the Officers' Mess, we never see any other officers. No one ever explains who is on duty when all four of them are off at the same time. The same PFC is always on KP when we see the mess tent.

Corporal Klinger wears dresses, but he is never demoted from corporal, and he pulls KP and walks guard duty, which a real corporal should not do (and which Radar, at the same rank, never does).

All of these series try to give the impression that they are about something new, about people doing real work at real jobs in the real world. But they are at heart no different from *The Adventures of Ozzie and Harriet*: Ozzie never went to work, and the contemporary series characters never go to work either. The importance of their situation is not that they work somewhere but that *they have a home there*. The producers have merely substituted stable adult families, about the size of traditional families, and have dropped those families into offices and other work areas instead of into the average living room they use in *Happy Days*. The "family" members make a self-contained and self-supporting unit within that situation, a unit that rarely has contact with other persons who in the real world would be necessary for the work to continue. They have regular contact with outsiders; what they have no room for is contact with persons who should be there regularly, who are not outsiders, and yet who cannot be fitted into the family.

These artificial families are slightly larger than the average family and larger than the basic sit-com grouping of four, as in *I Love Lucy*. But not much. Mary Tyler More had six, a very small extended family and, in a world of regular divorce, about the size of almost everyone's dream family. Bob Newhart had five in the core family, with three others as regulars in his therapy group. *Taxi* has five in the central family (including Louie), plus two "uncles," Latka and Jim. *M*A*S*H* seems to have one of the largest casts in all of sit-com history, yet it had only eight, then seven after Radar left. These groups are, in fact, the size of the family we remember or wish we had had in the good old days.

Many series do not even bother to pretend the characters need any external force to hold them together. *Three's Company* gave us the three kids sharing an apartment, all perfectly innocent in their living arrangements no matter how it might look to the outside world, with a landlord who served as parent-figure. This was a bit unusual for its time, in that the Ropers provided both a father and a mother, but the roles were traditional, with Father worried about the son's masculinity and Mom trying to be understanding. The titillation factors certainly helped the show's popularity, but the format was simply another version of the sit-com family. *Mork & Mindy* followed the same format, with Mork as kid and Mindy as Mom, at least in its first and most popular year. *Laverne & Shirley* moved in and out of the family format, depending on how important each episode made Laverne's father—he never checked up on the girls, as Roper did, but he was always there when they needed him. These people are all apparently unrelated yet are held together more strongly than most real families.

After television found these stable families, the common middle-class families of the past were all but driven off the air. By 1979, only one sit-com in the top 20 shows (*Happy Days*), featured a real family, and that was by then a family with grown kids. Only one other (*One Day at a Time*) even offered the single-parent variation. The rest featured either the family of work (*M*A*S*H, Alice, Archie Bunker's Place, WKRP, Taxi, Angie*) or artificial families with adult children (*Three's Company, The Jeffersons, Mork & Mindy*).

By the 1981-82 season, the family-of-work shows were wearing down. *Taxi, WKRP, Benson*, and *Barney Miller* all slid to the lower half of the fall ratings averages, so that it came as no surprise when they were canceled in the spring. Although *House Calls* also started the season strongly, along with *Alice* and *M*A*S*H*, its ratings began to sag after cast changes and internal dissension became public, and it too was canceled. Many new family-of-work series failed to find audiences—*Making a Living, Open All Night, Lewis & Clark, Best of the West*—but none failed so miserably as the only new series to try to reproduce in terms of the 1980s a real family in a traditional sit-com family format—*Maggie*. The artificial families provide all the advantages of real families without any of the disadvantages. Characters get emotional support and stable relationships, and the networks get stability because the characters depend on one other and no one can grow up and move away. (Or if they do go away, as on *M*A*S*H* and *Three's Company*, the empty slot can be filled without distress to the audience.) Television has found its perfect family.

This is such solid appeal for producers and audience alike that the only current comedy sketch show, and the only show to use any material remotely related to traditional plots and themes, is also built around the artificial sit-com family. *The Love Boat* is essentially *Love, American Style* in disguise, but the disguise is important. Each week we see several episodes involving strangers who are in love and who actually might change their lives. But each of these episodes is carefully buffered by the continuing characters on the boat. In some episodes these characters have plots of their own, in others they only serve the guests. But the continuing characters take an all too familiar form: one kindly but authoritative patriarch (the captain); three adults who work as a wonderful family, somehow seem to run the entire boat by themselves, and both support and defer to the captain; and one nice but cranky older man, perhaps an uncle (the doctor). Each week provides a visit with the sit-com family, which remains stable and familial. The humorous episodes that involve things like love and change and chaos and challenge all involve outsiders who disappear at the end of the episode, sometimes in midocean, never to be seen or even mentioned again. And even here, even on a boat whose sole purpose seems to be promoting the union of male and female, there is no sense of celebration in that union, as in the traditional comedy endings. Each couple's story is cranked out and thrown away as quickly as possible, excluded from the world of the regular characters as soon as it is convenient and legal for the crew to do so.

One of the most striking, and disturbing, aspects of the family's role in the sit-com is its intense exclusivity. The problems that occur in each episode must be solved, as in any dramatic form, but since the goal is a return to the way things were before the problem arose, the persons who cause the problem, if they are not already in the family, must be excluded and driven out of the basic situation. On *Bewitched*, Samantha was occasionally visited by her Aunt Clara, also a witch, whose major characteristic was that she could not get her spells right. She was a charming old woman, and audiences seemed to like her, but she kept messing things up. At the end of every episode, Samantha would have to find some way to correct the spells Clara had cast; when she did, Clara was sent packing and everything returned to normal. This solution was not any different in practice from what Samantha's mother often did, but Samantha's mother was a regular who appeared almost every week, while Clara was an occasional guest and was sent away in disgrace at the end of each episode in which she arrived. She just caused too many problems ever to be part of the regular family.

But Clara was a special case—she was after all a relative and something of a semiregular. In most series, the people from the outside who cause problems are overcome and excluded at the end of every episode, if their problems are in any way likely to upset the status quo. Bob Newhart has regular patients and others. The regular ones, significantly, are in his therapy group; the others get their problems solved in the half hour and disappear, never to return again. Mary Tyler Moore's boyfriends always leave or get rejected by the end of the episode. Occasionally, a character establishes unexpected popularity and the producers decide to make him a regular. At that point the stranger becomes a part of the family. The classic case is Fonzie on *Happy Days*; once it was clear that he was a critical factor in the show's ratings, he did not just become a regular, he moved in with Richie's family, contrary to all characterization and rationality. But in terms of the formula of the sit-com, he could not comfortably be a regular and an outsider simultaneously. He had to be in the family if he expected to be around for more than a few episodes.

This exclusionary attitude is often disguised by the happy endings of the episode. Problems do get solved, and none of the outsiders and upsetters charges off swearing revenge on the lot of them. But the changes of mind, the solutions to the problems, all happen to the outsiders, not to the family members. The mechanic does finally fix the car, the Army drops the court-martial charges, the boyfriend agrees with Mary that they would not be right for each other after all. But no new unit that has room for them is formed. The old unit, the old family, continues without regard for the outsiders and their problems.

This has made the characters of the sit-com defensive rather than aggressive, and reactive rather than active. In many cases, their reactive nature is so complete that the characters become almost completely passive. Things just happen to them, and they do the best they can in the circumstances. In *All in the Family* Archie's goal in life is to go to work, come home, read the paper, have dinner, watch TV, maybe have a couple of beers with the guys, and go to bed. A great day is a day in which absolutely nothing happens. Bob Hartley says in an episode of *The Bob Newhart Show* in which he is called a fuddy-duddy by everyone he meets, "I'm not opposed to change—I just don't like for things to be different," which might be a motto for the sit-com heroes. There is a strong sense in all the sit-coms of circling the wagons and fighting off the savages who want to upset the world. Almost no one wants to go out into the world, to do, to see, to make waves. Even when they leave their real homes, as we have seen, they quickly find and form new families that are stronger and more defensive than the biological ones they had as children.

The sit-com could be built quite differently around the person or personality of a comic or the comic's character. The hero could wander the country, finding adventures in a new place every week. *Get Smart*, a parody of the spy genre more than a sit-com, did that for a while with some success, but there are no others. The comic could operate from a fixed place but in a mixture of modes and situations, as Jack Benny did. The comic could just play a series of interesting characters, or offer a variety of funny things, as Ernie Kovacs and the comedians of silent film and sound shorts did. But the sit-com hero does not. In the sit-com format he seeks a safe place and tries to hide there.

It is difficult to speak of a hero in such circumstances. The hero ought to *do* something, even if it takes an enormous amount of prodding. But the sit-com hero tries by every means possible to avoid doing. This has done some very strange things to the characters who have populated Western comedy. In most cases, the sit-com has turned the comedy on end, and the aggressive, active heroes of the past are now the characters who must be driven out, while the defensive characters who used to represent the forces that must be changed now are the heroes.

At its most symbolic level, television comedy has dispensed with the comic destroyers. The comedy has traditionally expressed its energies through the impulse to make a mess of things, to attack authority and destroy its symbols of power, especially its property. In the history of television series comedy, only four principal characters ever did damage to the world, despite the tried and true humor available in such routines. Lucy in *I Love Lucy* (and often in her later series), Maxwell Smart in *Get Smart*, Gilligan in *Gilligan's Island*, and occasionally Gomer Pyle in his own series, *Gomer Pyle, USMC*, are the only characters who could physically wreck a room just by walking into it. A few others made messes of various jobs or situations, but these messes are remarkably few and far between. Such characters as Barney Fyfe of *The Andy Griffith Show*, who would have been destroyers in films, now show a remarkable reverence for physical property; though their ignorance may cause complex confusions, things can always be straightened out and put back as they were. Whenever the possibility of some kind of destruction does arise, as with Aunt Clara's or Jeannie's spells, the right magic is always found to prevent the damage before it actually happens.

As the anarchic and destructive impulses were eliminated, so was the traditional character who most clearly embodied those impulses, the Fool. The list of television Fools is almost exactly the same as the list of destroyers, although Lucy would only occasionally fit in that category. To those might be added Norton on *The Honeymooners* and Jethro on

The Beverly Hillbillies. Like the classic Harlequin, these characters were at sea in the normal world, and when they began scheming, the audience could be sure that everything would go wrong, one of the basic identifying characteristics of the Fool. But these are all old, almost ancient series characters; Maxwell Smart, of *Get Smart*, was the last, and he was canceled in 1970. The Fools had already begun to fade long before, and both *The Beverly Hillbillies* and *Gilligan's Island* had been canceled because they drew the wrong audience—older people who remembered and liked the older traditions.

Sometimes the sit-com hero meets a Fool, but the Fool is an outsider. If the Fool appears regularly, he is never accepted by the other characters but instead is the subject of insult and ridicule. Most often Fools appear only randomly, as Aunt Clara does on *Bewitched*, and when they appear they make such a mess that the hero or the principal characters expel them from the unit. The characters who get to stay are the fixers.

Even less visible, if that is possible, is the Scoundrel. Only one sit-com scoundrel in the mold of W.C. Fields or Groucho Marx exists, Sergeant Bilko, and *The Phil Silvers Show* left the air in 1959. *F Troup* tried to revive the character, but the show lasted only two seasons. The cheats and con men, the rogues and rascals of history, simply do not exist on television comedy. If they should by some happenstance wander in, they are immediately shut out of the family. Fonzie on *Happy Days* could have been one—he had all the traits—but the series opted to place him as protector and second father to Richie rather than as a con man for the gullible, which he appeared to be in the early episodes. Hogan of *Hogan's Heroes* combines many of the Scoundrel characteristics in a strange TV characterization. He serves simultaneously as scoundrel and as father. When dealing with Colonel Klink, a traditional braggart soldier and pompous nincompoop, Hogan is a Scoundrel, producing plan after plan to trick the commander and win the war. But all the plans are developed as father-protector for his little family, the other prisoners who share his hut. Hogan is not only the ranking officer in the hut, he is the only officer. And he actually runs the camp—that is part of the joke. He is the real commander, the man who sees that no one escapes and that all the rules are followed. But he runs the camp not only on the strength of his wit, as a real Scoundrel would, but also on the strength of his rank (he is a colonel), an authority recognized by all the forces of the society he represents as well as by the enemy. Thus,

Hogan serves as a bridge between Sergeant Bilko and *M*A*S*H*, the last vestige of the comedic Scoundrel grafted onto the rising father/officer/hero, in the same way that *Hogan's Heroes* is a bridge, one of the first family-of-work series to appear (winning the war is the work that holds this artificial family together, and they are amazingly competent at this task).

The only serious appearance of the traditional Scoundrel in the two decades since *The Phil Silvers Show* has been in the melodrama, in James Garner's characterization on *Maverick*, which was later revived in the cops-and-robbers format of *The Rockford Files*. After the early success of these series, a number of similar shows appeared, especially Robert Wagner's several series, but despite the humor of several of them, there can be no doubt that they were intended to be melodramas in form, and they cannot by any stretch of terms be considered comedies. For at least twenty years, nothing normally seen as a comedy on American television has featured the Scoundrel—one of the most basic of all comic characters and certainly one of the most important of all characters in terms of plot solution in comedy—in anything but minor, occasional appearances.

Only the Innocent has made any regular appearances in the sitcom, but even there, the character has been subtly but importantly altered. The sit-com innocent is a far different character from the one that figured in so many comedies of the past. Some traditional Innocents, the Clampett family of *The Beverly Hillbillies*, did appear for a while and achieved tremendous popularity. For nine years the Clampetts proved that there was a TV audience for the old American fable of the rube from the farm who comes to the big city and shows up the city slickers. Continuing a line stretching back to the Yankee introduced in Royall Tyler's *The Contrast*, the first performed American comedy, Jed Clampett and his brood brought the pleasures and outlooks of the natural man, coupled with good old American integrity, to the capital of money and glamour. Week after week, his innocence and integrity and common sense won through in situation after situation. Mr. Drysdale kept trying to educate him, and he kept refusing to learn.

The rube character has been particularly potent in American theatre and film and has appealed to people in the city as well as in the small towns of the Midwest and the South. Even the city slickers get to laugh, because almost everyone knows more than the hillbilly; whatever he does, he provides a lot of laughter. At the same time, he satisfies the need for a mythical success of innocence and a justification of America's own national innocence and ideals in a cynical, vicious international order. But after nine years, *The Beverly Hillbillies* was canceled. The ratings had begun to slide, as they must for any show that has been number 1, but they did not slide so low as to merit cancellation under previous standards. The show became one of the earliest victims of demographics. Ratings surveys became more refined in the late 1960s, and in 1971 CBS wiped out many programs that still showed good ratings because the shows attracted the "wrong" audience for the advertisers. The *Hillbillies*, it was found, appealed primarily to a rural and an old audience. The younger audience of the cities, people under forty with money to spend and those who had been raised on television, could no longer accept such a set of characters. Only people whose tastes were formed in the traditional comedy felt any identification with the Innocent on television. Since them, no male Innocents have appeared as regulars (until Mork, whose innocence was soon taken away from him) and *The Beverly Hillbillies* apparently were the last of the tradition.

Most of the change in the character of the Innocent comes from the sit-com's promotion of the family to the central position in all activity. In the family, there are only two genuine categories, parent and child, and the main characters of the sit-com usually fill one of those two roles in the family of the show. One of the jobs of the parent is to educate the child, and for that the child must be innocent of at least part of the ways of the world. *The Adventures of Ozzie and Harriet, Father Knows Best, The Danny Thomas Show,* and *The Donna Reed Show* all gave us real children with parents who guided them as they grew up. After a while, these lovely families shifted to the single-parent families, such as *The Partridge Family, Family Affair,* and *One Day at a Time,* with somewhat wiser children. Now shows feature grown-up families and children who are equal to their parents. But in all of these series, the children defer to the parent figure. They may argue, they may fight, they may resist, but ultimately the parent turns out to be right. In the television comedies, the innocence of the children is not a protection for them, but rather a problem. Because they are young, they make mistakes and cause problems, they make a mess of situations, and the parents have to show them the proper way of doing things and to clean up the messes.

The traditional Innocent is often described as a child in an adult's body, but he is innocent because he is pure, not because he is young. He makes a mess of things because he knows a higher right than do his parents; usually the mess results only because the parents do not respond to this higher right themselves and must be circumvented. In the sit-com, the parents solve the problems because they know the right, which the young do not quite understand.

This was clearer in the early days of the form. Hiding behind the never-never land morality of fifties and sixties network television, the sit-com family was always perfect, much better than any real family could ever hope to be and an example to us all. Populating a land of tree-lined streets in sleepy little towns where families never faced any bigger problems than whether the kids could stay out later than ten o'clock on a school night or whether the girls might ask out the boys first, those perfect parents taught their own children (and America) the way to perfect, stable, responsible, problem-free adulthood. Such series began to fade in the later sixties, not because their message was fading in power but rather because it became increasingly difficult for an audience to believe in families that lived in such cotton-wool country. No longer could we believe that Jim Anderson of *Father Knows Best* could never lose his job, never see a black family move into the neighborhood, never see Bud mugged or Kathy's lunch money extorted. A normal family where the parents really could solve all the problems seemed to make sense only in nostalgia, as in *Happy Days*.

But as the sit-com began to notice the real world in its themes, especially under the prodding of Norman Lear, some odd changes in family relationships began to occur. One of the responses to this change was to make the two-parent family disappear, while another was to shift all the children into adulthood even though they continued to live at home. At that point, the children ceased to be innocent at all. Those who were adult in body were generally wiser and more aware of the world than their parents, as on *All in the Family*, where Mike and Gloria, although tending toward bleeding-heart liberalism, were at least aware of forces in the world that grew from fact rather than pure prejudice. Those who were still physically children ceased to be emotional children most of the time. Since these children were primarily in one-parent families, they had to share the role of spouse for the parent. But like JJ on *Good Times* and Gary Coleman on *Diff'rent Strokes*, they were also street wise and tough and knew the angles. How they knew these things was unimportant, but in many cases they seemed to be acting as parent-guide for their own parent. Americans have always had a weakness for little children who shall lead them, but the child figure who has shown us the way in the past has always been a child who led the adults to purity, good-heartedness, faith, and hope. In many of the seventies sit-coms, the kids led the way into the modern world, which is a far different role.

When the stable adult artificial families established themselves, the child of the fifties sit-com returned as an adult. But it was always as a part of a familial situation, in which the innocent characteristics were carefully controlled by a parent figure. This control is clearest in those series with women as principal characters, *I Dream of Jeannie* and *The Mary Tyler Moore Show*. Both women were young and were in circumstances unusual for television, that is, they were neither wives nor mothers; both were in their ways career women. Both were in some way innocent of the "real" world, Jeannie through all her years in her bottle and Mary through her years as the traditional small-town girl now moving to the big city. But they are treated in quite revealing manners. Jeannie casts spell after spell to help her "master," but she always has to remove the spell and put things back. Sometimes the spell is wrong, sometimes it is useful, but in either case, Larry Hagman acts as a father rather than a lover and makes her stop even when she tries to help him out of a mess; she is controlled and protected and, if there were such a thing as a sequence in the series, gradually educated so that the effects of her innocence can be minimized.

Mary Richards is about the nicest character ever seen on television. Everyone comes to her for advice. But when she has a problem, sooner or later she goes to Mr. Grant, a curmudgeon who gives her the most cynical, world-weary advice available. And she is almost always successful when she follows that advice. The standard episode that involves Mary is built around someone who is taking advantage of Mary's good nature, often but certainly not always a man, and is demanding more from her than is fair for someone to demand. Mary's struggle is to learn to be nasty, but she eventually succeeds. If these things ever carried over from week to week, there would be a gradual progression from innocence to cynicism, but since we start each new episode with the same old Mary, that movement is never obvious enough to upset the audience. Mary, however, is much cattier and nastier to Sue Ann Nivens toward the end of the series than she probably would have been if the character had been introduced earlier; Phyllis provided some of Sue Ann's irritating characteristics but without drawing the same responses from Mary.

Mary's career can be compared with that of her only direct predecessor, Marlo Thomas on *That Girl*. There, as Ann Marie, Thomas also played a sweet young girl who went to have a career in the big city. There she had numerous adventures, even found a steady boyfriend, but she had no father figure to guide her, (her real father visited only to complain about her independence) and consequently she stayed as sweet and open to adventure as she had been when she first arrived. She never had a Mr. Grant to tell her what to do when things got too bad. *That Girl*, seen in retrospect, was one of the most daring of all sit-coms, in that it came closer than any other series to using the traditional comedy characters in a form that made the characters consistently active and energetic; it even came very close to the marriage at the end. It is doubtful if the show could have succeeded had the Innocent not been a woman, but this series was the traditional character's last gasp. Although many series followed its lead in giving us single women, none placed them either in serious opposition to their parents or living outside the safety and protection of an artificial family.

At the same time that the traditional heroes were disappearing from the sit-com, the forces of social order against which they were so often in temporary revolt were moving into the position of sit-com hero. Most striking is the role of the policeman in television sit-coms. Before there were police there were soldiers and justices, and there were, all in all, no persons more detested in comedy, except occasionally the fathers themselves. When police arrived in real life, they became buffoons in comedy, for important reasons. As the visible symbol of law and order and the protection of existing society the policeman was an automatic blocking agent to almost all comedic impulses. Everything comedy is for, the policeman by definition is against. The earliest comic appearances of the police in American films were the Keystone Kops, as blithering a set of nincompoops and dunderheads as comedy has ever known, incompetent in the smallest assignment. My memory provides one lone example (though there are certainly others) in the history of Western comedy in which the comedy's hero is a policeman, Charlie Chaplin's *Easy Street*, and that example is a short subject. Television comedy in a very short span of time has provided three major policeman heroes, on *The Andy Griffith Show*, *Carter Country*, and *Barney Miller*.

In similar fashion, where comedy in the past has dealt with the military, the heroes with whom the audience was expected to sympathize have always been the enlisted men, usually that lowest of the low, the buck private. In television's most potent military comedy, *M*A*S*H*, the heroes are officers, and there are no privates with whom to sympathize. Every one of the regulars is at the very least a noncom. In *Private Benjamin* the lead character is an enlisted person, but it remains to be seen whether that series will last for any significant time. Not only are the *M*A*S*H* heroes officers, but they are also doctors, characters who were the butt of comedic derision long before (and long after) Molière raised the ridiculing of doctors to a high art. They are joined by principals on such series as *The Bob Newhart Show*, *House Calls*, and *The Donna Reed Show* (where the husband was a doctor).

Where the vicious, often ignorant pedagogue was held in comic contempt, in the sit-com the teacher is admirable. In the pedant's place is the kind and sensitive teacher, full of warmth and understanding, to whom students turn for guidance when they have problems. This particular branch of the tree was established by *Our Miss Brooks* at the same time as *Mr. Peepers* was closing out the last of the ineffectual teacher figures, and it continued in numerous series such as *Room 222*, *The Bill Cosby Show*, and *Welcome Back, Kotter*. In a curiously persistent American strain, these teachers are still not allowed actually to know anything—Cosby teaches physical education and Kotter some kind of permanent homeroom that never lasts for more than five minutes and in which the subject can be dropped at the slightest sign of something more interesting to discuss. They are just nice guys, and everyone admires them for it.

Finally, there are the businessmen. Most of the Plautine fathers were businessmen of some kind, and most of Molière's fathers were also businessmen, not nobles. Traditionally in the comedy, a successful businessman almost by definition has to be someone the young people could not trust. Again, the sit-com reverses this arrangement, making the most likable and fatherly of heroes successful men of business: Jim Anderson of *Father Knows Best*, Howard Cunningham of *Happy Days*, Mike Brady of *The Brady Bunch*. It is probably significant that we have yet to see a hero in Big Business, but the small-town, independent businessman, which comedy has traditionally defined as the most dangerous opponent, has become the kindliest of principals.

These are the characters of the *commedia*, but they are not the heroes of the *commedia*. These are the roles played by Pantalone, il

Dottore, il Capitano, and Pulchinella. The most widely viewed and most powerful medium of entertainment in the country dedicated to the common man and progress on the strength of one's own wits and innate goodness has produced a comedy in which Pantalone is the hero and in which the common man and the natural man are the villains, if they appear at all. It is an incredible transformation.

Especially revealing is the way the sit-com has treated the working man. Almost everyone works on TV, at least since Ozzie Nelson, but the number of what could be called working-class heroes is extremely limited, and their roles have been curiously limited as well. In the successful series, we usually see such characters at work, not at home. Even though Alice has a son, we usually see him only as he passes through the coffee shop in *Alice*. For the most part, when we do see them at home, these lower-class characters are childless, like the Cramdens in *The Honeymooners*, or their children are already grown, as in *Petticoat Junction*, *Sanford and Son*, and *All in the Family*. *Good Times* is the exception, allowing us to see working-class parents act like parents, the only successful example since *The Life of Riley* went off in 1958. Most of these working-class parents are treated in a way that is quite different from the way in which the other parent figures are treated. Archie Bunker is Chester Riley with anger is Ralph Cramden with current topics, and all three never accomplish anything; all are guarded, protected, and shepherded by their wives. They are so ineffectual that they often assume the position of another child, a spoiled brat, in their own households, to be alternately mollified and protected from themselves. It is only in such lower middle-class television families that the mother has the last word. Like Edith Bunker, they may have to be pushed very hard before they put their feet down, preferring to let the childish men have their way if possible, but ultimately Mother knows best in these families. Where Father has made more money, where he has become a true middle-class figure, Father knows best. He may defer to his wife because he agrees with her or, like Ricky in *I Love Lucy*, he may defer to her wishes occasionally because he loves her, but when the real decisions have to be made, Father makes them. It has been almost axiomatic in comedy that the poorer a principal character is (at least temporarily), the more likely he is to become a comic hero. Even this is upset in the sit-com.

If there is a single characteristic that unifies almost all of the sit-com heroes, it is prosperity. Many have been comfortably middle-class, often living in modern suburban homes, as on *The Dick Van Dyke Show*, *Father Knows Best*, *The Brady Bunch*, and *Happy Days*. When they live in the city, they live in their own homes, as do Maude and Archie Bunker, or in comfortable apartments.

There is a process used in the making of commercials that seems to be reflected in the placement of comedy series. A standard pattern in the commercial is to determine the social status of the potential customer, then to illustrate the use of the product in the home of someone just a step or so higher on the socioeconomic ladder. This upscaling is assumed to make the product more attractive and desirable without making the consumer feel the world it represents is totally beyond reach. In the same way, the homes of sit-com characters seem to be always just a bit better than they could afford in the real world, given the salaries and backgrounds they are supposed to have. Jim Anderson of *Father Knows Best*, an insurance salesman, lives in almost exactly the same home as Doctor Stone of *The Donna Reed Show*. This upward mobility dominates even the supposedly tightly structured and class-defining world of the military. In *M*A*S*H* the pigsty atmosphere of Hawkeye's tent is intentional; the Swamp would be clean and comfortable if he wanted it to be, but he likes the boyish sense of freedom that comes with not having to pick up his clothes every day, or perhaps that comes when Mom is not there to pick up for him. And every one is an officer. Even the enlisted men are officers. They play poker in the officers' tent, they eat with the officers, and they even use the officers' club. Nobody on the show is ever a social inferior, no one (except the Koreans) is poor, and none of the regulars ever seriously tries to make it any different. Mary Richards lives in a one-room apartment, but it is a one-room apartment large enough for three rooms, and the furniture is neither standard furnished-apartment-motel-modern nor typical working-woman-scraping-to-get-by. Publicity materials made much of her clothes being bought off the rack, but the rack they came off of is not to be found in Sears or J.C. Penney, which is where her assumed salary would place her. Even the poor, as in *Good Times*, seem to be just a bit better off than their real-life counterparts. The Bunkers' home seems plausible, as does the apartment on *One Day at a Time*, until you look at an older series like *The Honeymooners*. Standards have changed over the years and in many cases cheap products disguise themselves a little better now than they used to, but there was no doubt with the Cramdens that you were seeing two people who were just scraping by and who would be in bad trouble if Ralph ever missed a paycheck, a feeling you never get from even the poorest sit-com principals since then.

In those few series where both adults work, there is rarely the feeling that they work because they have to. On *The Bob Newhart Show* Emily Hartley teaches because she wants to, but her money is superfluous; it is mad money that can be used to buy five-hundred-dollar watches or spur-of-the-moment weekends in San Francisco. For the most part, if there are two adults, only one of them has to work, which is an increasingly rare situation among even the upper middle-classes of the real world today.

This upscaling has done some odd things to the sit-com's representation of reality, which also in some ways reverses the traditional comedy. Where comedy's endings were artificial, a matter for wish or dream rather than for probability, the sit-com's episode endings tend to be more realistic. Most situations can be dealt with, and most of the problems sit-com heroes are asked to handle can realistically be solved in some way (although rarely in twenty-two minutes). For those that cannot be solved, those larger issues that the Norman Lear and to a certain extent the Mary Tyler Moore production companies introduced, the sit-com heroes find no solutions. Like most people in real life, they do the best they can in the face of these problems, from teenage sexuality to racial bigotry, but they do not find solutions, even temporary ones, that alter the problems. No matter how brilliant the *M*A*S*H* surgeons, some of the patients die, something that would rarely happen in traditional comedy. This is certainly a perception of at least some parts of reality.

And yet, in many other areas, the sit-com seems to avoid the minutiae of daily life that the traditional comedy has relished. Characters go to work, but they do not work there, certainly not with the attention to detail and the excitement in the equipment and tools of the trade that Harold Lloyd exhibited in his department store job, Laurel and Hardy at the carpentry shop, and Buster Keaton at his many mechanical jobs. And one could watch years of families at home in sitcoms and never see them do the one thing that almost every family does at home—watch television. Watching people watch something is not very interesting dramatically, so it makes sense to devote little time to the activity itself; however, 97 percent of American homes have at least one television set, and most make that set the central piece of furniture in the family's main room. Archie Bunker was the first sit-com principal to arrange his furniture around the TV, and even there it is only from Archie's chair that anyone can actually see the set. Any film comedy from the thirties that had a normal living room showed immediately the importance of the radio to the family, whether we saw it turned on or not. But in many television series you have to search in the little nooks and crannies of the room to find the TV set, which ought to be even more dominating physically.

Most sit-coms continue to be concerned with the mundane world of daily family life—of dinner tables and children's toys, school assignments and relatives who impose—and within that world they are quite specific (although they carefully exclude brand names for obvious commercial reasons). But the world with which the family comes in contact is treated much more vaguely and imprecisely than comedy traditionally has treated it.

Because the sit-coms exists in a time-warp, because it has to be comprehensible at any time period, in reruns and later in syndication, it has lost almost all contact with daily events in the outside world. Topical allusions have almost disappeared. Mary Tyler Moore's *newsroom* lived and worked through the entire Watergate scandal and never mentioned it. Characters live in specific cities yet make no specific local references and the producers shoot nothing beyond the credit sequences on location. References, when made, are generally to the past, not the present. *Happy Days* and *Laverne & Shirley* make far more specific references to the social and cultural events of the late fifties and early sixties than did the shows made during that time, because the past is fixed. The references are purposely old, so they cannot be out of date when the show in rerun, or even when the first showing finally comes around. It is impossible to divorce completely a regular series from the world in which it is written, of course, and there are numerous uses of current cultural concepts and ideas that may turn out to be fads, but there is a curious lack of specificity to many of these references. The bristling topical allusions that fill the clowns' mouths in Shakespeare and Jonson and by which modern scholars date the plays are missing, replaced by soft and nebulous comments; the scholar who tries to work from a script of an average sit-com will have as much trouble dating the show as does the viewer watching it in reruns today. The reversal of comedic traditions is not nearly so complete in this area as in the others we have examined, but it is nonetheless in process.

In order to reach the authority, the professional status, and the prosperity he displays, the sit-com hero must of course not be young, which the lovers have always been. To be married, to have children, to act as a father, all require some maturity and thus mitigate against youth. Even within such requirements, however, television often seems to make sit-com heroes older than they would need to be in the real world. Part of this aging process is accomplished merely by casting. Almost no one in films or television, whether comedy or any other genre, ever plays his real age; performers are consistently cast as five to ten years younger than they really are. Whenever age is mentioned, which is rarely, the performer is said to be just a bit younger than he looks, which in turn is just a bit younger than he really is, because performers have to maintain a youthful appearance to compete as actors. But for the most part, age is not mentioned, and the resulting number of forty- to fifty-year-old parents with children younger than ten is remarkable. Even outside the traditional family, characters seem too old for their situations. When Mary Richards started her series, she was said to be in her early thirties, a figure corresponding to Mary Tyler Moore's own age. But no one seemed to wonder why she was doing at thirty-two what other people in America do before the age of twenty-two. What did she do back in the small town, where she was not married and did not work, that kept her from looking for a career or coming to the big city until after she was thirty? Traditional comedy edged toward youth as defined by the social standards of the time, but though Restoration lovers were older than Jacobean ones, for example, they were still no older than the age that was accepted for marriage in their societies. American television comedy edges its characters toward maturity, so that they are just a bit older than might be expected. Alan Alda has gray hair by the fifth year of *M*A*S*H*, but he was already thirty-six when the series began: if his character Hawkeye had been that age, he would have served in World War II or would have established a full practice, neither of which is ever suggested.

Finally, the heroes of television situations are competent. Pantalone was competent at getting money, but not at being a father. The hero of television comedy is competent at everything, but especially at being a father. At their jobs, they are always competent, or at least it is so claimed. Hawkeye and friends are brilliant surgeons; even the odd man out, Major Winchester, the replacement for the nearly incompetent Frank Burns, is a brilliant surgeon as well. Bob Hartley is an excellent psychologist, Mary Richards and Lou Grant are good at their jobs (although their ratings never go up), and Barney Miller and his men are all good cops. At home they are even more competent. There are no unsuccessful parents in the sit-coms. From *The Adventures of Ozzie and Harriet* to *Happy Days*, the parents always find the right thing to say and to do when a crisis arises. The more "modern" parents, in the mode of Norman Lear's *One Day at a Time* and *Good Times*, hesitate a lot more and often have much more serious problems. But they eventually solve them too. Even though these shows allow fights between parents and children, which the fifties happy-family shows did not, the children always turn out fine. No parent produces an idiot child, an immoral child, or a juvenile delinquent on television, no matter how close the temptations may come. The parents are just as competent as the bosses at work.

In Hawkeye, an almost perfect television comedy hero appears. His heart is in the right place, but he rarely has to do anything more than talk. Seeing the series stripped in reruns, in some cities as often as four or five times a day, one becomes impressed by how much Hawkeye relies on his mouth. He is a whiner more than a doer, a complainer but not a changer. Arthur Berger once said that a typical sit-com hero is "not so much an actor as one who is acted upon, and is generally a victim of circumstances," [6] which certainly describes Hawkeye. A draftee, he rails against the system but never takes advantage of it when it offers him routes of escape. He is competent, a fine surgeon with a superb bedside manner, the kind of doctor most of us would love to run into. But beyond that, he mostly talks. After the elimination of the nurses, and especially Cutler, in 1973, he even talks about his sex life. We see a lot of activity with Burns and Hot Lips; we even see one clear fall from grace for B.J.; but except for the one desperate episode with Hot Lips, we see few if any episodes in which Hawkeye is not rejected or interrupted or somehow thinks better of it. He talks a good flirtation but does not seem to actually sleep with anyone.

The principal characters of the sit-com—it is still difficult to call them heroes—may be parents or they may be children. Where there are real children, the principals are usually parents, and where they are parents, the dominant figure is usually the father. When the stable families of adults began to dominate, the principal characters sometimes acted as parents (Bob Hartley, Alice) but more often they filled the role of child in the structure (Mary Richards, Hawkeye). They defer to, respect, and respond to authority. They operate defensively, through the family-type unit, to protect the stability of a world constantly threatened by outside forces over which they have little or no control. Having forsaken the traditional comic plot and the aggressive and progressive impulses of that plot, the sit-coms have also forsaken the traditional comic heroes and their characteristic roles. As a result, they have also been forced to surrender a number of the most fundamental weapons of humor in their comedy.

The most basic weapon in the comic arsenal was exposure of the blocking characters to public ridicule. But in the sit-com, the characters who used to be exposed are now the central characters, the ones the audience knows, understands, and likes. There is nothing to expose except those things we already know, and while there may be a certain amount of pleasure in seeing Frank and Hot Lips humiliated for the thirteenth time, this device is limited. Only outsiders can be really overturned, but the very fact that they are outsiders limits their potential threat and the amount of humorous release in their downfall. Very often we are reduced to the continued exposure of problems for characters, like the people in Bob Newhart's group therapy sessions and Barney Miller's crime victims, whose problems are very real, which is different only in degree from visiting asylums to laugh at the inmates.

Henri Bergson has described three classic methods of developing humor in comic situations: repetition, inversion, and double meanings.[7] The sit-com has rejected or significantly altered the uses of most of these. For example, we find a lot of humor when characters repeat themselves unnecessarily, when they act as usual even when circumstances require different responses. It is funny when Howard always shows up for dinner at Bob and Emily's on *The Bob Newhart Show*, when Mr. Roper complains about Jack in the girls' apartment on *Three's Company*, or when Klinger appears in his forty-seventh dress on *M*A*S*H*. At the same time, it is also comforting, for repetition is the very foundation of the sit-com form. Every episode returns to the basic series situation, and the characters keep doing the same kinds of things. After a while this becomes not a humorous device but a proof of continuity and stability.

Inversion, when a character suddenly reverses himself to humorous effect, is rarely used, although one might expect it to be used constantly. When it does appear in a nearly pure form, it seems to stagger the television community. The most famous case of comic inversion of the past decade is the episode of *The Mary Tyler Moore*

Show when Chuckles the Clown is killed, stepped on by an elephant, while wearing his peanut costume. Everybody makes jokes except Mary. After telling everyone else to take this seriously, Mary goes to the funeral and gets the giggles. This was a well-written and well-performed episode, but from the awards, the critical comments, and even a few public appearances by the writers (unheard of on American television), one might think Molière had returned to the world. Unfortunately, it was merely that this simple, traditional technique of inversion had been used so rarely in recent TV sit-coms that when it was carefully developed and then well executed, it looked like a new and brilliant work of imagination. The outsiders in a sit-com cannot invert for comic effect, because we only have a few minutes of exposition in which to establish their characters, not enough time to establish a pattern from which the inversion can be seen as something different and funny. Only characters about whom we know enough to have certain expectations can be inverted—which means the series regulars—but they cannot be inverted too often or the pattern of repetition that holds the series together might be broken.

That leaves only double meanings. The classic form of this is the mistaken identity, but it also obviously includes such things as the double entendre. Double meanings do not disrupt the format; they actually strengthen it. The challenge that might upset the equilibrium does not even have to be a real challenge. As long as one of the characters *thinks* that something is happening, a situation can be developed, but since the assumption can be seen to be mistaken, the balance is easily restored as soon as everything is explained. This device is extremely common in the French sex farces of the nineteenth century, in which the wife thinks the husband is unfaithful when he really is not. *I Love Lucy* used the device regularly, and most sit-coms since have made frequent use of it. After *All in the Family* brought in more "mature" subjects, especially sex, which had been taboo in the sit-com before then, the "I thought you really meant..." situation was joined by the snigger-snigger situation, all part of this same comic device.

This device depends to a great extent on an assumption of childishness on the part of the characters. A good, mature adult would not and should not jump to conclusions and, with experience, would know what the other persons were really doing, saying, and meaning. But a child can misinterpret. When in the traditional comedy the figures of authority and power managed to misinterpret events, this was a form of their exposure and could become funny. However, in the sit-com, characters who do this are usually in childlike positions in their worlds, even when they may be physical adults. Howard Borden thinking that Bob and Emily are breaking up is essentially the same as one of the Brady kids running away from home because he thinks he is not wanted anymore, since Howard is just an overgrown kid in Bob's family. In the sit-com, then, we use the classic device to laugh not at a weakness or an ignorance that had disguised itself successfully until now behind a powerful exterior but rather at a genuine ignorance in the weak and unprotected mind of the child or the childlike figure. This is a cruel perversion of the old device.

It would of course be foolish to suggest that comedy had never allowed audiences to laugh at the weak and the ignorant. The very popularity of the Innocent and the Fool as comedic heroes immediately gives the lie to such a statement. Comedy has also provided a small but noticeable strain of humor at the expense of the ill and the handicapped, like the young man with the missing palate in Feydeau's *A Flea in Her Ear*. Most of the time, however, those weak and ignorant people have had the opportunity to turn the tables in the course of the play, and in a regular comic inversion they become stronger than their tormentors, or stronger than the audience had originally thought them to be. For the most part, the laughter at the weak has been aimed at those people who pretended to be strong, those who ought to be able to take a little public ridicule. After all, it is no one's fault but his own that the miser is a miser, and the character who pretends to be sick when he is not is perfectly deserving of the laughter. This is not, however, the way the sit-com for the most part choses to work. In Sheridan's *The Rivals*, when Mrs. Malaprop dropped one of the terms that are named for her, she was a rich, powerful, mature woman who had control of a young woman's fortune and future, and she dropped those terms precisely because she pretended to an education and wisdom that she did not in fact have. When the audience, and some of the other characters, laughed at her, they were laughing not at the ignorance but at the pretension behind the ignorance, the hypocrisy that was now exposed for all to see and hear. When Archie Bunker drops a malapropism, he is simply repeating something he overheard and does not understand, probably from the TV, but he is doing so because he has no other word. He is not pretending to be college educated and well read; in all his arguments with his son-in-law about right and wrong, he may claim more brains but he never claims more education. What we are asked to laugh at is not his ignorance exposed behind the facade but his ignorance, period. This is a small but critical distinction, for it serves to underscore the completeness with which the sit-com has overturned the comic traditions.

Because the sit-com is dominated by family life, and most of the activity comes from those characters who act as children in the family unit, it is only logical that eventually the sit-com would have to resort to the humorous devices of children—practical jokes, name calling, and insults. Most of these devices can be traced to *All in the Family*, although the other seminal series of the seventies, *The Mary Tyler Moore Show*, certainly used them. There were a lot of comedy series in the fifties at which people laughed—*Jack Benny, Burns and Allen, You Bet Your Life, Your Show of Shows, Amos 'n' Andy*, to name only a few—but toward the end of the decade something happened. The family sit-com took over and, with very few exceptions, the goal of the family sit-com was a chuckle and a warm glow, not a belly laugh. By about 1970, these sit-coms were worn out and audiences were on the verge of turning away, as the ratings records show. Then came *All in the Family* in 1971. While the press and intellectuals discussed the political and social implications of the program, they missed the single most important factor in its success: unlike most other situation comedies of its time, it made the audience laugh. When compared with *Mayberry RFD, Nanny and the Professor, The Brady Bunch, Family Affair, Arnie*, or almost any other sit-com of 1970, it seemed like the reinvention of *I Love Lucy* or *Amos 'n' Andy*. The sit-coms had reached that state by a complete exhaustion of the resources of their limited formula. In a world in which family stability is king, the ancient heroes are the villains, and the father is always right, humorous possibilities are obviously restricted. TV sit-coms had been so busy being nice that they were on the verge of forgetting even how to be funny.

All in the Family and its many followers, however, primarily discovered and delivered name calling and the insult. For a decade following, no successful show could be complete without at least one shouting/insulting match per episode, and the critical response to the show could be predicted relatively well by the intelligence, calmness, and variety of the insults. Mary Tyler Moore and Bob Newhart ranked very high on critical scales, because they rarely had to raise their voices for their insults. *Laverne & Shirley* ranked much lower because of the shouting, the predictability, and the forced quality of the insulting matches. Insults were not new to TV comedies; Ralph Cramden on *The Honeymooners* and the Kingfish on *Amos 'n' Andy* had certainly dropped their share of abuse on an undeserving world. But they were new to an audience that had had a steady diet of wonderful families, where the parents were trying to train their children to have good manners and quit name calling and insulting people they did not like.

Insults have long been a weapon of humor and a traditional part of all comedy. However, they have been for the most part only one of many humorous weapons, and a weapon used primarily at the lower end of the social and intellectual scale. When mixed with the enormous range of other humorous devices, the insult provided a useful portion of any comedy. The contemporary sit-com rarely provides this mixture, relying on an almost inexhaustible variety of ways to insult characters for the laughs in its episodes. "Up your nose with a rubber hose" from *Welcome Back, Kotter* is a representative catch-phrase for everything from *M*A*S*H* to *The Jeffersons*; the difference from show to show lies only in the wit of the insult and the name.

These are the weapons of children, and it is significant that they dominate so many shows where adults in an artificial family group play the role of children or where the father in a real family is far more childish than the children, as in *Sanford and Son* and *The Jeffersons* (the Jeffersons soon misplaced their son, since George could provide enough childishness for several families). But they are the weapons of children precisely because they are also ineffectual weapons. "Sticks and stones may break my bones, but words can never hurt me" is essentially true in the world of the traditional comedy. Calling Shylock names and heaping insults on his head make no difference in what he does in *The Merchant of Venice*; you have to beat him at his own game if you want to overcome him, and you need either the protection of the gods or a ready mother wit, which Portia has in plenty, to do that. Insulting the fools who want Jonson's alchemist to help them will not deter them; only by giving them the proverbial rope with which to hang themselves can you expose them and prove themselves to be what the names and the insults cannot prove. Insults are defensive, not aggressive; people resort to them when, like little children, they can think of nothing better to use against those who frighten them. They are funny when well done, for there is an art in invective and it is no small art, but it is only in the world of the melodrama and Spanish cloak-and-sword tragedies that the insult has an effect, most often prompting revenge and the death or downfall of the original insulter. That the sit-com must depend so completely on insults for its humor shows how little of the weaponry of the traditional comedy it can command.

In its pursuit of stability, the sitcom, a form in which the goal of all activity is a perfect defense that prevents any change, has been forced either to surrender or to alter those forms of humor that might promote some change. It keeps only those comic devices that are most defensive and ineffectual and shifts their aim onto the characters who used to be the heroes of the comedy—the young, the natural, the inventive adventurers who looked for progress in their comic societies. The only progress the sit-com accepts is the progress that makes the family unit more nearly perfect, more respectable, and more safe. How *M*A*S*H* gradually found and substituted more satisfactory children and a father has already been discussed, but a similar process can be seen in almost any sitcom. New characters are permissible, but only when they both fill an empty slot in the family unit and improve on the previous occupant of that slot. If an improvement cannot be found, then no replacement is made. Mary Tyler Moore's weatherman is never replaced, nor is Radar when he finally leaves *M*A*S*H*. There is no room for new people, never an all-inclusive welcome as at the ending of the traditional comedy. Nowhere is this more clear than in the "endings" of the situation comedies.

The ending of the traditional comedy is the promise of a new life, a celebration, a wedding, a possible baby, a new and better world. The only ending that the sit-com allows is death. Because the series format is designed to last forever without significant change, obviously no ending is planned. But series still must end sometime, and they end in most odd manners. When they go off the air, they just do not come on one day. Those series that do choose to make an ending always do so by making a change that destroys the situation. But there is no particular promise of something better or different; if anything, the ending is very sad. The tearful exit of *The Mary Tyler Moore Show* is the most memorable conclusion, but it only expresses something inherent in all comedy series. When the traditional comedy ends, there is no weeping in the house; if it has succeeded at all, there is elation and happiness in the audience, a feeling that things have been put right, at least in the world of the imagination. When a television comedy ends, for its fans something has gone wrong with the world. There is no sense of completion but rather an interruption, like a heart attack in a loved relative that removes him from one's world. It is sudden, inexplicable, and final.

This applies even to individual characters. The sit-com has an inexplicable urge to exclude permanently anyone who leaves the family in any way. Characters and actors are merged in an unusual way, as will be discussed later, but this merging means that when an actor quits for any reason, the character also quits. In the world of theatrical comedy, when one actor leaves the run of a play, he is simply replaced by another actor. Even films, despite their apparent permanence, can be remade with new casts; if they could not, such shows as *M*A*S*H* would never become TV series. But only a handful of sit-coms have ever changed actors in a character's role. Richard Deacon replaced Roger Carmel on *The Mothers-in-Law*, which did not last, and Penny Parker replaced Sherry Jackson as the daughter on *The Danny Thomas Show* for a year. Only two shows made successful cast changes: Dick Sargeant replaced Dick York for the last three years of *Bewitched* and Larry Keating replaced Fred Clark in midepisode on a remarkable *Burns and Allen Show*. Most of the time, an actor gone has meant a character dropped off the edge of the world, never to be heard from again. In recent years, there has been an odd urge to make the figurative death literal, the unnecessary killings off of Henry Blake and Edith Bunker being the most disturbing examples. Most others just disappear without explanation and without further reference from the remaining characters.

The sit-com lives under the ax. There can be movement inward but never outward, because "out there" is dangerous. The ratings ax is obvious, and when it falls, a series can die almost in midsentence, cut off without another word, another thought, another activity. But the fear of this ax aimed at the show's neck seems to infuse the attitudes of the shows themselves. Despite all the good spirits and humor and fun inside the family units, there is a persistent paranoia about life outside. Archie Bunker verbalizes it, but almost all of the series express it in some way, in their refusal to move, to change, to include additional people, or to maintain contact with anyone who dares to leave the circle. This inwardness is reflected in the individual episodes as well as the series as a whole by the finality with which Mary drops her boyfriends, Fonzie chases off the bullies, Mork learns his lesson, and Bob cures his nongroup patients. It follows through in the way characters are "spun off" for their own series and then lose all contact with the people of the series from which they came, a process that has intensified since the triad built around *The Beverly Hillbillies* family was killed in the great 1971 CBS schedule massacre. The sit-com operates in a world of

Us and Them, and there is room for only so many of Us and no more. If you cannot be one of Us, you automatically become one of Them and we will have as little to do with you as possible and will try our best to keep you and your effects as far from our little family unit as possible. This is not the world of the old comedy simply adjusted to fit a new medium. Films made that adjustment and found new variations that continued the plots and impulses of the traditional comedy, but television did not. After a few years of exploration, it settled on and perfected a new kind of comedy, which is a *new* comedy in almost every aspect. The situation comedy as it has evolved on American television has rejected more than the traditional comedy plot. Not only does boy not pursue and capture girl, he does not pursue *anything*. The principal fundamental situation of the situation comedy is that things do not change. No new society occurs at the end. The only end is death, for characters as well as for the situation itself, the precise opposite of the rebirth and new life promised in the celebrations of the traditional comedy. The series may come on every week for no more reason than that it is convenient for the network and the sponsors, but the messages that accompany those weekly appearances are the messages of defense, of protection, of the impossibility of progress or any other positive change. As a new comedy, it even has to destroy the ancient heroes and even the humorous devices with which they fought their good fights in the past. That such a change occurred is curious, but that such a change occurred in the largest mass medium known to man, in the most progressive and changeable society in Western history, and was immensely popular, is almost incredible. Everything the traditional comedy stood for, at every level of art, psychology, philosophy, and myth, has been overthrown in this New Comedy of American television.

4 • Movies and Other Mass Media

The year is 1914. War threatens in Europe, but America is secure and essentially unconcerned, its only real interest in European affairs being the continued influx of immigrants who were coming increasingly from central and southern Europe. The nation as a whole seems not only healthy but somehow innocent, like the big, awkward, square-faced girl wandering down the path in the flickering grey images on the screen. Her real name is Marie Dressler and she is in fact hardly a girl, forty-five years old under the strange and heavy make-up, but for the moment in the movies she is an innocent farm girl named Tillie.

Tillie meets a fellow with a funny mustache who is really Charlie Chaplin, on the edge of stardom, before he has discovered the little Tramp character. A real city slicker, he knows a sucker when he sees one, and with a little charm he convinces her of his love. Tillie steals her father's money, and she and Charlie run away to the wicked city, where Charlie meets Mabel Normand, an old girlfriend who is considerably more attractive than Tillie could ever hope to be. He gets Tillie wildly drunk, steals her money, and runs away with Mabel, leaving the chastened farm girl to slink back to her father. But the story does not end there; Tillie's uncle dies and leaves his fortune to her, and she returns to the city in wealth. Charlie discovers this and reappears, convinces Tillie of his contrition, and marries her. Mabel tracks Charlie down in Tillie's mansion, and when Tillie finds her there, the outraged wife begins to shoot up the house. At that point the uncle returns, for he was only missing and not dead. In the confusion of Tillie's anger, the police are called, and Tillie, with pistols blazing, chases Charlie, Mabel, her uncle, and the police into the Pacific. When they are all finally rescued, the women realize how Charlie has taken advantage of them both and, as Charlie is taken off by the police, they shake hands and go off together.

This confused and rather awkward piece of film became *Tillie's Punctured Romance*, Mack Sennett's first attempt at a long comic film feature. Before this work, most humorous silent films were only one reel in length, roughly ten minutes. *Tillie* was six reels long, about an hour, depending on the speed of the projectionist's cranking. Preceding D.W. Griffith's *Birth of a Nation* by several months, it was one of the first feature-length American films as well as the first feature-length comedy from any country. And it did remarkably well in the movie theatres and halls across the country, not as well of course as Griffith's blockbuster would do, but certainly well enough to indicate that people were more than willing to pay a bit extra to see longer humorous movies. Yet among the many curious aspects of the feature, one of the most curious is that it had no immediate successors. Chaplin did not make another six-reeler until *The Kid* in 1921, Harold Lloyd did not make one until 1922, and Ernst Lubitsch's *The Marriage Circle*, at eight reels the first genuine sophisticated film comedy in America, did not appear until 1924. Despite the growing audiences for movies and the increasing popularity of the film comedians themselves, the filmmakers were very wary of a film comedy any longer than a vaudeville sketch.

Part of the reason for this wariness can be seen in *Tillie* itself, for the film raises a number of problems that persist in films and film criticism into the present. It is an extremely disorganized piece of work; in fact, it looks like two completely different short films spliced together for no other reason than that they share the same casts. Given the way the Sennett operations worked, the film might very well have been assembled in precisely that manner. Nothing connects the two portions— Tillie's uncle is unmentioned before the bequest, and Charlie's loss of Tillie's original money is never explained—and the ending is incomplete and unmotivated. Film comedians through Jerry Lewis and John Belushi consistently experienced the same problems of how to connect their various routines and how to know when they had come to a point that could be a real ending. Many solved the problems just as awkwardly and artificially.

In the terms we have used here, *Tillie* is not a comedy at all, despite its general recognition as the first comedy feature film. It was a comedy by casting: Chaplin, Dressler, and Normand were all comedians, so the film was a comedy. In fact, it is, even for the times, a rather old-fashioned melodrama with humorous routines that, seen from the present, are decidedly unfunny. Chaplin was the villain, the seducer who defiled womanhood for filthy lucre, and Marie Dressler was the country bumpkin, the innocent maid who was lured away by the guiles of a silver-tongued city slicker but reformed when she saw the error of her ways. She let him come back, but only as a husband, so that she could remain pure. The film demonstrated that a long modern-dress melodrama could be translated to the screen, to compete with the adventure and spectacle films, if it used occasional spurts of humorous business to extend the length and keep the audience happy. Consequently, it encouraged the development of the six-to eight-reel feature, but it convinced the comics themselves that they would need a more viable model before they could surrender the security and the profitability of the shorts. Even when comedies were adapted from the stage, they tended to be changed to melodramas, although few made the violent changes that Griffith did when he converted a quaint Yankee hillbilly comedy called *Way Down East* into one of the most famous sinful-daughter-thrown-out-into-the-snows-of-winter melodramas in history, without even a pretense of humor.

The film comedians faced some very serious problems, much more serious than later mass media faced, because film was something new. It was the first real mass medium. Print had made information available to many, but the newspapers and magazines were always hampered not only by the general illiteracy of the public but also by the distances over which the printed material had to be distributed. These problems limited the practicality of print media in such a way that most localities still had very little contact with other parts of the nation or the world. Theatre, of course, communicated to large groups, but only to those who could fit into a single room for a single performance. It could take years for a play to work its way around the country, by which time the original experience would be significantly altered. With film it was at least theoretically possible that every person in the country, or even in the world as long as the film was silent, could share the exact same experience. If enough prints were made, they could even share that experience at the same time. And film spoke to illiterate and literate, to old and young, to rich and poor, to sophisticates and simpleminded alike. There had been absolutely nothing like it, and the people who made the movies had to invent an entirely new way of ordering experience in order to exploit the new medium.

Much of the early film work was pure naturalism, pictures of people and animals and machines doing various things, in which the novelty, and the interest, as with Dr. Johnson's performing dog, was that the pictures existed at all. Within a very short while, however, the audience had accepted that pictures could move, and the novelty wore off, just as it would do some years later when sound was introduced, and again after color and wide-screen processes were popularized. Producers were forced to find some way to hold the audience's attention beyond novelty, so they turned to the stage for stories, for styles, and for performers. For the most part, this solution did not work. Despite the use of such stage stars as Sarah Bernhardt, neither famous nor obscure plays on film attracted or interested film audiences. Although film seemed dramatic in relation to its audience, the conventions and devices of the stage seemed to make little sense on film. Even when sound was added, films of stage plays always seemed a little stodgy and out of place, and most turned out to be very poor movies unless heavily revised.

The initial experiments made by the moviemakers involved the simple substitution of reality for stage scenery—real trees in real woods, with real trains, real horses, real rivers, and so on. This helped only a little. Not until the development of the close-up did film begin to find its own grammar. But once the close-up was accepted, the whole editing process—with changing viewpoints, intercutting of scenes, and a variety of shots—gave movies a language that completely eliminated their dependence on stage materials for either content or inspiration.

If, as Marshall McLuhan says, the content of any medium is another medium, then the content of films became the novel or the short story, not the play. Not only are most films adapted from narrative rather than dramatic materials, but also the very arrangement of material is borrowed from the written story. Movies are pieced together in sentences, each shot demonstrating one thing and one thing only, just as the novelist lays out his story on paper, and the meaning of those shots is developed sequentially, one thing after another, just as in the written story. On the stage, the audience sees action and reaction simultaneously. As one character speaks, the persons to whom he speaks are present, visible, and within our area of concentration; their expressions are part of the simultaneous experience. In the film we see that kind of simultaneous experience only if the filmmaker wants us to; most of the time, we see a shot of the speaker, then a shot of the reaction from the listener, two separate and discrete pieces of information, two sentences that we take in sequentially and then reprocess to comprehend as a simultaneous experience.

The standard film formula for establishing a scene, the long shot/medium shot/close-up sequence, is the standard method of the nineteenth-century novelist, visible in the beginning of most of the chapters of Dickens, Balzac, Flaubert, Hardy, and hundreds of others long before writers began to shape their books for an eventual movie sale. Although the nineteenth-century theatre adapted an enormous amount of its material from the novels of the day, from Harriet Beecher Stowe's vigorous *Uncle Tom's Cabin* to Mrs. Henry Woods's saccharine *East Lynne*, playwrights were never able to lay out scenes in a novelistic manner. Except for the fact that feature-length films are conventionally ninety minutes long, many novels could be made into movies almost without adaptation, simply by following the novel as written. The point can be easily demonstrated by almost any of the eight-to thirteen-hour adaptations for television brought over from England in recent years which have had the time to follow the books in detail (some, like *Brideshead Revisited*, based on Evelyn Waugh's novel, are almost word-for-word adaptations). The shots as well as the dialogue are already in the original fiction.

This made a unique set of problems for the comedians and humorists who were working in films. As we have seen, the comic traditions of the novel and of the theatre had been far different from each other. Most important, comedy had always been the most public of all art forms. Because it used humor in some form as its basic weapon, comedy had to have groups of people immediately present to laugh as well as to share the important communal myth implied in all the basic comedy plot variations and heroes. The storyteller's tradition, which the novel had transferred to print media, was much more personal and private. The storyteller communicated in a one-to-one relationship, speaker to listener, writer to reader. As a new medium, film shared both the public, communal nature of the theatre and the private, personal world of the novel. Audiences viewed together, but in darkened theatres, sharing in the darkness a sense of personal identification with film characters that had not been possible in the theatre. A film shown in an empty theatre is essentially the same film as the work shown in a full theatre, but a play shown before an empty house is far different from the work that a full house sees, and never more different than when the work is a comedy. Years later, radio and then television would provide the sounds of artificial audiences to augment the private experiences of their home audiences, but the early filmmakers had no access to sound technology. For the most part, humorous filmmakers wandered around, trying a bit of one thing and a bit of another, for about twenty years. As the melodramas expanded and dominated the marquees (and the profits), as the short comic films were relegated to supporting status on theatre billings (and rentals), comedy was forced to expand its length for its own economic survival.

When it did so, it returned to the basic plot of theatrical comedy. It did not have to do so. Film was a new medium, and film comedy could have developed its own formulas and forms; all other genres did. Film could have adopted the comic novel as its inspiration, with its almost random sequence of funny events along a journey through life. Given that such a form would have been easy to produce and that the rest of film borrowed heavily from novelistic traditions, it is more than just remarkable that film comedy rejected this form. In fact, few famous comic novels past or present have been adapted for films. Henry Fielding's *Tom Jones* was eventually filmed, but no one has yet tried Laurence Sterne's *Tristram Shandy*; adaptations of Dickens have not included *Our Mutual Friend* or *Martin Chuzzlewit*; Thomas Berger's *Little Big Man* did reach the screen, but not Saul Bellow's *The Adventures of Augie March*, J. D. Salinger's *Catcher in the Rye*, or John Barth's *The Sot-Weed Factor*. When many other novels were adapted they became melodramas, often rather turgid ones at that, without any of the humor of the original source, from the various film versions of Thackeray's *Vanity Fair* through Faulkner's *The Hamlet* (buried in *The Long Hot Summer*) and Joseph Heller's *Catch-22*. At least one strand of this method of organization did persist, however, in the almost obligatory Army film.

Many comedians have made a military comedy, and in most the structure is provided by the experience. The film begins when the comic gets drafted or joins up and ends when he gets out or the situation significantly changes. In between are whatever adventures occur as the comic civilian comes in contact with the strict military regime. Chaplin's *Shoulder Arms*, Laurel and Hardy's *Great Guns*, Abbott and Costello's *Buck Privates*, and Martin and Lewis's *Jumping Jacks*, Bill Murray's *Stripes*, and Goldie Hawn's *Private Benjamin* all share the same structure, varied only to demonstrate the unique talents of the individual comic. The same structure was used in more critically respected military comic films as well, such as *No Time for Sergeants*, *Mr. Roberts*, and *M*A*S*H*. But outside of these military features and a handful of similar job-oriented features designed to show off the individual comic, like Lewis's *Bellboy*, filmmakers seem uncomfortable with this form.

So do audiences. For example, *Duck Soup* is now considered by most critics to be the Marx Brothers film *par excellence*. It is the only one of their features in which they completely surrendered the role of helper to a set of young lovers and adopted the form of the random adventure. In the theatres of the time, however, it had the lowest gross income of any of the Marx Brothers features to that date, so low in fact that there was considerable speculation that the team might be completely washed up in the movies. They did manage to get out one more feature, the blatantly traditional *A Night at the Opera*, which became their most popular and profitable film.[1]

The other mass media all developed their own dominant, and in general unique, forms of comedic organization. Newspapers and magazines, once teletype made serious syndication possible, developed the short random essay, of which Will Rogers was the acknowledged master, and later the four-panel comic strip. Radio developed a varying mixture of verbal comedy and music, often built around a fixed place but often with very little plot. Examples include *Duffy's Tavern*, and the series built around Edgar Bergen and Charlie McCarthy, Jack Benny, Fred Allen, Jimmie Durante and many others. TV of course, developed the sit-com. Moviemakers returned to the traditional comedy. That this was not an automatic decision, that it was made with some difficulty, can be seen in the time it took the comedians to accept the old plot as the best way to shape and organize their longer work.

Most of the film comedians came to movies from the music hall and the vaudeville houses, not from the legitimate stage. Sandwiched among the singers, jugglers, and animal acts, they had learned to use and to hone their four, five, or ten minutes (if they were stars) for maximum humorous results. When they moved to films, the limits of the one-reeler form were no limits to them—they kept changing places and sometimes changing clothes and doing the same pratfalls and routines they had always done. Some, the more successful ones, realized that there were new opportunities; Chaplin, Lloyd, Keaton, Fields, and others kept expanding their material and exploring the possibilities of the new medium. But plot was rarely an interest for them. All they really needed was a framework in which to do their routines, and melodrama or parody provided frameworks in many ways more profitable than did the traditional comedies.

Funny characters within the melodrama had been a consistent part of theatrical life throughout the nineteenth century, and many a comedian's career had been enhanced when he became the funny guy whom the hero met along the way or the hero's sidekick. Such characters had been common in all serious drama since the Renaissance that had not fallen under the spell of the French neoclassicists, and included Shakespeare's Falstaff, Gravedigger, or Porter at the head of a long list of what is often called comic relief. Sometimes these relief characters would almost overwhelm the rest of the work, as Falstaff does, but the presence of funny characters, even of major proportions, does not automatically mean that we are seeing a comedy. Many of the stars, once the star system developed, provided their own comic relief, acting as a hero in the melodrama or adventure who also did funny things that helped endear him to his audience. On stage, Dion Boucicault's Irish plays often allowed him to provide some of his own comic relief while ultimately defeating villainy. Many of the character comics of the silents did the same when they made longer features, especially Charlie Chaplin.

Chaplin, seen from the present, is an enigma, a very confusing character. He was the first and most famous of the great film comics, the man who made silent films world-famous almost single-handedly. He was the king of comedy for many people and is still the man most intensely studied and discussed in film histories and studies of comedy. At the same time, the acclaim, the nostalgia, and the canonization have all served to cloud any real perception of his work, especially at feature length. When we wade through the piles of adulation to see the movies themselves, it often turns out that in his feature-length films Chaplin was very uncomfortable with comedy and often rejected not only the comedic plot but also the use of humor for anything more than occasional relief from a sea of sentimental pathos.

When seeing Chaplin from a distance, the younger critic has some difficulties with him that people who saw him in first runs or who knew

113

about him through the constant admiration of parents and older friends do not seem to share. In a way, seeing Chaplin's films today is rather like seeing the films of D. W. Griffith; one can recognize their historical importance and their influence on later works without enjoying or particularly admiring them. Like Griffith, Chaplin seems to belong to another time, another world, which has little to say to the present. His films, despite the attention and acclaim he received in his own day, may become the equivalent of the works of Sir Arthur Pinero and Dion Boucicault, or Colley Cibber and George Colman. One can see the imaginativeness in Griffith's *Birth of a Nation* and at the same time see what was not so apparent at the time, that the film was a throwback not only in its racial stereotypes but also in its conceptions of plot and society: it reflected a world view that was already on its way out, even as it was being made. In the same way, one can recognize the grace and charm of *City Lights* while at the same time recognizing that it has little to do with comedy and a great deal to do with "The Little Match Girl Meets Horatio Alger."

The world of Chaplin is very much the world of Alger's books, a world in which the hero establishes his pluck and his good heart and is rescued by some lucky fortune. Despite the myth of pulling yourself up by your bootstraps associated with Alger's works, in the books themselves hard work only establishes the hero's worthiness; the success comes from a sudden bequest, an unknown benefactor, or perhaps a long-lost relative who dies and leaves our hero a fortune. Chaplin's world is also one of great sentimentality, in which the little guy is good *because* he is little (except, of course, when he has found the windfall, which he will probably give away), in which girls are always blind or frail or orphaned, and in which old ladies would always bake cookies if they were not starving. It is, in effect, the world of the Victorian social melodrama, of Dion Boucicault's *The Streets of New York*, John Walker's *The Factory Lad*, Tom Taylor's *The Ticket-of-Leave Man*, and various versions of *The Drunkard*, and it was already out of date while Chaplin was working, a point that may have been at least partially evident to him.

It seems important to note that, during the Depression, in the decade of the greatest economic distress and most widespread poverty the country had known, in a time when the common man was more desperate and depressed than ever before or since, the one man in the entertainment industry who most personified the resilience, inventiveness, pluck, and ability to survive and prosper in the worst circumstances, at the height of his creative powers and financial strength, managed to make only one film. That film, *Modern Times*, even if the lack of speech is disregarded, seems to be rooted in 1919 rather than 1936, its marchers more a part of the era of the Wobblies and the red scare than of the CIO and the great lock-in strikes, its hero a wanderer by choice rather than necessity, except when he has to feed the orphan girl. The whole business of the orphans' home appears to be some weird throwback to Dickens.

Chaplin's first feature after he developed the Tramp character was *The Kid* (1921), a domestic melodrama of the most obvious order. Edna Purviance leaves her illegitimate baby in a car that is stolen; the crooks leave the baby on a garbage pile, where Charlie finds it. Unable to give the baby away, he raises it, until the kid gets sick. The doctor reports the kid's existence to the authorities, who try to take the kid to an orphanage, but Charlie grabs him out of the truck and they hide out together. Edna is now famous and wealthy and offers a reward for the kid. The owner of the flophouse where they are hiding recognizes them, steals the kid while Charlie sleeps, and returns him to Edna. Heartbroken, Charlie dreams of a heaven where he can not find happiness either, only to be awakened by a cop who miraculously takes him to Edna's home to meet her and the kid again. While there are humorous touches, such as the inventive baby furniture Charlie devises or Charlie repairing the windows that the kid has broken "by accident" to make a living, the dominant device is tears, tears in the audience's eyes to match the tears flowing from the one memorable image of Jackie Coogan penned in the orphanage truck like a pet dog and being driven away from the brokenhearted Chaplin. Despite Chaplin's presence, the film was no more a comedy than was Wallace Beery's version of the same basic story as *The Champ* ten years later or the hundreds of long-forgotten poor-orphan features being cranked out at the same time in other studios without the authority of Chaplin's presence or skill as a director.

The same tearful perceptions permeate most of Chaplin's other features: in the Little Match Girl world of *City Lights*, in the faded old star talking endlessly about the beauty of a life lived through tears and pain to the girl who wanted to commit suicide in *Limelight*, in the poor little barber's escape from the forces of evil in *The Great Dictator*, in much of *The Circus*, and even in *The Gold Rush*. Whatever his awesome skills as a filmmaker and a comedian might have been, the forms within which he chose to place his comedic routines were the forms of the melodrama, where his humor served primarily as a release from the tensions and sentiment of his tear-jerking story lines.

Many of the film comedians continued in this vein, although most tried to avoid the pathetic, almost bathetic, stories that Chaplin preferred. Most chose to do funny versions of basic melodrama genres. Abbott and Costello's credits cover the territory in their titles: *Abbott and Costello Meet the Mummy/Captain Kidd/Frankenstein/The Invisible Man*; *Abbott and Costello Go to Mars*; *Comin' Round the Mountain*; *Ride 'Em Cowboy*; *Hold That Ghost*; *Pardon My Sarong*. But many an actor not famous for being in comedies made funny versions of these various melodrama genres as well. Yet no matter how funny Jimmy Stewart might be in *Destry Rides Again*, the plot line is the same as *Shane*; no matter how you laugh at Peter Ustinov in *Topkapi*, the heist is still the center of the film and the story the same as *Seven Thieves* or *Rififi*. If *The Crimson Pirate* is a comedy, so is *Captain Blood*, and no matter how delightful William Powell, Myrna Loy, and the dog may be in *The Thin Man* series, they are still solving murder mysteries. Thus, one of the dominant strains of film humor ends up in the service of the melodrama, often with the comedian's role greatly expanded yet still within plot structures and myths of that much-maligned yet persistently popular form of dramatic and literary entertainment.

These same genres of the melodrama often provided the comedian with subjects for another popular kind of material, the parody. Many a comic has made his audiences laugh by simply exaggerating some work that was currently popular or by ridiculing the clichés of a whole body of similar works, from Aristophanes sending a character to Hades to find a good playwright to Johnny Carson making Colonel Sanders jokes. Film comedians were quick to take the opportunities when they came up, and there are innumerable parodies of films, plays, and books. Most of these parodies were short films because it is very hard to sustain parody for any length of time, and most have disappeared as their subjects have faded from consciousness, in the same way that Beaumont and Fletcher's *The Knight of the Burning Pestle* and Henry Fielding's *Tom Thumb* have disappeared from the theatrical world as their subjects faded away. Some feature-length parody films have succeeded, and should not be ignored. Mel Brooks has made a career from these parodies, ridiculing the western in *Blazing Saddles*, the monster movie in *Young Frankenstein*, the Alfred Hitchcock thriller in *High Anxiety*, and so on. But they are all ephemeral because they make no sense and provide no humor unless the audience shares a full knowledge of the material being parodied. Just as their material depends on another genre, so does their form, and they are all organized around the ideas and characters of the genres on which they depend. Thus, although they are an important and persistent form of humor, they are not really a part of the comedic tradition.

Many of the silent comedians moved only gradually toward the traditional comedy plot, by way of the melodrama versions that had borrowed parts of that comedic tradition. It is to melodrama's adaptation of the basic comic plot that we probably owe the disrepute of the happy ending today, for much of melodrama grafted on the boy-gets-girl aspects of the plot. Melodrama, however, differed from the traditional comedy in several ways, not the least of which was its concern for morality. The social problem or the blocking character in the traditional melodrama is an evil that must be overthrown or, more often, completely destroyed. In the comedy, characters may be wrong but they are only rarely evil (Molière's Tartuffe being a possible exception). The "fault" of the father in Plautine comedies, for example, is that he wants the same girl his son wants, and for exactly the same reasons; the father is socially unacceptable because of his age, but not evil or wicked or less moral than the son with the same lusts. In the American melodrama, however, the older man who wants the girl wants her only to get her land, or to tempt her into drink and a life of prostitution for his own profit; or perhaps he simply wants her because she is too pure and must be destroyed to make his own villainy palatable. Whatever the reasons, the villain of the melodrama rarely wants the girl for the making of children.

Most often in the melodrama, the girl is little more than a prize for the hero after he succeeds in saving the town, capturing the villain, or doing his great deed for any number of reasons unrelated to the girl. It may be simply the code of the west or the code of chivalry, doing deeds because they are the right things to do. It may be the only way for our hero to make his fortune. Or he may find that he has no choice in the matter: surrounded by Indians or Nazis or whatever villains are at hand, he must win simply to stay alive. But rarely does the hero oppose the melodrama's villain simply because they both want the same girl; instead, other issues, usually moral issues, are at stake.

Once the hero has won, if he has survived, melodrama writers generally shower him with the prizes of the age—happiness, success, and a smiling woman with open arms. Such endings are often so awkward, unclear, and obviously gratuitous that they cheapen the artistic values of all melodramas. They also have made all happy endings suspect. Comedy's lovers are quite different, but they are still lovers who rush into each other's arms at the final curtain, and it is easy to treat one ending as cheaply and casually as you treat the other.

This fear of the boy-meets-girl basis of the comedy brought on by its overuse in the melodrama has led to some strange positions among contemporary intellectuals and literary figures. The editor of one recent short-story collection, *Familiar Faces*, even apologizes in the foreword for including a boy-meets-girl story with a happy ending.[2] Why this has occurred is the subject for a psychologist to consider, but there can be no doubt that it has occurred. Because it has caused critics and scholars to belittle or ignore the traditional basic comedy plot, it has disguised the fundamental changes being made in our perceptions of the world through the television situation comedy, and made it all but impossible for us to perceive much of importance about the comedy itself.

Melodrama, of course, had many other plots as well. Once the question of good and evil enters the plot, the hero must do the right thing or he cannot be the hero. Thus, we have melodramas where the hero gets the girl as he dies, or she declares her love for him as she dies. Sometimes he gets the girl but gives her up for her own good, a very popular plot in the movies especially (see *Casablanca* and almost any western). And sometimes there is no girl involved at all; there is an adventure, or a battle, or a test for the hero, and the reward is his success, or good for its own sake, or even his death while saving the town or the family. But the melodrama for the most part shares some of the interests of the comedy, which makes it possible for many comedic performers to move from one form to the other, as well as confuses much of the criticism of the works produced, especially in the movies.

The biggest problem the silent comedians had with the adoption of the comedy plot lay in their own personalities. Many of them had developed characters who were not socially acceptable for the girl. Chaplin, again, provides the most complex example of the problem. After he developed the Tramp, as a wastrel and wanderer, he had little to offer a girl within the Victorian moral code of so many of his films. The inventive rascality that endeared him to his audience also made him rather dangerous as a suitor. Since his code and the morality of the time rarely allowed him any short-term alliances with the virginal heroines he preferred, he often found himself surrendering the girl for her own good, as in the short entitled *The Tramp*, where his character made his first fully recognizable appearance. There we begin to see the "classic Chaplin finale,"[3] as Uno Asplund describes it, with Chaplin jauntily walking off into the sunset, cane atwirl, having sentimentally sacrificed himself and his own happiness again.

However, the "classic" Chaplin is not always the most common one. When he places the character in situations that allow him to have some respectability, or at least economic potential, he often becomes a romantic hero and gets the girl for himself. This can be seen in such shorts as *The Immigrants*, where his vagrancy is shared by Edna Purviance, since they are both immigrants, and *Easy Street*, where the Tramp becomes, of all things, a policeman. In his feature *The Gold Rush*, Charlie must strike it rich before he can get the girl (a theme more common with Harold Lloyd), and in *Modern Times*, the girl is as much a vagrant as he and they *both* walk jauntily into the sun, his cane still atwirl. As the little Jewish barber in *The Great Dictator*, his dream is a nice barber shop and the lovely Hannah. Although a lot of conflicting comments have been written about *City Lights*, and particularly about the final frames, in the print I have seen there is little doubt that the girl not only recognizes Charlie but accepts him as well.

The ambiguous nature of the Tramp's relations with women is most noticeable in *Modern Times*. What is a reasonably intelligent viewer supposed to make of Paulette Goddard in that film? She was nearly twenty-five when the film was made and she looks it. The film even accepts her physical maturity, giving her a job as an attractive dancer who draws male customers. Yet we are also asked to accept that she is a child running from the orphanage, a female version of Jackie Coogan perhaps. Thus, when she and Chaplin join hands and walk off into the sunset, is it a kindly fellow leading the kid off for another adventure together or has the "dirty little man" finally found himself a lover who is not too good for him? The second interpretation makes it a very old-fashioned comedy, while the first makes it an even more old-fashioned orphan-in-the-storm melodrama, as soapy as a Gene Autry western. But it cannot be both simultaneously: the situations are mutually exclusive.

Buster Keaton and Harold Lloyd were much more handsome in their public personalities (although behind his Tramp costume there were few in Hollywood better looking than the real Chaplin). They were able to shift their basic personae into roles as lovers and often got the girl at the end of a long comedic pursuit, at the end of the feature. In many cases, they began the feature in pursuit of her as well. In *Safety Last* Lloyd is in the city where he makes the famous climb only because he is trying to make enough money to get married to the cute little girl he has left behind. Sometimes the relationship with the girl is a bit nebulous, as in Keaton's *The General*, and it is difficult to tell whether he gets involved in the war because of his job or whether he gets involved to prove his worthiness for the young woman he loves, who has temporarily forsaken him. But there is a tendency in all of these films to move toward the traditional comedy plot.

For some reason, most of the "famous" comics of silent film were unable to accept comedy plots in which they could not get the girl, and they resisted the position of helper in working out the basic plot until sound films came along. Meanwhile, Ernst Lubitsch was proving with such films as *The Marriage Circle, Kiss Me Again,* and *So This Is Paris* that the traditional comedy not only could work in film but could often be more intelligent and sophisticated, as well as more cinematic, than most of the supposedly serious features with which it competed. When sound came, the ground had been prepared, and the movies accepted almost completely the traditions and characters of the traditional comedy plot, led initially by Lubitsch again with his Maurice Chevalier/ Jeanette MacDonald operettas.

Throughout most of dramatic history, one particular variation of the comedy plot dominates at any given time. The Restoration concentrated on lovers who were scoundrels, for example, while the French at almost the same time concentrated on the characters who blocked the lovers from their union. Jacobean England liked women who pursued the men, while Victorian England and Second Empire France preferred older men who pursued the virginal female. Because the movies were so new, and so desperate for material to fill the thousands of theatres in the country (and ultimately the world), American filmmakers borrowed from almost every variation the theatre had taken hundreds of years to develop. Although the possibility existed to develop a unique form of comedy, the traditional comedy and the flexibility of the traditional plot structures and characters made them irresistible to the new medium. The result was a second golden age in film comedy, which has not received the critical attention that the silent era has received, and which produced examples of almost all the dominant variations in Western comedic history.

Those comedy films that dealt with lovers and the nature of love reproduced all the Shakespearean variations. Feuding lovers were especially popular, from the spectacular *Twentieth Century* through *The Awful Truth* to *Philadelphia Story* and the excellent films made by Spencer Tracy and Katharine Hepburn, to mention only a few of the most obvious examples. Wandering lovers were not as prominent as might be expected, given their possibilities, but there are notable examples. The most common form is very simple, where the girl next door loves the boy, who is lured away by a blonde siren but realizes his mistake and returns to the girl who always loved him, as Mickey Rooney returns to Judy Garland in *Strike Up the Band*. Some extremely sophisticated variations of the serial lovers occur, such as the daring *ménage* in *Design for Living*. An apex of complexity can be seen in *Midnight*. Don Ameche falls in love with Claudette Colbert, who is hired by John Barrymore to steal Francis Lederer from Mary Astor (who is Barrymore's wife); Colbert is successful until Ameche pretends to be her husband and forces her to get a divorce (although they are not married), in the course of which the judge refuses to divorce them and Colbert and Ameche decide they really are in love.

The variation of pure love separated only by circumstances beyond anyone's control occurs as well, though not as often, because beliefs in magic and angel interference are less prevalent than in earlier periods. Usually a couple discovers for some reason that their marriage was not legal, as in *Mr. and Mrs. Smith*. Later, especially in the 1940s, when a raft of ghosts and angels return to earth, we get a number of these plots, the most notable being *The Ghost and Mrs. Muir*, in which Gene Tierney falls in love with a ghost and stays faithful until they are united by her death. Quite often these films require the cynical city lovers to take a physical detour into Arcadia, as do so many of Shakespeare's lovers, to rediscover their own innocence and find love, as does Barbara Stanwyck in *Remember the Night* and *Christmas in Connecticut*.

The fading love variation that involves married couples, developed in the French bedroom farces, is a most important strain, from the young-married comedies like *Eternally Yours* and *True Confessions* to the sophisticated and complex divorce comedies like *Philadelphia Story* and *The Awful Truth*, in which scandalously divorced couples wander away only to return eventually and remarry their original spouses.

The other major strand of stage tradition put the emphasis on the lovers' problem, often personified by particular persons. For most of the stage plays, the person was a parent of some kind, but that character often dominated the entire play. Films used this variation a great deal but often chose to make the blocking character less important than the characters who overcame him yet who were not themselves the lovers. This is the variation chosen by most of the great comic teams. In *A Night at the Opera*, Allan Jones and Kitty Carlisle are lovers blocked by the jealousy of the Great Rodolpho, who is aided by Sig Rumann as the impresario. Enter the Marx Brothers, who promise to get Jones to America, help him make his career, and in the process get him to Carlisle. Most of the film is devoted to some of the Brothers' finest routines, but they are present only to aid in overcoming the obstacles that separate the lovers. This position is the one most often seen for Laurel and Hardy in their features, as well as for Abbott and Costello. It is a noble tradition, tracing itself back to Plautus's wily slaves, through Molière's Scapin and Sgnarelle, but it is not a position central to the structure of the comedy itself. They are present as helpers for the lovers, often dominating the lovers because they are much more interesting, but still merely helpers to the basic plot.

Since the thirties were a time of terrific social and economic unrest and considerable questioning of most social and economic institutions, it should come as no surprise that many films made their blocking characters stand for particular social figures and values. The problems for the lovers in these films are caused by the problems various characters and their policies make for society as a whole, rather than specifically for the lovers. The primary examples are of course Frank Capra's films. In *Mr. Smith Goes to Washington*, the hero finds cliques and corruption rampant. In *Mr. Deeds Goes to Town*, the hero discovers that money is a problem in itself and tries to give it away to help those suffering from the Depression. In *Meet John Doe* the problem is again social: political corruption growing from the Depression threatens to develop into an American fascism. The thread that holds all of these films together, however, is the girl's realization that she loves the hero and their eventual embrace in the final frames. Even so, they illustrate how closely the comedy and the social melodrama are connected. Especially in *John Doe*, Capra loses much of the humor and respect for the opponents that lightened the earlier films, and there is no doubt that we are dealing with a real villainy. Like Chaplin, he mixes melodrama, sentimentality, and comedy in such a pleasant blend that it is always debatable where one ends and the next begins.

Other writers and directors used social problems for their comic plots without wandering quite so far into the melodramatic aspects. Preston Sturges, for example, looks at the economic problems of a young couple trying to get married in *Christmas in July*, gives them a big prize from a contest, then takes it away again to show the fatuousness of business and the greed of the average man, but he does it without villains or evil. In *Sullivan's Travels*, his hero even ends up on a chain gang, but the conclusion reached, once he is returned to the love of Veronica Lake, is that it is important to make people laugh. Many movies, particularly in the thirties, were concerned with the problems of the Depression, of lack of jobs and lack of money. Yet consistently the filmmakers chose to frame the story in terms of the boy-meets-girl plot, from *Easy Living* to *My Man Godfrey* to *My Sister Eileen*.

As already noted, the traditional heroes were widely represented in all these comedies. Innocent, Fool, and Scoundrel all were a part of the comedy world that film borrowed and adapted from the traditional stage, and filmmakers used the same comic devices and weapons that the comedy had always used to attack the same forces the comedy had always attacked. There were, of course, some peculiarly American variations, not the least of which were an insistence on matching male Innocents with female Scoundrels and the widespread, highly sophisticated dependence on comic teams as characters who helped to make the mess and then straighten it out again.

As might be expected in a nation whose mythology celebrated the common man, the natural man, and democratic principles, the comedies were most often designed to expose and ridicule people with social pretensions. One might expect, particularly during the Depression, that the rich would be the principal target, but it was not that simple. The rich were regularly attacked, but not for being rich or even for spending gaudily. Rather, they were assaulted only when they tried to pretend they were better than other people.

My Man Godfrey is the most spectacular of the film attacks on the rich through humor, but certainly not the only one. We are introduced to rich people as unfeeling swine, crawling through a Depression shantytown in their evening clothes in search of a "forgotten man" for a scavenger hunt. Then we see the rich family, the best of whom is a

123

father who may be good at heart but who has little head for business and no control of his wife and daughters. The wife is artistically pretentious, devoting herself alternately to her pets and to her protegé, a mad Russian *artiste* who never produces any art but does eat a lot and acts like a pet gorilla when called upon to entertain. One daughter is a selfish bitch, the other a scatterbrained idiot. Their butler Godfrey, their forgotten man, is the son of another rich family who is out to prove his own worth without depending on the family money.

What makes such film caricatures more than merely attacks upon the rich is the addition of a relatively new, and generally American, twist. All of the problems of the family in *Godfrey* are caused by the pretensions of the women. Eugene Pallette, the father, is a good guy underneath all this folderol, which becomes clear as soon as he falls on economic hard times. The wife is the one who needs paintings she does not understand, a phony protegé, and the trappings of wealth and status. In an overwhelming number of American film comedies, the pretentious, hypocritical character who blocks the lovers and who must be overcome or reformed is a female, the mother rather than the father. Margaret Dumont personifies everything the Marx Brothers were in revolt against, and it is always her interference in something she does not really understand that catapults them into the prominence that allows them finally to destroy her.

Even more than pretentiousness, respectability in American films belongs to the women. In theatrical tradition, respectability has been for the most part a male role, the middle-aged man upholding his position in middle-class society. Mrs. Malaprop in Sheridan's *The Rivals* is a notably rare exception. Shakespeare's characters, or Jonson's, rarely even have mothers. None of Molière's major hypocrites has a wife. Partly as a result of the public morality of the Victorian era, we begin to see some powerful female blocking characters (Lady Bracknell, for example, in Wilde's *The Importance of Being Earnest*) in European comedies by 1900, yet still surprisingly few. But in American plays they begin quite early, as evidenced by Mrs. Tiffany in Anna Mowatt's *Fashion*. Mrs. Stonington and Miss Merriam in Clyde Fitch's *Captain Jinks of the Horse Marine* set the tone for the women who later populate the movies in their eagerness to condemn things they have not seen and cannot hear, a tone that has solidified by the time of the awesome menagerie of mature Phillimore females in Langdon Mitchell's *The New York Idea*. The same phalanx of respectable women drive Mae

West out of town in *My Little Chickadee* and appear in most of her other features.

In films, these pretentious women were everywhere. Topper's wife, W.C. Fields's wives in *The Bank Dick* and *It's a Gift*, and all of the various Laurel and Hardy wives are only a sample of the women who hold their men down and prevent them from doing the right things in order to the proper things. And if there is a twerpy son in an American comedy, a respectable matronly mother cannot be far behind, as witnessed by Ralph Bellamy in almost any of his movies, particularly *The Awful Truth* and *His Girl Friday*. Sometimes this woman is a spoiled rich bitch, like the girls in *My Man Godfrey* or Claudette Colbert in *It Happened One Night*, but she is rarely spoiled or supported by her father: it is Colbert's father who tries to get her to leave her upper-class lover in favor of Clark Gable.

For all these women, the worst pretense, or at least the most visible sign of their pretense, is artistic. The opera and symphony come in for inordinate amounts of comic assault, perhaps even more than modern painting. Mr. Deeds is all in favor of music, as long as it is good American masculine music, as produced by the town band in which he plays tuba, but he will not give a cent to the opera or the symphony, whose supporters are all portrayed as foreigners, pompous matrons, and effeminate city types. Museums, for which such women are always raising money, are of course stodgy, boring, and wasteful, frequented by the same character types as the opera. One of the oddest versions of this theme occurs in *On the Town*, one of the finest of all film musicals, especially odd since the film is based on a ballet. In the course of the story, not only does Ann Miller throw away her glasses and her museum ticket to run off with Jules Munschin, but Vera Ellen is convinced by Gene Kelly that it is wrong for her to want to be a ballet dancer when she could be a housewife instead (although it is all right to be a hootchy-kootch dancer at Coney Island).

Aside from this tendency to shift the basic attack from the father figure to the mother figure when possible, the film comedies followed the lead of the ancient comedies. Policemen and military men (except draftees) were stupid, incompetent, and often cowardly; teachers and intellectuals were either pedants or ineffectual, absentminded twits with no perception of reality; politicians were inept or corrupt; and businessmen were to be trusted only if they were absolutely incompetent, like W.C. Fields or Laurel and Hardy. Many of the heroes were destroyers, as seen earlier, and they destroyed the property with which these respectable characters tried to maintain their public propriety and authority.

Such traditions did not transfer to film automatically. In many ways, as we have seen, they developed in the face of contrary traditions in basic film grammar and other genres of the movies. Despite the use of the film medium and techniques and a film grammar, television comedy has consistently rejected those same traditions, and much of the film business experienced the same problems television producers would later share. The biggest problem was how to get people to come and pay money to see a movie before they knew what was in it. This problem has of course been known in the theatre, but not in the same way. Most European theatres had always had some subsidy for their work, from the Greek festivals through the English Tudor companies supported partially by noblemen to the Comédie Française and other national theatres. In America, where theatres operated without subsidies almost from the beginning, the search for attractions was constant and encouraged the development of the star system. But throughout much of the nineteenth century, for example, the theatrical nights were long and a new play would be billed with a familiar work until it was clear the new one could be popular; as many as half of the regular offerings were "classics" that people came to see over and over again. After some real hits appeared, the theatre began to shift toward the long-run system, in which a play ran as long as people would pay to see it and no one worried what was happening in other theatres or to the people who had already seen the hit. Film producers opted to take advantage of their ability to enlarge the screen image and chose larger theatres rather than long runs, but this left them with the problem of filling the large theatres regularly, getting the people to come back every Thursday, so to speak. This is not much different from television's need to deliver viewers every night.

In television in America, the viewers paid no money directly, but they still had to be delivered in a predictable manner for the advertisers who did pay the money. It would have been logical for the filmmakers to develop some series, similar to the television series, with not only regular stars but also continuing characters who could guarantee a regular, predictable, and therefore profitable audience. And in fact many moviemakers did so. Most of these series, however, were not comedic. Most were melodramas, usually from the minor, B-picture studios. Boston Blackie, Bulldog Drummond, Sherlock Holmes, Nancy Drew, and Charlie Chan headed an almost endless list of regular detectives seeking and destroying the forces of evil, while the Three Mesquiteers, Hopalong Cassidy, the Cisco Kid, and Gene Autry did the same amid the sagebrush, and Tarzan, Bomba, and Jungle Jim protected the jungle. Comparatively few of these series involved regular humorous characters and, although most of them were profitable, only one, the Andy Hardy films, had the widespread popularity that could be fairly compared to that of a popular sit-com today. Blondie, Ma and Pa Kettle, Francis the Talking Mule, the Dead End Kids/East Side Kids/Bowery Boys all made their regular profit, but little more.

Those comedy series films borrowed from the techniques and attitudes of traditional comedy in some ways. In almost all cases, the continuing characters *did* things—Ma and Pa Kettle went places, had adventures, and looked for things to do, just as the Bowery Boys or Maisie in her ten features with different jobs and locales did. Only Andy Hardy and Blondie stayed home the way the sit-com heroes would do, safe and secure within the carefully defended world of the family. In their way, these few movies (thirteen Andy Hardies, twenty-eight Blondies, eleven Henry Aldriches, and a few others) laid the groundwork for the sit-coms of television, but they were hardly the dominant strain in film comedy.

Thus, the sit-com's growth and domination of television is not an automatic response to the problems of a mass medium, or even to America's peculiar economic attitude toward the performing arts in general. Moviemakers had numerous opportunities not only to reject the theatrical traditions of comedy but also to produce and sell material in the series format. They did not do so. Only American television has so consistently rejected the comedic tradition.

5 • The Sit-Com's New Audience

In Preston Sturges's *Sullivan's Travels*, an odd little scene appears. After being mugged and having his identification stolen, Sullivan, the famous movie director who has gone out in disguise to find the real America, winds up on a southern chain gang. One day, without warning, the men are taken into a backwoods church and seated, still in their chains, at the back of the congregation. Instead of a sermon, they see a Walt Disney cartoon. As the incredulous Sullivan watches, all around him the broken and miserable convicts, along with the poor, shabby sharecroppers of the congregation, begin to smile and then to laugh, and their faces begin to show an almost transcendent glow of happiness and well-being. Finally, even Sullivan begins to laugh, and he promises himself that, if he ever gets out of this mess, he will remember. Since it is a comedy, Sullivan is finally rescued and returned to Hollywood, where he swears he will never again try to make serious, "meaningful" pictures, for he has learned that the highest good to which the artist can aspire is to make his audience happy for a while.

Although one can certainly argue with such a simplistic statement of the idea, the point has some validity. After all, most of the great playwrights of the West, at least until the twentieth century, have written comedies as either the main body or a significant portion of their work. Shakespeare, Molière, Jonson, Sheridan, Shaw, Lope de Vega, Goldoni, even Corneille felt no shame in writing comedies, and they certainly did not impoverish the world's literature by doing so. In spite of a persistent critical assumption that comedy is merely a passing entertainment, a way to while away the night that may be pleasant and even intelligent but must always be ephemeral, comedies have shown surprisingly sturdy physiques. If Oscar Wilde's reputation rested on *Salome*, he would be remembered only as the central figure of a minor Edwardian scandal, but with *The Importance of Being Earnest* to his credit, he appears in every anthology and is constantly before audiences a century later. There is hardly a "serious" play between *King Lear* and Henrik Ibsen's *A Doll's House* that can be seen today except as a curiosity piece, while dozens of comedies stay alive and lively.

Much more important, however, is the situation that caused Sullivan to reach his decision. In his search for a serious subject, he found instead the audience, and he was forced to realize the part they play in the artistic work, a part that he had previously equated only with the buying of tickets. Of all the performing arts, the comedy is most dependent on its audience. The reliance on humor as a major part of the conflict within the plot, the communal good spirits and reunification of its societies, the strong leanings toward active use of song and jokes all require a large, active, and responsive audience. As we have seen, this requirement in turn has made the comedy the most public and communal of all artistic experiences and the most expressive of the social and natural impulses of a living, growing community. A comedy is successful immediately, or it is rarely successful at all—Congreve's *The Way of the World* is, I think, the only comedy more highly regarded and more frequently performed today than when it was written. Thus, any study of comedy must also include a study of the audience that shares in that comedy. Even in this, television in America has produced something new.

American television is a business medium. Programming is only incidental to the business of television, which is selling advertising. If network programmers and local station managers felt that an audience would watch, they would program twenty-four hours of commercials each day. No income is provided through programming. Producers of individual shows do not pay rent, as they would in a theatre, or guarantee a "nut" (a minimum for daily "operating expenses"), as they would in a movie theatre, nor do they offer the various kinds of buy-back options given to book and record stores. The networks pay the producers for programs and receive absolutely no money from the producers or

129

from the audience. All proceeds derived from television broadcasting are derived from the sale of advertising time. To make money, the broadcaster has to provide an audience for the advertiser that the advertiser believes can be provided in no other way. Programs are the barkers for the real programming, the ads.

Many critics have realized this and have demonstrated the effect of such an organizational approach on "quality." Phrases like "lowest common denominator" or "twelve-year-old mentality" are common in such discussions, and in some cases the descriptions are obviously true. But the programming is not particularly different from that being offered to the public in other media; certainly the Broadway musical comedy is often aimed at the lowest common denominator, and the average movie shown in the average drive-in would fit a similar description. Even books service the twelve-year-old-mentality market, as evidenced by recent tomes on the Bermuda Triangle, Rubik's Cube, and diets, as well as the Harlequin Romances, and the junior high vocabulary (and approach to sex) of many current best-sellers. In its search for an audience, television programming differs in approach from most other media in modern America only in its success. Television has found a genuine mass audience.

A few rough computations can show how successful television has really been. The most successful film in history, in terms of money made at the box office, has been *Star Wars*. In the first year of its release, it made $126.4 million in rentals at the box office. Given the peculiar nature of Hollywood accounting procedures and the rather random manner in which box office receipts are counted and reported to the public, there is no way to know if such a figure is accurate, but for purposes of illustration it is the best figure available.

When a movie plays a theatre, the theatre owner receives some guarantee for his expenses, and then the owner pays a rental fee that equals a certain percentage of his receipts over and above his deducted expenses. The amount of that rental fee varies from picture to picture, but a potential hit usually elicits a higher rental because the theatre owner can expect to make extra money from the additional crowds who will patronize the concession stands. For a popcorn burner like *Star Wars*, which draws not only enormous crowds but enormous numbers of young people who are heavy eaters and drinkers, the rental percentages may go as high as 90 percent (although few people will talk for the record about this). But, to be conservative, let us assume that the figure of $126.4 million represents only 75 percent of the actual gross receipts for the film. When *Star Wars* was released, first-run ticket prices were $4 in most cases (theatres sold a lot of less expensive children's tickets, but in many larger cities theatres charged $5 or more for adults). That would mean about 42.1 million tickets were sold.

Many of those tickets, of course, were sold to repeaters, people who saw the film two, three, or even five times. If only 10 percent of the sales were to repeaters, then about 38 million people actually saw the film in its first release in Canada and the United States. If there were more repeaters (and personal experience suggests that more than 25 percent of the audience may have been repeaters), then as few as 32 million actually bought tickets for the most popular film of our time. No small number by any measure other than television's measures.

In the 1977 TV season, by contrast, *Laverne & Shirley* averaged a Neilsen rating of 32.1. That means that an average of 32.1 percent of all TV sets in the country were tuned to this show on an *average* Tuesday night; at least half the time, even more were tuned in. In 1977, there were more than 74 million households in the country, with an average of 2.91 people per household, and 97 percent of those households had television sets. Thus, about 23 million households were watching *Laverne & Shirley*, with a potential audience of some 67 million people. Not everyone in a household watches the same show, of course, but in most homes, if anyone watches a program, everyone watches the same program, and these homes tend to be the ones with larger families. However, to be conservative, we can estimate this average viewing audience as 50 million people, although it was probably considerably larger.

In other words, anywhere from 67 to 100 percent more people watched an *average* episode of *Laverne & Shirley* than bought tickets during an entire year for the most popular movie ever made. The actual *Star Wars* audience, when translated into TV terms, would have shown a rating of 16 to 18 points. In 1978, NBC started canceling series whose average ratings were below 18.6, and in 1979, when it was sinking to third position in the ratings race, it still canceled anything with an average rating below 16.9.[1] If *Star Wars* had appeared on television with only the same audience it had in the theatres, it would have been immediately canceled for poor ratings; such is the enormity of television's (and the sit-com's) audience.

It should be remembered that this is still a minority audience, a point that many writers overlook. It is, however, an enormous minority audience. And, in the aggregate, the TV audience is the first real mass audience in history, at least since the medieval play cycles. The networks set out to deliver an enormous audience to their financers, the advertisers, and for the most part they have succeeded. This success has come more consistently and more dependably with the sit-com than with any other type of entertainment.

No one in the past has ever been able to deliver an audience in the way that network television has done, but almost all have depended on comedy to provide the most regular, dependable, and numerous audience available under the circumstances. Precisely because the comedy has been successful, it has tended to live with a certain amount of critical disrepute. With its vulgarity, its sexuality, its celebration of life and of irresponsibility, it has persistently outraged the forces of decency, stability, and order. Respectable people simply did not frequent the comedic theatre, where they had to mix with the vulgar riffraff who came to the comedy to overcome vicariously those same respectable people who controlled most of daily life.

Just as respectable people did not frequent the comedy, respectable scholars and critics did not study it. Aristotle told us that comedy was an imitation of lower types, but then the rest of his *Poetics* was lost, and most critics decided they did not need to know any more about the subject. For every serious statement on the comedy, there are hundreds on tragedy; most of those which deal with comedy either attack the form for debauching lower-class minds that ought to be more carefully protected or defend the form from those attacks by arguing that the comedy really shows those lower-class minds what they ought not to do with their lives. It is simply understood that no serious writer produces comedy except to make a buck and that Shakespeare, for example, resorted to comedy only to keep the scum in the pits happy enough to let him get on with the *real* stuff in his plays. Even Shaw, who certainly was not above using every trick of the theatre and every twist of the comedy tradition to make his points, and who should therefore have known better, seemed convinced that titles such as *As You Like It* proved that Shakespeare thought his own work was garbage and was trying to disown it.

In the twentieth century, this attitude has begun to change for a variety of reasons. Essentially, it has become obvious that the ancient tragedy of the noble classes no longer makes the least bit of sense. Now critics have decided that comedy is really tragedy and is very serious business, so serious that the modern "comic" writer must avoid laughter, romance, progress, and most of all any significant box office appeal. This peculiar viewpoint probably has been the result more of the work of one man, Charlie Chaplin, than of any other single influence.

Because of Chaplin's sentimentality, pathos, and tendency to moralize, many writers and critics and scholars who had traditionally dismissed comedy from serious study recognized that something else was going on in Chaplin's films besides "just" entertainment. This is why so many recent works on comedy devote so much attention to Chaplin, and in a very real sense this is the primary reason why so many recent works on comedy even exist. Without this sentimentality, which many have seen as tragedy, our understanding of the nature of comedy, in the sense of why we laugh and what we laugh at, would be much different today. More than any other person, he made both film and comedy acceptable scholarly and critical material. This is probably a mixed blessing, but there is no doubt it has made a fundamental impact on the way we think about our world. Chaplin did so by finding a way to wed brilliant humor to the old sentimental melodrama, in much the same way that Shakespeare used Falstaff in his histories or the Fool in *Lear*. Nonetheless the traditional comedy itself, without the support of the sentimental melodrama or the contemporary, ironic, middle- and lower-class version of the tragic forms, continues to live in critical disrepute. Neil Simon may cry all the way to the bank, but he is not accepted as a "real" playwright, for no particular reason except that he writes comedies to which people insist on coming.

That such attitudes should be common is not really surprising. Scholars and critics are part of the world that has been attacked by the comedy and comedians throughout history. The professor is scarcely one of the comedy's heroes, which is only natural. Part of the scholar and critic's position in life is the protection of standards, of proper ways that have been preserved from the past and are looked upon by society as important for respectable and intelligent people's lives. Comedy is uninterested in the past and uncaring of the present, its eyes firmly on the future. Only in the last twenty years in America has it been possible to see the scholar as a force for change; in every other Western culture (and in America until the sixties), the scholar has been the guardian of the past, trying to live in a world of fixed, never-changing facts, philosophies, and languages. Comedy is not likely to attract the praise of such people.

And yet, there is the problem of all those "classics" that insist on being comedies. What are the critic and scholar to do with them? In general, the common solution is to define them away. The classic comedies are "literature," somehow a different kind of comedy than the comedy we see around us. In general, critics have settled on three types of comedy: high comedy, low comedy, and farce, with comedy of manners high or low depending on the critic. High comedy is worthy of study and appreciation because it is the only "real" comedy. The other forms are not just lesser forms of comedy; they are something else entirely and should not really be considered as a part of comedy by serious critics.

This view can lead some writers into some very strange positions. George Meredith, for example, wrote an enormously influential essay on comedy in 1877. After pointing out numerous sensitive and socially desirable traits to be found in dramatic comedy, he then declared that there had been only two writers of genuine comedy in history—Menander and Molière.[2] That only two such writers had ever existed is remarkable enough, but even more miraculous is that, at the time Meredith was writing, not a single play from Menander had been found or was even thought to exist to support his contention.

Most critics are not as extreme as Meredith, but most continue to try to avoid consideration of the vast body of works in the comedic tradition. Underneath the various definitions and assumptions, however, the avoidance of most comedy by critics is based on attitudes toward the audience rather than toward the material itself. One way we can define high comedy, for example, is as the kind that no one writes any more, which can safely be read in the study away from any real audiences. Terence used to be a favorite example, but most of the classics can join him now. Low comedy is the kind they do write now, which never is as good as it used to be, while farce of course is merely debased low comedy with unsophisticated characters for unsophisticated audiences. Another approach to defining these categories is through laughter. If the audience nods sagely, and especially if only the sages nod sagely while the rest nod on the edge of sleep, then you have true high comedy. If the audience chuckles appreciatively, occasionally muttering in recognition, you have comedy of manners. If the audience laughs out loud and repeats the jokes, you have low comedy. If the audience screams and rolls in the aisle, especially if people you would not associate with scream and roll in the aisle, then you have farce.

These distinctions seem to be pointless, generating much more heat than light. In this study, all comedies are comedy, and all ought to be equally acceptable here.

The point to be made is that comedy is not much studied, and when it is studied, it is often poorly studied, because comedy is rarely separable from its audience. When the "wrong" audiences seem to respond to certain works, then the "right" people tend to ignore or belittle those works. In the process, they not only miss a lot of potential pleasure but also often miss the point entirely. Meredith, for example, could not have made his absurd statement about Menander (and could not possibly have been supported in it by so many others in following years) had he not been far more concerned with trying to convince people of what comedy *ought* to be than with trying to figure out what in fact it *is*. Meredith wanted to encourage the production of comedies in which "our public might be led to try...finer meat,"[3] something much more delicate, more intellectual, more moral, and less popular. To such people, there are good comedies (the ones they like) and bad comedies, and unfortunately the large audience, particularly of the lower orders, seems always to prefer the wrong ones.

These problems simply do not exist with other kinds of works, at least not before the modern painters managed to convince large numbers of people that nothing that was popular could also be real art. No one would take seriously a claim that *Hamlet* is a terrible play simply because it has been produced so often, or that it is not worthy of serious study or consideration because it was a sell-out when Richard Burton played it last. Yet one would have to look long and hard to find the anthology or serious critical study of modern theatre that includes Kaufman and Hart's *You Can't Take It with You*, Joseph Kesselring's *Arsenic and Old Lace*, Noel Coward's *Private Lives*, Ann Jellicoe's *The Knack* or even Joe Orton's *What the Butler Saw*, much less Neil Simon's *Barefoot in the Park* or Jones and Schmidt's *The Fantasticks*.

Thus, if we are to understand the changes that are in process in the sit-com, we must examine not only the programs but also the audience and the audience's perception of the programs, far more than critical perceptions of those programs.

The most remarkable aspect of the American television audience is not its quantity but rather its uniformity. A successful TV program usually cuts across all economic and cultural lines in the country, drawing its audience from all groups in society with almost equal success. "Something for everyone" generally translates into success in some form with everyone. The demographic breakdowns of the Neilsen ratings which are generally not nearly as widely reported as the overall ratings, reveal some surprising information. In most cases, they show that there are very few differences in the tastes of all segments of the American general audience.

Rose Goldsen, for example, has given some demographic breakdowns for the 1973-74 TV season. No matter how the groups are arranged, they all share at least 60 percent of the same favorites in their top 10 programs. Persons with a high school education, with a college degree, and with only a grade school education all selected *All in the Family, The Waltons, The Friday Movie, Sanford and Son, Maude,* and *M*A*S*H* in their ten favorite programs. If income, rather than education, is considered, the same results appear: people making over $15,000 watched *Maude, All in the Family, The Friday Movie, The Waltons, M*A*S*H,* and *The Sunday Mystery* in their top 10, exactly the same as people who made less than $10,000 and those who made between $10,000 and $15,000.

Although it would be comforting to claim that the remaining four favorite programs were more intellectual or sophisticated in the richer or better-educated groups, this was not the case. College graduates, for example, included among their favorites two *additional* sit-coms that the grade-school-educated groups did not view as often. The most significant difference, however, was sports. College-educated groups and those making over $15,000 at the time placed *Monday Night Football* among their favorite programs, while those with less education and money favored *Gunsmoke* and *The Monday Movie,* both of which featured somewhat sophisticated "adult drama," far more stimulating and "intelligent" than the football games.[4]

However, the point is that the mass audience is a uniform mass audience. Television's lowest common denominator is also its highest common denominator, and its sixth-grade mentality reflects just as accurately the interests and pleasures of its college-graduate mentality. Successful television series are successful across the board; they appeal to every large social group simultaneously. When they are unsuccessful, they are unsuccessful across the board. In that same 1973-74 season, college graduates who made over $15,000 did not suffer disproportionately when *Adam's Rib* was canceled, because they did not watch it significantly more than grade-school-educated factory workers did.

Although the details of such demographic breakdowns have obviously changed in the decade since these figures became available, the general shape has not. A successful television program must be attractive to almost all groups or it cannot provide the numbers necessary to reach hit status. Since the sit-coms persist as the most popular form of television programming, it must be assumed that now, as at any time in the last two decades, a successful sit-com appeals in a significant way to almost every group in the American populace.

How that audience perceives the programs it watches is an important, and for the most part unexamined, question. Researchers know who watches what programs, but no one knows why they watch, nor what it is they think they see when they do watch. This ignorance is not unique. Considering the importance of audience perception and reception to theatrical material of any kind, we know practically nothing about audiences of the past or present. The first known serious study of the "typical" Broadway audience, for example, was not made until 1967.[5] For some currently unfathomable reason, scholars know a great deal about eighteenth-century London audiences and almost nothing about any others. Whatever studies do exist, whether scholarly or the local survey designed to find markets or potential donors, the final results are generally only demographic: they tell us who comes, who does not, what they can pay, even what they wear, but not what they see, hear, and respond to. Writers as well as producers are thus forced to guess. After all the estimates, all the ratings, all the advertising demographics, the program, like the play or the movie or the book, has to be thrown out and allowed to live or die in front of that amorphous mass called an audience. An observer can guess at what a particular show offers that is attractive to its audience, but it is only a guess. An enormous number of people may watch Archie Bunker to ridicule his bigotry and simplemindedness, but possibly even more are watching because they are glad someone who sees things the way they do finally got on the TV. Ultimately, one must say that the forms of entertainment have certain apparently popular characteristics that must illustrate the perceptions of the audiences who make the shows popular and profitable. In the case of the sit-com, which is such a revolutionary form, certain inferences must be drawn from the evidence. However, at this point, they are clearly inferences and assumptions, not provable fact.

One of the oddest changes brought about by the sit-com is a new relationship between the actors and their audiences, which in turn suggests a new audience perception of the actor's role in the comedy. Sometime during the 1770s, Diderot began to examine the acting of his day, eventually formulating his famous paradox of acting: the best actor is the one who feels the least emotion and moves the audience by remaining unmoved himself.[6] For the comic actor, this defines one of the fundamental positions of all performance—to make them laugh, the comedian should not laugh himself. This paradox, however, also reveals the persistent dichotomy of audience perception of the actor.

If an actor can move the audience by being unmoved himself, then he and his role are two separable entities, each unique and compartmentalized. What he does tonight in performance has no bearing on what he may do tomorrow in performance, or at home for dinner. Yet the very fact that such an apparently obvious position must be not only stated but also debated, restated, modified, and developed over the centuries since its statement indicates that a significant proportion of the audience assumes the actor and his role are one and the same, synonymous and inseparable.

Although it is difficult at any time to tell how any single audience perceives the different aspects of any individual performance, it seems relatively certain that most people, throughout most of Western history, certainly throughout the eras of professional actors, have perceived the performances in essentially the same manner. There are stories of people who, seeing their first play or their first movie, rose up from the audience and assaulted the villain; in my local community theatre not so very long ago, a man left the audience to put out a fire on stage, apparently convinced that the actress on stage was blind and could not see the fire. However, that such things are noticed at all indicates the rarity of their occurrence. The great theatre riots of the past have been caused more often by perceptions of actors, as at the Astor Place Riot, or of the literary aspects of the plays, such as the *Hernani* riots, than by audience response to the momentary events of the performance itself.

For the most part, audiences recognize actors as actors. They know it is not the real world there in front of them. And yet, it is equally obvious that most people do not recognize the play the actors are in. They hold the performers somehow personally responsible for the contents of that play. At one end of this scale, there are the people who write letters to Morris, the talking cat who appears in cat food commercials, assuming that he not only does his own voice but writes the lines as well; at the other end, there are supposedly the most sophisticated and certainly the most experienced audience members, the critics, congratulating actors on performances "so much better than the material," as if they could perform without something to say provided by the writer. Many, if not most, members of the audience think, even as they recognize the actor, that he is somehow making it up as he performs.

For the actor in a comedy, this is an especially difficult problem. Spontaneity and timing are so critical to the success of the humor within the performance that the actor *is* "making up" part of each performance. When the actor succeeds, however, when his performance delights the audience, he is in danger of being forced to repeat it ad infinitum. We sometimes forget that Queen Elizabeth not only asked Shakespeare for Sir John in love but also asked for the actor to play Falstaff again. Actors call this typecasting, but for many people, it is more than being typed, it is a process of being specified precisely. For every Clayton Moore happy to spend his life playing the Lone Ranger there is a George Reeves committing suicide because he is not allowed to play anything but Superman.

For the comic actor, there are then two basic ways in which the audience may perceive him. First, he may be perceived as an actor, as a person who acts and happens to be in a comedy today. He may be in another comedy tomorrow, or he may be in a tragedy; if he is in another comedy, he may play a character much like today's, or he may play someone completely different. But he is an actor first, a comic second. (In actual practice, this is an extreme position. Only the most powerful stars in any period are ever allowed to play against type. Some periods define type more loosely than others, but the typing remains reasonably stable. Only stars play Romeo today and Lear tomorrow. For the rest of the company, the old man always plays the old men, the juvenile always the juveniles, the friendly fellow always has a role that requires the appearance of friendliness. If, however, the audience perceives him as an actor first, whatever his type, then he will play variations of that type in all kinds of plays and films.)

Some comedians are so successful in their performance, or so limited, that they develop a specific persona for themselves. This persona then becomes their public character and, whenever they perform, they are expected to look like and sound like this particular persona. The audience may call the comedian by the character's name, or they may say, "Oh, good, here comes old Will Kemp now," but either way, they expect something predictable from the performer on sight. If an actor is lucky, this makes him a star, and he can build a profitable career off that persona.

This approach can best be illustrated by the *commedia* troupes. There, the actor and the characters were so closely entwined that many of the actors were called by character names, and many of the character names were based on the famous actors who played them. Since much of the performance was spontaneous, the actor had to be personally aware of the kinds of things his character could and could not do, so actors played the same characters as often as possible. When new stories came along, they just moved the same old characters to the new story and went on, always alert to the possibilities for inserting one of their famous routines somewhere in the performance. Audiences for the most part perceived actor and persona as one.

The other tradition can be demonstrated in the repertory systems that grew up in England and other countries when the traveling troupes settled down into fixed theatres. At that point, the performers were required to develop a much greater variety of material. No matter how inspired their comedy, or how many variations they might be able to ring up on their basic plots, they could not survive on one kind of play alone when they had a fixed, limited audience to draw from. Thus the Elizabethan and Jacobean theatres provided a varied set of plays, as listed in *Hamlet*. Because no one likes to pay actors for not working, the actors had to develop the flexibility to play that entire list, so that the company could be held to the smallest practical number of performers. The actors had to be, as Thomas Middleton described them in *The Mayor of Queenborough* (V,i), "comedians, tragedians, tragi-comedians, comi-tragedians, pastorists, humourists, clownists, satirists. . .from the hug to the smile, from the smile to the laugh, from the laugh to the handkerchief." That they survived indicates that the audience was willing to accept them in a wide variety of roles and personae, to see them as actors first and comedians second.

In the nineteenth-century American theatre, both perceptions of the performer in comedies existed simultaneously. The actor as actor existed in most of the legitimate playhouses, where a modified form of repertory playing continued. Because the power of the star was more intense than it had ever been, many of the supporting players were severely typecast, but stars who were willing to push their range found no problems in getting their audiences to allow them to do so, within some obvious limits. Richard Mansfield, for example, played the lead in Edmund Rostand's *Cyrano de Bergerac*, Clyde Fitch's *Beau Brummel*, Shaw's *Arms and the Man*, and Ibsen's *Peer Gynt*. All of these roles are relatively virile leading-man roles, but they still provide a significant range of tone and style. Even among those who specialized in comedies, the range of roles was often spectacular. Henry Placide played five hundred different roles and was considered to be unequaled in *three* different types—middle-aged gentlemen, drunken servants, and simple country boys—at the same time. John Gilbert was praised for both Sir Peter Teazle in Sheridan's *School for Scandal* and Caliban, the monster, in Shakespeare's *Tempest*, and Dion Boucicault played Wah-no-tee the noble Indian in his own play *The Octoroon* as well as Myles-na-Coppaleen the quintessential stage Irishman in *The Colleen Bawn*.

At the same time, a number of actors were making remarkably successful careers as one-role comedians. Most notable was Joseph Jefferson, who, after years of other roles, found his métier most completely in *Rip Van Winkle*. Many others left the confines of the legitimate stage for other pastures, the vaudeville, where they toured the country as comedians with their own acts, living for years off not only a single character but also just a very few minutes of material. For them, the persona was their regular performance, always the same no matter where they went, in new material or old.

When filmmakers looked for comedians, they drew from both perceptions, simply by luring as many performers away from the stage and the vaudeville as they could. Each performer brought with him the perceptions of role and the attitudes toward performance that he had held with success on stage or observed in the success of others.

Shorts, the staple form of early film comedy, tended to use the approaches of the sketch artists and comedians of vaudeville first. Most of the famous comedians of silent films are persona comedians, actors who are perceived by their audiences in a single guise. Fatty Arbuckle, Charlie Chaplin, Buster Keaton, Harold Lloyd, Stan Laurel and Oliver Hardy, Charlie Chase, and Harry Langdon all achieved success only after each settled on a persona with identifying features and a recognizable, repeatable personality. For all practical purposes, this recognizable persona was essential to success in the shorts, once the film companies began to identify their performers in credits. It continued in the sound shorts as well, most clearly shown by W. C. Fields, the Three Stooges, and Laurel and Hardy, whose best work was for the most part in sound short subjects.

So successfully have certain of the persona comics been identified with silent comedy that it often seems as if they made the only comedies of the time. A number of successful feature-length comedies, however, featured actors perceived as actors rather than as comedians. The most famous were made by Ernst Lubitsch, beginning with *The Marriage Circle* (1924), though there were innumerable others at other studios and with different directors. The actors for Lubitsch illustrate the audience's willingness, even at the height of the persona comics' fame, to accept comic stars as actors, who might even appear outside of comedies. Monte Blue, for example, who played in such comedies as *The Marriage Circle* and *So This Is Paris*, also appeared in many melodramas, including D. W. Griffith's *Intolerance*, as a heroic figure. Jean Hersholt followed his harrowing performance in *Greed* with a kindly, genial comic role in *The Student Prince*, and Mary Pickford of course played almost everything.

In the sound features, the ability of the actor to succeed in a number of different kinds of roles and films was expanded. Some of the persona comics continued: Chaplin, Lloyd for a while, and Keaton in a somewhat different persona. Fields, if anything, found much greater success with sound, but few new comics achieved lasting success as specific personae until Abbott and Costello and then eventually Jerry Lewis. Throughout most of the thirties and later, the actor perceived as actor dominated feature-length comedies.

The most striking and varied example is Cary Grant. In his early years, he was cast primarily as a pretty face, often as the other man in a love triangle. But as early as 1933 he indicated his possibilities when he was successful as the seducer in the melodramatic and slyly humorous *Blonde Venus* and as the pure Salvation Army leader trying to reform Mae West in *She Done Him Wrong*. After *The Awful Truth* demonstrated not only his own comic ability but also the willingness of the audience to accept him in comic roles, he made a series of spectacularly successful film comedies, many of them classics of the genre. At the same time, he played melodramas, especially for Alfred Hitchcock, and straight adventure films as well, all of them not only well played but well accepted at the box office. There is no doubt that the audience always saw him as "Cary Grant" when they watched him, but there is also little doubt that they accepted and believed that Cary Grant could do a lot of different things in a lot of different ways, as, for example, Buster Keaton or Harold Lloyd or even Charlie Chaplin could not.

Throughout his career, Grant provided a remarkable series of contrasts in his public appearances. In 1940, he played the quintessential newspaperman-scoundrel, Walter Burns, in *His Girl Friday*, followed that with the witty, debonair C. K. Dexter-Haven of *Philadelphia Story*, and in 1941 went to the mysterious apparent villain and wife murderer of *Suspicion*. In 1948, he was an angel for *The Bishop's Wife*, the perfect upper-middle class executive attempting to build his dream house, and a male war bride. Even within the comic roles themselves, the variety he established would be phenomenal had he never been used by Hitchcock or visited a melodrama like *Mr. Lucky*. His characters and performances vary from the witty comedy of manners of *Philadelphia Story*, very sophisticated and European, to the raucous, high-energy, rapid-fire American rascality of *His Girl Friday*; from the gentle, almost wistful, middle-class comedy of *Room for One More* to a farceur's handbook in *Arsenic and Old Lace*. As such, they illustrate the willingness of the audience to accept Grant as a personality rather than a persona, and to accept and feel comfortable with a perception of him that allowed him a remarkable latitude in roles and styles of performance.

Had Grant been unique, he could be dismissed as the exception that proves the rule, but he was matched by most major film stars of the time. Henry Fonda moved from childlike innocence in *The Lady Eve* to the pleasant integrity of *Mr. Roberts*, from the lower-class Tom Joad in *The Grapes of Wrath* to the heroic Wyatt Earp in *My Darling Clementine* or Abraham Lincoln in *Young Mr. Lincoln*, to the crazed troop commander of *Fort Apache*, all without disturbing his audience. James Stewart was Mr. Smith and Destry, but he was also successful as a series of near-psychotic characters in his westerns with Anthony Mann, as the happy drunk in *Harvey*, and as the small-town hero of *It's a Wonderful Life*. Gary Cooper did *Meet John Doe*, Sergeant York, and *Ball of Fire* back to back in 1941 and continued a varied, successful career until its end, when he made *Love in the Afternoon*, with its delicious comic seductions of little girls, and the soap opera *Ten North Frederick*. Nor were the women confined to categories, as shown by the varied careers of such performers as Claudette Colbert, Ginger Rogers, Carole Lombard, Barbara Stanwyck, and Miriam Hopkins. There were always limits, of course, beyond which performers could not go and still maintain any audience credibility, because there are always some roles that an actor does not have the talent to play well, but within those limits most of the audience did and could perceive such actors as

143

personalities who could somehow be different people in different types of performances from feature to feature.

Audience expectations often did confine a performer to a specific genre without confining him to a specific persona. In romantic tragedy, no one was more convincing than Greta Garbo. When she finally did a comedy, *Ninotchka*, she showed herself to be an accomplished romantic comedienne, but the film was marketed as a freak show—"See Garbo laugh!!!" The audience simply refused to let her out of her original genre more than once, and *Two Faced Woman*, the second comedy, was such a disaster that Garbo chose to close out her career rather than repeat continually the same old films. A number of comedians without specific personae nevertheless did find themselves confined to comedies. Danny Kaye, Bob Hope, Martha Raye, Red Skelton, and Donald O'Connor all played a variety of characters, but all had to remain within comedic films. Such limits probably had less to do with particular abilities than with the audience's perceptions. Audiences and critics alike are surprised when a comic like Burt Lahr appears in a Beckett play and when a tough guy like Lee Marvin does a comedy role in *Cat Ballou*. The limits a successful performer reaches over a long career explain how the audience perceives him as much as they explain his own inherent talents.

At any rate, film audiences tended to see film comedy actors in much the same way as stage audiences had viewed actors throughout the history of stage performances. Some were seen as specific personae and were welcomed and applauded as long as they stayed within the confines of their persona. Others were seen as actors who could vary their characters, types, personae, and styles to a certain degree. Television, however, has changed even this. The comedic actor who comes to fame in television comedies faces a new perception. For the first time in Western tradition, significant numbers of the audience appear to be losing sight of the actor as a distinct personality.

In the stage traditions there have been two general methods of seeing the comedy performer—as an actor capable of many styles of performance within a general type or as a particular persona who was expected to demonstrate the same appearance and general characterization in a variety of situations. There is a third way to perceive the performer, one which has occurred only rarely. He may be perceived by the audience as existing only in the character, as being "real" rather than "acting." This is, on stage, extremely rare. It requires a complete lack of sophistication on the part of the audience. Once an audience member has come back to the same building, looked through the same curtain, and seen something different from what he saw on his last visit to the theatre, he cannot ever again ignore the theatricality of the event, no matter how realistic the presentation. In the same way people seeing movies for the first time are often reported to think they are seeing not only pictures of real people but events in real time as well, despite the editing, changes in perspective, and even lack of color. But once the viewer has seen several movies or has seen the same actor twice, he is aware that he is seeing an actor. Not even the Astor Place Riots, America's most famous and bloody audience uprising, which eventually killed twenty-two people, was caused by events in the play. It began with people who thought that Edwin Forrest was a better Macbeth than William Macready, not with people who thought Forrest *was* Macbeth and that Macready was an imposter.

Until recently it has been possible for one type of television viewer, even with considerable viewing experience, to perceive the performers in this third way. Regular watchers of the daytime soap operas tended to accept the characters they watched as real people rather than as actors playing real people; many lost the perception of the actors almost completely. This was encouraged by the circumscribed life of the soap opera performer. Since a regular worked every day, he had little time for outside appearances. For the most part, the field was staffed either by actors approaching middle age who had been passed over in other fields, were tired of the awkward existence of the stage actor in New York, and were thus pleased to settle down for a while, or by young actors who were eager to have a paycheck and a credit of any kind. All of these actors were unknown to the television audience, so they provided unknown faces. At the same time, they appeared every day in the same circumstances and at the same time, further encouraging the audience to regard them as neighbors rather than as fictive characters played by actors. Since the soap opera was a disreputable, if lucrative, child of the medium, with limited audience appeal (so it was assumed), little publicity material was given to the public to help them identify the performers.

This has changed in the past few years. There are now magazines about the soap opera stars, and many of the performers appear on the covers of general fan magazines. Regular public appearance tours are made to shopping centers and fairs across the nation. Many of the more prominent actors have shown up on numerous network and local talk shows, discussing their roles and their personal lives away from the shows. These changes have tended to shift audience perceptions back into the more traditional modes for all but the most ignorant viewers. Regular watchers still become deeply, emotionally involved in the shows and in the lives of the characters, but they are now just as likely to discuss the actor as to discuss the character over their coffee cups.

Comedy has traditionally resisted this third perception, probably because of the humor. The man who makes us laugh is special and we do not let him hide. The comedian may wish we knew the real person, but we know him as an actor in every performance. No matter how many names he may adopt, how many times he may change his place, as soon as he does a pratfall or cracks a joke, we know he is "only" acting. At that point, we may see him as a specific persona or as a more general actor type, but we still see him as an actor.

When we look at the careers of the performers in situation comedies, we notice something curious. Only one performer has ever starred in two successful comedy series in the thirty-odd years of television situation comedy—Lucille Ball. Only one other moved from a major supporting role in one successful series to a starring role in another—Mary Tyler Moore, who was the wife in *The Dick Van Dyke Show* before she began the show that carried her name. Two others almost made successful changes. Wayne Rogers was in the first three seasons of *M*A*S*H* and returned for *House Calls*, which had very high ratings in its first two years but was canceled after its third. Bob Denver starred as Maynard Krebs in *The Many Loves of Dobie Gillis*, which did last four years although it made major format changes in the last two; he also starred in *Gilligan's Island*, which lasted only three seasons and is not considered successful in the terms used here in spite of its strength in the rerun market. Ted Knight, formerly of *The Mary Tyler Moore Show*, is off to a good start in the ratings with *Too Close for Comfort*, but so were *Rhoda*, *Phyllis*, *The New Dick Van Dyke Show*, and *House Calls* before their collapse, so it is a bit early to declare the show a success. The number of television comedians who have had an actual career in television comedy can be counted on one hand.

Some performers have gone to other genres to sustain their careers. Jackie Gleason returned to the variety show from which *The Honeymooners* had begun, but most left comedy completely. Robert Young became everybody's favorite doctor in *Marcus Welby*, and Buddy Ebsen became a senior-citizen private eye on *Barnaby Jones*. Larry Hagman, after a considerable dry spell, became the man we all loved to hate on *Dallas*. Most, however, have simply failed to find the parts and the audiences necessary to give them regular and profitable television careers. Some, like Jane Wyatt or Donna Reed, gracefully retired. Others found careers in other media. Barbara Eden, for example, used her considerable singing and dancing abilities, which had been untapped in her series, and established herself as a potent Las Vegas showroom performer. Some comedians try to go on to bigger things, especially to stardom in movies, but they have had minimal success. Few TV stars have succeeded as movie stars, and the records suggest that no TV comedy stars have done so, although many have tried, such as Mary Tyler Moore. Many performers have tried to return in new series, often with painful results in both the ratings and in personal egos. Some then settle for guest appearances, an occasional TV movie, and summer stock musicals in the Midwest, often quite remunerative arrangements. But, with the few exceptions mentioned, no one succeeds twice.

The difficulty of stardom in television situation comedy can best be illustrated by the career of Dick Van Dyke, as genuine a TV star as there has been and a man of recognized talent and professional experience. Van Dyke has appeared as a regular in eight series, half of those summer replacements (in the days when there were summer replacements) or quiz shows in the 1950s, before he reached star status. In 1960 he was a principal in the Broadway hit *Bye Bye Birdie*, a role he would repeat in films in 1963. His Broadway success led to *The Dick Van Dyke Show* in 1961; that he had achieved some prominence is indicated by the title of the series. That show started slowly but by the 1962-63 season had moved into the top 10, where it stayed until dropping to number 16 in 1965-66, when Van Dyke and the production company agreed to close out the series while it was still both popular and a high-quality product. In those five years, Van Dyke's portrayal of Rob Petrie had established him as one of the most pleasant and talented comedic actors in television, while allowing him occasional chances to demonstrate his considerable abilities as a song-and-dance man. He appeared to have an enormous potential in film.

His film work, including a contract with the Disney studios, where his most prominent role was in *Mary Poppins*, had begun while he was still in the series. Immediately after the series, he made the excellent *Divorce, American Style*, playing a character similar to Rob Petrie. This film was followed by another musical, *Chitty Chitty Bang Bang*, an enormous disappointment at the box office. Not all of the blame could be placed on Van Dyke, but much of it had to be, because he was the film's only star with any box office clout. *The Comic* allowed him to salute the silent comics and to engage in slapstick and a gritty, challenging characterization simultaneously. It was probably his best film role, but again the box office results were disappointing. Then came *Cold Turkey*, which sent its producer, Norman Lear, firmly back to television, where Archie Bunker would give him more influence and money. Van Dyke, meanwhile, reappeared on TV in *The New Dick Van Dyke Show*. As so many others would do, Van Dyke had tried to capitalize on his television exposure and popularity to build a more lucrative and varied career in films, and as so many others would also do, he had failed to produce the ticket buyers. So he went back to TV comedy.

Unfortunately, success eluded him again. The new show did not catch on. It finished its first season as number 18 and went down from there, not finishing in the top 25 for 1972-73. A certain sign of ratings problems, a change in the format at the end of 1972-73 moved the character away from Tucson but produced no improvement in the ratings for 1973-74. The show was canceled. Van Dyke was having additional problems at the time with alcohol, but those problems were not a factor in the show's lack of popularity because the public knew little about them until he made *The Morning After* in 1974 and began discussing his alcohol problem in public. By that time, the series was already dead.

He and the network then tried a variety show. He obviously had the ability to carry one, and as such shows go, this one was not bad. But it met with even less success than the sit-com had done. It was canceled after three months, an ignominious ratings failure. In 1978, he reappeared as a regular on *The Carol Burnett Show*. His appearance was in part an attempt to boost the sagging ratings of Burnett, who nonetheless was canceled at the end of that season. Yet no matter how his position was defined, he was in fact a regular supporting player on someone else's show, along with Tim Conway, another hit series regular (*McHale's Navy*) who had found movie success only with Disney and had failed in both a second sit-com and a variety show. Though now better paid and better recognized, Van Dyke had gone back to his 1958 career, when he had done exactly the same thing for Andy Williams. Eventually he toured the country with *The Music Man*, taking the lucrative but still depressing route taken by so many faded movie and TV stars, playing musicals across the Midwest at fairs and in the big convention center theatres, a kind of year-round summer stock.

That he never "succeeded" as a movie star is of little import to this study, except as his failure served to send him back to television. Much more important is that he could not "succeed" a second time on television. And if Dick Van Dyke, a highly versatile comedy performer, could not find an audience in a second series, how much more difficult must it be for more limited performers such as Tim Conway, Bob Crane, Don Knotts, Don Adams, Barbara Feldon, Dwayne Hickman, and Gabe Kaplan? Van Dyke did not just tell jokes; he was an actor, a singer, a dancer, a skilled mime, an intelligent pratfaller, and a very pleasant personality. Even so, the audience rejected him in the very medium and form that had made him famous and popular to begin with. Some explanation should be found for this phenomenon.

Two theories suggest themselves. One says that the audience simply sees too much of the performer of a successful comedy series. Coming as he does into the home every week, he is like a relative come for a visit. When he has overstayed his welcome, when the audience has lost interest in his activities and is looking for a little variety, they ignore him until he leaves. Thus, each series, comedy or other, carries the seed of its own destruction in its very popularity. It will, if successful, stay on so long that people will get used to it and take it for granted, assuming it will always be there while they go off to temporarily more fashionable entertainments, at which point it will be canceled. Then, when the performer tries a new show, the audience will simply see him as old-fashioned and turn him off.

A second theory says that styles change, and styles in humor are no exception. The performer who does a particular kind of humor is out of work when that humor has become old hat.

Unfortunately, there are problems with both explanations. Many movie comedians have had long careers. Though many fell by the wayside when styles of humor changed, especially the silent comics after the coming of sound, many more did not. Chaplin made successful films for more than forty years; Laurel and Hardy had over twenty successful years, as did Jerry Lewis. Those who did not get tied to specific personae often had extremely long careers, among them Cary Grant, Fred Astaire, Gene Kelly, Jack Lemmon, and Henry Fonda. Obviously, with many actors, the audience does not tire of their faces, no matter how long they have been watching them.

In sit-coms, however, there are factors that suggest a new relationship has developed between actor and audience which did not exist before the new form of comedy. A number of people have had remarkably long careers in television, often in television humor, as long as they have managed to avoid the situation comedy. Bob Hope, of course, is remarkable—forty years in films, radio, and television, and a still undiminished stature—but many others have stretched series into runs of almost twenty years or have had several successful series. Arthur Godfrey, Jackie Gleason, Ed Sullivan, Raymond Burr, and Johnny Carson, among others, suggest that it sometimes takes an awfully long time before the audience gets tired of a performer.

In the same way, the successful long runs of shows in the syndication markets suggest that it often takes a very long time before people tire of a particular style of humor. *I Love Lucy* is for all practical purposes *still* a regular series. It has appeared in almost every city of the country at least once every day and sometimes more often since it ceased weekly production in 1957. *The Brady Bunch*, of all things, seems aimed at a similar immortality, as do *Bewitched*, *Green Acres*, *I Dream of Jeannie*, *The Odd Couple*, and several others. Obviously, certain styles of humor do not go out of fashion on television; they are repeated not just in style but in totality in regular, all-pervasive reruns, which significant numbers of people watch. Why did the people who happily watched repeats of *The Odd Couple* refuse to watch Tony Randall in *The Tony Randall Show*, yet watch Jack Klugman in *Quincy*? Why did the people willing to sit through tenth reruns of *Hogan's Heroes* refuse to watch *The Bob Crane Show*? They obviously were not tired of Bob Crane. Why did the people who had memorized *Gilligan's Island* completely ignore Bob Denver when he played the same kind of character on *The Good Guys*? If they had been tired of the type of humor, they could not have continued to watch the earlier series. Why did they watch *The Dick Van Dyke Show* but not *The New Dick Van Dyke Show*?

Part of the answer lies in the basic formula, the new plot, of television situation comedy. Another part lies in the kind of heroes the actors portray within that plot. Both are developed in a consistent manner, devoted to stability and resistant to change of any kind. By implication, within those structures, the performer himself is dedicated to stability and resistant to change. He is not supposed to be different. Every line he says, every episode he does, every season he survives, is dedicated to the proposition that, when the audience next sees him, he will be exactly the same as the last time they saw him. Exactly the same.

Simply being similar is no longer sufficient. He must be *exactly* the same, say the same kinds of things, in the same places, with the same look. Even the surroundings must stay the same. It sometimes seems that the most important event in a sit-com character's life is getting new furniture. When a series has been on long enough that the sets start to look a little tired, or when even dyed-in-the-wool fans start asking why Mary has never moved out of that one-room apartment despite her raises and promotions, new furniture or a new apartment is an obvious solution. But most series make a very big thing out of new furniture or a move. It always occupies at least one episode, and sometimes more, and it is done either in the very first episode of a season or the very last, to minimize the effect on the audience.

Thus, the actor is gradually perceived by much of the audience as inseparable from his surroundings. This perception is similar to the traditional view of the persona comedian, yet different in an important way. The traditional persona comedians were trapped by their audiences into specific characterizations. Often their careers were very tightly structured, and they lost much of their audience when they ventured into characterizations that looked different from the persona that had made them famous. However, within that persona they could do *anything*. Chaplin's Tramp could be many things—a tramp, a new immigrant, a seducer, a gold miner, a circus performer, a vaudevillian, a barber, or even a policeman. He could not be all of them in a single feature or short, but from month to month and year to year he could change social position and physical place at will.

Even the most famous persona comedians were part of an ancient tradition dedicated to change. For them to play a new role in this month's short caused no problems for the audience. Previous roles had all *ended*. There was a solution to each role that left the character not only at a clear ending to that particular situation but also free to go somewhere else, if necessary. If he happened to get the girl, then everyone knew that particular story was over. The next time they saw him, he might be pursuing a different girl, but the clear movement and ending of the previous works allowed the audience to dismiss them from their minds while viewing the new production. When the actor became a star, he was idolized by an audience, and his films or plays were seen and remembered intensely and intensively, but he was idolized as star,

151

as actor, as comedian, or possibly as a particular persona combining actor and character. But he was not tied to a particular place and time. The audience wanted to see what he could do if...They expected, almost demanded, that he be put into new situations, so they could see more of the person they idolized.

For the television comedian, the audience seems to demand less rather than more. The actor has a new relationship with the audience. They see him in the same place at the same time with the same surroundings and the same supporting characters each week, and over a period of time they come to build a very specific and precise set of expectations about both the surroundings and him. Eventually, the two merge into a single whole. The actor becomes inseparable from the role, and both of them become inseparable from the situation. Chaplin was Chaplin, Groucho was Groucho, Fields was Fields, and Cary Grant was Cary Grant, but Henry Winkler is the Fonz, and the Fonz is trapped not only in a particular look but in a particular place. He cannot exist in both the city and the country, as a doctor this week, a college professor the next, and a hobo the week after, or as a young punk and a sophisticated man of mystery. He cannot change, no matter how talented he may be, or how great his popularity. If he wishes to be funny, he must stay the same. If he is willing to give up comedy, he may be able to return after a few years in a different kind of series, but all odds are against his ever appearing again as a major character in another successful comedy series.

This perception of the unchangeable actor/character is both accepted and encouraged by the producers of the sit-coms. Sit-com actors are never treated as actors. As already noted, on sit-coms actors do not replace other actors—characters replace other characters. It would seem obvious to anyone trained in the perceptions of stage or film that, if Gary Burghoff is tired of playing Radar on M*A*S*H, a new actor should be found to play Radar. On television, however, the character completely disappears; if Burghoff is not Radar, no one will be. But the obverse must also become true: Burghoff must always be Radar, wherever he might try to appear otherwise. Sometimes this perception reaches absurd proportions, as do so many things in television programming. When Polly Holliday's character of Flo was spun off from *Alice*, her character was replaced by a new waitress who was very much like Flo. For the more observant, she was more than very much like Flo—she was in fact Diane Ladd, who had played Flo in the film on which the series had been based. But, since *Alice* was now a sit-com, the actress who had created the original version of the character could not play the character again; she had to be a new character (who was just like the old one, so she could fit into the family in the diner) because Flo and Polly Holliday were now one and the same, eternal and inseparable.

It seems significant that many performers are able to return in other kinds of series. All television series, at least in prime time, share a devotion to keeping at least the major characters the same from week to week, within very stable situations. However, other series do not for the most part share comedy's television plot. The two heroes may still be the same at the end of an episode of *Starsky and Hutch*, but their world is different; a few more cars have been wrecked and a few criminals have bitten the dust. The case has been solved, and there is an ending that at least minimally affects the whole of society. Like the western, in which the gunfighter rides off into the sunset after making Dodge a better place to live, the television melodrama often introduces the cop or the doctor or truck driver into a new world each week. He continues to work for a hospital or a city or out of his trailer, but these are his identification marks; he has to figure out each new problem as an outsider would and then interfere to fix things. In earlier days, this was made even more clear with a number of heroes who literally traveled, such as the wanderer of *The Fugitive* and the young men of *Route 66*. Within the general series concept, the character and the performer must meet a new situation each week and must find a genuine ending. This is what comedy used to do, but no longer does, at least on television. The hero of the television melodrama still dares something. He can change things. Some of this changeability rubs off on the actor playing him. Other factors, especially the distressing tendency of television executives to cast series leads who cannot act, may limit further careers after a series has been canceled, but the actor in a series other than a sit-com has a noticeably better chance of finding a successful second series. The actor in television comedy has, on the record of the last thirty years, almost none.

Some interesting parallels for this problem can be seen in the film careers of comedy actors who found themselves in successful film series. The most prominent of these is Mickey Rooney, who was for thirteen features between 1937 and 1944 Andy Hardy. He was also among the top 10 box office draws in all those years and, for three years (1939, 1940, and 1941), number one draw in the nation.[7] The Andy Hardy series was quintessential 1950s and 1960s television, complete with a lovely middle-class home in a lovely, quiet midwestern town; a perfect father; a loving mother; precocious but wonderful, loving, and intelligent children; and a guarantee that when the credits came on the audience would know exactly what to expect. Rooney was not only a star but an obvious talent. Sometimes MGM seemed so intent on proving his talent that they devoted too much time to showing him off, especially in his musicals, where he played Andy Hardy-type characters who had to put on a show. But there was no doubt the kid could sing, dance, do comedy, tug a few heartstrings, and even turn in a solid straight performance when necessary.

But after World War II, Rooney was too old to be a teenager and could no longer play Andy Hardy. He kept finding work, and he kept being treated and billed as a star, but he quit dragging the people to the box office. Finally he resorted to a dismal attempt to revive the Hardy character in *Andy Hardy Comes Home* (1958), now back in the small town as the father of his own family. It too failed to attract audiences, and Rooney became a cameo star, an actor who is too well known to do character roles but not strong enough to carry his own picture, as in *Breakfast at Tiffany's* and *It's a Mad, Mad, Mad, Mad World*. He even tried television sit-coms in 1954 and again in 1964; both shows were canceled, the second after only thirteen episodes. A new sit-com in 1982 was canceled even quicker.

Similar fates met other, apparently less talented performers in other film series. Arthur Lake and Penny Singleton starred in the successful *Blondie* series, but neither established a career away from it. Lake eventually played Dagwood again on the failed *Blondie* TV series. Donald O'Connor, after years of near stardom in MGM musicals, got trapped into the Francis the Talking Mule series at the same time the musical business was dropping off; although he tried to establish credentials as a straight actor and as a character comic in *The Buster Keaton Story*, not many people bought it, and he went to the summer stock route. Some, like Leo Gorcey and Huntz Hall, in the incredibly long-lived Dead End Kids/East Side Kids/ Bowery Boys series, never seemed even to try to move out of their series. Of the real comedy series stars only Ann Sothern managed to maintain a career, partly because she never became a really major star and partly because the Maisie series left her free to be many different things at different times. Her later success on television was something of a follow-up on her earlier film series.

All of these performers had the same career problems as do most television comedy performers. The more successful they were in the initial series, the less successful they were in any humorous or comedic work that followed it. And all were involved in film series that, to varying degrees, reflected the formats and formulas, as well as the heroes, of the later television situation comedies.

Although it is difficult to be sure of anything involving the careers of actors, especially in a medium that is at most thirty years old, it seems clear that a new perception of the television actor has developed. In the television situation comedy, things do not change. After a while, the audience seems to expect even the actor not to change. When he appears in a new show, people who used to watch his old one look in out of curiosity but soon fade away. Often they can be heard discussing why he "is not as good as he used to be," without ever finding an answer to the question. When they tune in *The New Dick Van Dyke Show*, for example, they really expect to see the *old* Dick Van Dyke. And they seem to expect him to match the picture they carry from the previous series. The result is a strange mental tension, as the audience sees and hears two characters in two situations simultaneously, which often quickly causes them to get up to change the channel.

There is no explanation for Lucille Ball. She is unique. Perhaps she changed from *I Love Lucy* to the later *Lucy Show* without Ricky early enough in television sit-com history to beat the audience, settling in to the new series before the audience had settled its expectations for the sit-com actor. Even so, it is striking that *I Love Lucy* is still being rerun across the nation, but that *The Lucy Show* has had relatively few takers.

Mary Tyler Moore is a bit more easily explained. Although she was prominent and identified in a successful series, she was clearly a supporting character. Moreover, she changed her looks *significantly* before returning to the second series. Moore went through three changes: production shifted to color, which gave everyone a slightly different look; her hairdos changed to such an extent that she really did look like two different people (as Laura Petrie, she had been a queen of starched hair; the more natural Mary Richards hairdos completely changed her face); and her voice dropped in pitch so that she sounded more mature than the squeaky flibbertigibbet she had been. Most important for Moore, however, was probably CBS's decision to ride out the slow start her series had, so that she could find a new audience for her new look.

Mary Tyler Moore and Lucille Ball apparently got lucky. Others as talented somehow mistimed or misplayed their later series attempts, and these few are still the only ones to overcome the peculiar dual vision problems of their audiences.

As things stand now, the actor in a successful television comedy starring role should seek as much money and public acclaim as possible while the series is a hit. Chances are his career will be over when the series is over. Some will find careers in other genres or other media, but most will simply disappear. The stability, permanence, and resistance to change that are built into the sit-com have combined to limit even the actors who perform this kind of new comedy. A new plot and new heroes have also made a new relationship with the audience.

This new relationship has also seriously affected a small but extremely important part of that audience, which often receives little attention: the people who write the shows. In the early days of television, the comedy writers were the people who had been raised on, and in many cases trained in, movies, plays, vaudeville, revues, and radio. The variety and imagination of early television comedy series of all types illustrate the wealth of stimulation and training such youthful experiences encouraged. Today's television writers, however, have been raised in and trained on television. As the sit-com gradually overwhelmed all other types of comic work on the networks, it of course came to dominate the conscious and unconscious training of a new generation of writers and producers, for whom the sit-com became the traditional way of doing things. This influence in turn spread back into other forms, so that new plays and movies began to resemble extended sit-com episodes. The form of the sit-com has come to seem so natural and so obvious that most "creative" people in the business seem incapable of imagining any other form of comedic production or of using the traditional characters or methods when they appear by accident.

One of the striking changes in comedy on television since the rise to dominance of the situation comedy is its debilitating loss of sophistication, though this loss has been disguised in a wave of self-congratulation following the rise of *All in the Family*, when television comedy is supposed to have come of age. Discussions of sophistication in television at present tend to be limited to themes. Shows that deal with such "adult" or controversial topics as abortion, drug use, race prejudice, women's equality, or street crime are thought to be more sophisticated than fifties sit-coms, especially if the show seems to favor the more daring side of most arguments on those topics. Such sophistication is only a matter of political or social daring and has little to do with the way the topics are actually presented to the audience. Sophistication in any art form lies not so much in topic as in execution—Shakespeare's *A Midsummer Night's Dream*, with its poetry and its four-level plot, is a far more sophisticated work than Brian Clark's *Whose Life Is It, Anyway?*, even though it is about silly young lovers and fairies in the woods rather than euthanasia and personal rights. In those terms, television comedy is one of the least sophisticated forms of public entertainment ever to disguise itself under the name of comedy.

Any new form begins at a primitive level, so it seems a bit presumptuous to point out the lack of sophistication in television situation comedies. And yet, it was little more than twenty years from *Gammer Gurton's Needle* to *A Midsummer Night's Dream*. The real beginning of the television situation comedy is open to debate, but the premiere of *The Goldbergs* in January 1949 is as good a date as any. The thirty-three years following the construction of the first English theatre produced Shakespeare, Jonson, and numerous compatriots. Similar periods of theatrical development in Spain produced Lope de Vega, in Italy Carlo Goldoni, in ancient Rome Plautus, in ancient Greece Menander. In the motion pictures, a similar period produced the films of Chaplin, Keaton, Lloyd, and hundreds of others, including the early sound comedies of Lubitsch and the first Fred Astaire/Ginger Rogers musicals. In general, whenever a new medium, a new form, or even a striking new variation within an older medium has appeared, an intensive period of eclectic experimentation follows, in which the producers borrow from everything else to find out what the new medium or form can be made to do, often producing what could be called a golden age that lays the foundations for all subsequent developments in the form. Television comedy somehow has reversed even that tradition; its most sophisticated examples were its very first examples. Within its first thirty years, rather than finding new ways to expand the form, it has devoted its creativity to eliminating as many subtleties and as much sophistication as possible.

The most dramatic illustration of this loss of sophistication can be seen in the use of shifting points of view. Many of the earliest comedy series were transferred from radio. Ozzie and Harriet Nelson began there, as did Burns and Allen and Jack Benny. *The Jack Benny Show* spent fifteen years on the networks yet never quite settled into the confining structures of the situation comedy. For one thing, there was never any question that Jack and his family were *performing*. Shows consistently began with Benny in front of a curtain, sometimes with introductions, sometimes with monologues, sometimes with people coming up out of the audience to do something with or to him. Dennis Day might sing in his "house" or he might come out front to talk or sing. Sometimes the performers even took bows. And you could never be sure where a sketch would go. Usually it involved Jack's family life at home, but you could never be quite certain, especially since his little resident company brought over from radio, particularly Mel Blanc, might play different parts each week.

Probably the most complex and sophisticated of all the comedy series in the fifties was *The Burns and Allen Show*. Not only did George Burns and Gracie Allen use the curtains as Benny did, with monologues and routines and direct audience address, but they also built a complex series of overlapping layers within each episode, which has rarely been matched even in the most complex feature films or avantgarde novels. This series made a short reappearance in syndication recently and was amazing in many ways. A typical episode illustrates the point.

Gracie needed some money, as wives in fifties comedies often did, and George did not particularly want to give it to her. As the show began, they both appeared on their front porch and did a routine directly to the camera audience. Then they went into the living room and began a "normal" sit-com scene. Next, we cut to George sitting upstairs in his office watching Gracie's plot on his own TV, which he turns off to turn to tell us his plan to thwart her. Then we cut to Gracie, who is now watching George on her TV, and she explains her plan to us. When everything is solved, the curtain falls and George and Gracie appear to do their final routine in front of the curtain for the studio audience. Thus, at one point we have a film audience watching a "live" audience watch a real man and wife on a stage playing an imaginary man and wife at home, where he watched her watch him on their television sets. And even more important, all these layers had to be understood by the home viewing audience before the plot of the episode could make any sense. Compared with this kind of complexity, a play like Pirandello's *Six Characters in Search of an Author* is a piece of cake. Only a handful of films, such as *Sherlock Jr.* and *8½*, have even attempted this type of viewpoint variation. Yet despite the obvious success of the Burnses, no sit-com in today's television makes even a minimal attempt to work in such a complex manner. Whatever sophistication such series have, it is social rather than structural or artistic sophistication.

The variety show, once the staple of television comedy, which rivaled and sometimes outdrew the sit-com, is gone too. Some say this is a result of the generational splits in musical tastes, which are certainly a factor. Only in contemporary country-western music are there singers who appeal across the age groups, but few country-western singers have become cross-cultural stars as well. So there are few musical hosts or guests who can consistently deliver high ratings. But the classic variety shows were loved and remembered more for their comedy than for their music. Carol Burnett on her own show and on Garry Moore's gave TV a sketch comedienne fully equal to Lucille Ball; her guests had little to do with the show's popularity. Flip Wilson, Jackie Gleason, Milton Berle, Red Skelton, Steve Allen, and even in his own unique way Dean Martin all headlined variety shows that were watched for their comedy sketches and characters more than for their music. Burnett's show has even been syndicated in thirty-minute versions with the music cut out. And, towering over them all, from 1950 to 1954, *Your Show of Shows*, the program everyone points to when discussing the golden age of television. All of these shows were sketch comedies, very like the silent shorts, with several jokes, a few stories, some music and dance, and a handful of one-reelers each hour. In the 1960s, *Laugh-In* combined the repertory company concept of *Your Show of Shows* with the visual imagination of Ernie Kovacs's early series, almost eliminated sketches, and proved you could have a popular humorous show with nothing but nonstop jokes; but again, there were no followers. And now, as I write, there is only one variety show, *The Barbara Mandrell Show*, being broadcast in prime time, and it has decided to close down at the end of the season.

There are a number of possible explanations for the death of the variety show. Changes in musical taste, as well as the continuing cultural fragmentation of the country as a whole, are certainly important factors. But more than anything there seem to be no sketch writers left, or no people doing the hiring and firing who can recognize and use sketch writers when they see them. The often inept outlines on *Saturday Night Live* illustrate the problem. Promising, often brilliant, ideas are stated, the audience laughs at the beginning, and then the sketch falls apart—no development, no movement toward anywhere, and no punch line, just a trailing off into a few titters and a commercial. There are always more promises made than delivered, and the expectation is always funnier than the result, the reverse of a typical silent short or a good revue sketch.

Without the full-length forms of traditional comedy and the inventive eclectic forms promised in the earliest years of the medium, television comedy of the last decade has settled into a single simpleminded formula. It has eliminated any flexibility in format or in performers and has even surrendered most of the arsenal of humorous techniques of the past. Shifting points of view are gone. But also gone with them are such basic artistic tools as paradox, allusion, metaphor, symbol, personification, and often even simple irony. One need not go further than one of the most critically maligned series of the early sixties, *The Beverly Hillbillies*, to see how much the supposedly sophisticated sit-coms of the seventies and eighties have lost.

Not only was *The Beverly Hillbillies* built around a set of traditional characters who have been part of the fundamental American myth, characters who have all but disappeared from the present world, but it also illustrated a kind of sophisticated foundation for its humor that is increasingly absent in television and films. Most of its humor was built on the conflict between cultures, which seems a simple foundation. However, to be successful, the humor assumes that the audience is aware of and can understand material from both cultures. Scenes in which an Englishman courts Grannie by quoting Shakespeare are not funny unless the audience recognizes the quote, just as scenes about etiquette with the Drysdales require the audience to understand both the concept and the details of etiquette (which much of a 1982 audience would be unable to do). The show also had a striking sense of genuine satire. Never the least bit subtle, it nonetheless was extremely aware of its world, particularly the California world, and it viewed the world from outside, the same way Ben Jonson had done. Especially through Jethro, who in true Fool fashion would adopt any big-city habit and carry it to its logical extreme, the series could deal with the way we lived, or the way we wished to live, completely without sentimentality. In the true sense of Henri Bergson (and of Ben Jonson and Molière as well), it held a distorted mirror up to our nature and attempted, through pure ridicule, to teach us the error of our ways. Very few American series of any kind have ever tried to do that; that *The Beverly Hillbillies* did it and did not close on Saturday night is demonstration not only of the strength of its traditions but also of the unconsciously expressed sophistication of a mass audience. Such a series seems all but impossible today. Who would dare make Shakespeare jokes? Who would even seriously satirize a recent book? Who would dare take something that we all take for granted, such as money, and follow an attitude about it to its logical and absurd conclusion, a genuine *reductio ad absurdum*? Only Mork, and only for a year. Every other series worries about the "human" elements, which is commendable, but at the same time such single-minded concern leaves no room for any shared cultural sophistication beyond parodies of TV commercials.

Even when, almost by accident, one of the traditional methods or characters of comedy suddenly appears in a sit-com, the producers seem not to know what to do with it, resulting in a mishmash that eventually leaves the audience completely dissatisfied. A recent case in point is the film *Animal House*. Often crude and certainly primitive and simple-minded, *Animal House* depended primarily on the magnificent scoundrel/slob/destroyer performance of John Belushi. It was almost completely dedicated to a release of the anarchic spirit of comedy in a form unseen on American screens since the Marx Brothers. It also, much to everyone's surprise, made more money than any other nonmusical film comedy in history.[8] As a result of all that audience and all that money, not one but *three* imitations of *Animal House* appeared as potential series, one on each network, in the spring of 1979. All three were disasters, in content, in humor, and in ratings, and all three were almost immediately canceled by the same people who had ordered them. The essential problem was simple but very real: faced with a model that was dedicated to anarchy in a form that was dedicated to stability, none of the writers, producers, or executives seemed to know what to do. No one either knew how to write in the manner made popular by the film or had the temerity to try to write in that manner. Trained on the series, faced with a concept that, no matter how potentially profitable, contradicted everything in the regular series concept, all production teams simply trod water and produced shows that did not even manage to get a laugh.

Even more disturbing was the record of *Mork & Mindy*. Without much planning or, according to the producer, even any detailed serious thought, Mork from Ork dropped in on the planet Earth. In the first handful of shows, he was an incredible character. More than anything else, he reminded one of the entire cast of *Laugh-In* in one body, throwing off jokes, puns, and allusions with stunning abandon. But he was also something we had not seen for many years on American television—a true comic Innocent. Smart enough to allude to almost anything, foreign enough to misunderstand almost everything, he was the ultimate foil for a crazy world, a cosmic Huck Finn adrift in the sea of modern America. We quite literally had not seen anything like him in almost a decade, and the country took him to heart more quickly and intensely than it had any television comedy character since Lucy. The show finished its first thirteen weeks at an average number 4 position in the ratings,[9] a phenomenal response for a brand new series, which had been surpassed only when *The Beverly Hillbillies* had surged to number 1 in its first season. And the people who put it together did not know what to do with Mork. Handed a character who was part of an ancient tradition, the single most widespread and widely developed character type in American comic traditions, in a shape that was at the moment the single most popular characterization in American television, they proceeded quickly and efficiently to destroy him.

Mork & Mindy's second season demonstrated so many mistakes that it is hard to single out a particular decision as the cause of the show's ratings collapse. First, the network changed its night, putting it opposite the still potent remains of *All in the Family*. That show, however, was undergoing the most difficult of all changes in sit-com history, a complete change of format on a scale that no series to that date had ever survived. Mork could and should have clobbered Archie, but he did not. Second, the producers changed the format too. Admittedly, the original format was nothing to brag about; it looked as thrown together as, by most current stories, it actually was. But the new format did not offer any new possibilities for humor. Mork's strongest point was that he was trying to learn about the world. His choices were severely limited in a small town and a small family. But the format change did not move Mork to places with more options. He did not go to a big city or a new apartment building; in a town supported by a major university, he did not even go to college. He just added a new, weirder family to replace the older straight one, and stayed in the small town. I can find no evidence of any previous show that was often number 1, except *Rhoda*, making a format change for the next season, and Mork's results soon matched Rhoda's. To change the format without producing any more promising comic possibilities than they did was little short of playing Russian roulette with five full chambers.

But most important and most symptomatic, they changed Mork's character. Mork was an Innocent. He was strange because he did not know how we did things here. He was still a child who would be educated out of his innocence, at least if Mindy had her way, but until that happened, he could expose our shortcomings by his purity and directness. For the Innocent to work in humorous situations, he must be the weird one. Only through the juxtaposition of his weirdness with the apparent normality of the rest of the world are the humor and failure of the normal world exposed, with comic and humorous effect. In the fall of 1979, we returned to find a new Mork, surrounded now by weird people who made him seem normal. Almost overnight, he was forced to assume the role of father to this strange family, which might have been good for somebody else but was insane for Mork. The result was that he quit being funny. The next year saw more changes, with new characters who still made Mork seem "normal," and eventually he and Mindy had to get married. In the fourth and final season, his figurative father position became literal with the birth of Mork's child, played by Jonathan Winters. At that point the series had come full circle; Winters was now the innocent that Mork had been when the series began, while Mork now had to serve as father-protector-educator, but it was far too late to save the series with the audience and the show was canceled.

Another factor, much more subjective, was that the scripts became appallingly bad. They were not funny, organized, thought out. Jokes were missing, the bizarre allusions were gone, the vigor and surprise had evaporated. Although many people claim that "quality" has little to do with success in television, it certainly has something to do with failure. Shows that the audience expects to be funny lose their audience when they do not deliver laughs, and *Mork & Mindy* stopped delivering laughs.

It seems obvious that the writers and producers of the show were very uncomfortable with what they had produced. They simply did not know what to do with what they had created. Given a non-sit-com hero who used a tremendously varied arsenal of humorous weaponry, they could not work with him. They tried to force him into more confining, more controlled television molds, even if it meant the loss of their audience and the destruction of the show. They could not cope with the material of traditional comedy.

Another sign of the atrophy of television writers and producers in the face of comedy can be seen in the made-for-television movies.

Hundreds have been made since the first in 1964, but again only a handful have been comedies. The magnitude of the failure to extend the comedic forms to feature length may be seen in a quick survey of a recent year. During the 1977-78 season, there were 164 made-for-television movies on the three networks during prime time. (There were not 164 different titles, because some shows, such as *79 Park Avenue*, played in several parts, but the equivalent of 164 different 90- or 120-minute movies were presented.) Of those 164 presentations, 2 were comedies. That comes to 1.2 percent. Those 2, for the curious, were ABC's *Three on a Date* and NBC's *Just You and Me*. Two others were western melodramas that the networks called comedy-dramas: *Kate Bliss* (about a female detective in the Old West) and *The Incredible Rocky Mountain Race*. One other production, *Sticking Together*, was called a comedy-drama but was essentially a pilot for an *Eight Is Enough* copy with a family of five orphans. Of all the hours devoted to feature-length presentations, barely 1 percent resembled comedy in either its traditional or its television guises, and less than 2 percent more even pretended to offer humor. [10] Similar results could be found for most seasons in the last decade.

In spite of the popularity of the sit-coms, the people who make them have not been able to produce feature-length versions with any consistency or success. Neither have they been able to shift their mental gears, so to speak, and produce more traditional comedies at feature length with consistency or success. They apparently do not know what to do with comedy in any form but the half-hour episode of the stable sit-com format. They cannot write longer, and they cannot write shorter. They cannot take advantage of a major film success, and they cannot even maintain their own successes when they accidentally go outside the established patterns of the sit-com formula. The situation comedy has wiped out all other traditional forms of comedy on television and has done so, at least for the moment, in the most deadly of all manners, by killing off the imagination of the people who produce and write them.

In general, the audience has been similarly led away from traditional comedy. Successes like *Animal House* are exceptions, and the traditional comedies of filmmakers like Woody Allen are usually quite limited in terms of actual audience. They make a nice profit because they are made cheaply and because the filmmaker is willing to play to a small but dependable audience, a minority.

There are some hints that the mass television audience might respond to traditional comedy if it were offered, but they are only hints. The first season of *Mork & Mindy* did draw a much better response than the many changed seasons that followed. The much maligned (often deservedly so) *Love Boat* still slips an occasional glimpse of the old plot and heroes into its sit-com framework. Most ironic, however, is the persistence of certain comedic character types but in new situations. Comic policemen are part of the world of melodrama on television, in *The Dukes of Hazzard*, with its daring youths who consistently make buffoons of the minions of the law. The Scoundrel heroes have also continued, again in the melodrama, not only in *Maverick* and *The Rockford Files* but also in *Switch*, *To Catch a Thief*, and the new *Fall Guy*. The Innocent even gets an occasional shot at glory on such series as *The Greatest American Hero*. As funny as these might be on occasions, however, they are still not comedies and are not perceived as such.

Much the same thing has happened in recent films. The stunning gross receipts of *Grease*, which is as traditional a comedy as it is possible to write—even with the rock and roll, Plautus would recognize it immediately—show that the large audience of the young can still respond to comedy now and then. But most of our film and stage comedy is now beginning to follow the lead of television sit-coms. The hit "comedies" of the second half of the seventies were either elaborate sit-coms, like *Same Time, Next Year* on stage or *Hooper* on film, or often hilarious elaborations on familiar melodrama formats, like *Smokey and the Bandit*, *Stir Crazy*, and *Nine to Five*. The television comedy has become the new tradition for an enormous portion of the American audience, and that is affecting not only television but all the other media as well. A comedy of change, of movement, of anarchy, and of instability offers little attraction to many who have come to understand comedy only in terms of the sit-com.

It is important to stress how complete and how sudden this change has been. Within one generation, a completely new form of entertainment, a new literary form perhaps a later generation will say, not only has been invented but has swept the field. Almost before our eyes, over two thousand years of tradition have been wiped out. Comedy as the Western world has known it is almost dead in the richest and most powerful nation of the Western world, and in its place has grown and prospered a new form that denies almost all the myths, heroes, and

165

relationships of the most meaningful and enduring tradition of our performed arts.

Such a change does not happen because of a single success. *I Love Lucy* or *All in the Family* did not cause this new form to appear, no matter how important they may have been in providing the models that so many others chose to imitate in the most imitative of all media. Nor did it come about because of some secret conspiracy hatched in the boardrooms of the corporate networks or the teeming advertising agencies who depend on ratings success to sell their services to manufacturers, no matter how popular conspiracy theories may be to people who criticize the industry. It happened because some peculiar circumstances made it possible and because the audience liked it, asked for more, and supported more when it appeared. The sit-com is not inherent in the medium itself; the rest of the world does not have it, at least not yet, although television is now almost universal. The sit-com as we have described it is still a peculiarly American phenomenon, which for the most part speaks only to Americans.

Of course, the United States is the only nation to have a completely commercial television system. The purpose of every broadcast is to provide something for everyone *at the same time*, and something that will get everyone to watch again on a regular basis. The need to guarantee an audience to advertisers causes programmers to seek stable forms. The very concept of a series is based on this need for predictability—for many other nations, the series as we understand it does not exist. There are regular time slots, usually for variety shows, which may continue on a regular basis for several years. But most other series are simply one long show broken into several segments, which will eventually have a clear ending, or continuing soap operas, which have no endings but which are continually changing situations and characters. Only in the United States in the last two decades has the concept of a regular TV series come to mean a regular, never-ending situation in which nothing ever happens.

Even in American commercial television, however, most series are not so stable. Although the goal is to guarantee an audience by guaranteeing to present what the audience expects, it is only in the sit-com that this goal has produced such total stability and repetition. Most of American television programming still does not reflect the stability of the situation comedy. Daytime programming is made up of news and talk shows, where the host may stay the same but all other participants change regularly and where each day's programming is to some degree unpredictable; game shows, which offer the same unpredictability in more limited form, because of specific rules (like the weekend sports on a simpler scale); or the soap operas, which have no end but which constantly change characters and situations and emphases throughout a "real-life" time progression. Despite the agonizingly slow speed with which they develop, the soap operas are in many ways the most sophisticated form currently on American television. They are the only programs where events *do* develop and where the audience needs to know what happened in the past. That is why they spend so much time repeating themselves, giving exposition to people who may have missed yesterday's episode but need to know what happened to understand today's. No prime time programming is structured in such a way except the occasional prime time soap opera like *Dallas*. At the very least, the soap opera still believes in cause and effect and, even more important, believes its audience can understand them, which is more than almost any prime time situation comedy can claim.

The prime time melodrama still retains many unstable factors. The only consistent characters are often outsiders who meddle in the lives of the "normal" people; they are heroes precisely because of their successful meddling. Those principals vary their locales and their problems from week to week, always meeting "new" characters and "new" situations. And the most significant proportion of melodrama-drama in prime time is not even in the series form; the movies and the made-for-television movies occupy most of the noncomedic time slots, with occasional variety specials. Where American television has tried the limited series, it has also been in the melodrama form, as in *Rich Man, Poor Man* and its various imitations.

Obviously, there is an audience capable of accepting variations in programming, or these programming features would not survive. It is only in the situation comedy that the search for complete stability is dominant. And television producers and programmers have tried other types of comedies. Variety shows have gradually disappeared because their audiences gradually disappeared. Comedy feature films have been shown, but their ratings are consistently lower than for any other types of features. Comic anthology series have even been tried, *Love, American Style* being the most successful example. But as the years passed, the audience left these types of comedy and moved to the situation comedy for their humor. It cannot all be blamed on the network executives. Though they certainly did not object to producing and scheduling the new form, the audience has made it happen. This is the kind of comedy we want at the moment.

The situation comedy *as a form* is successful because it tells the audience what the audience wants to hear, the same reason the traditional comedy as a form was so successful and persistent in the past. In its simplest terms, the old form said that change is life, and the new one now says that change is death. All the evidence available indicates that the contemporary American audience overwhelmingly prefers the latter message. How can that be? This is the land of opportunity, the one nation in the world dedicated to the proposition that anything can happen, and that the sun will come out tomorrow, if not this afternoon. Where did that all go?

A major part of the answer to that question lies in the nature of the American television audience. The new comedy is in effect addressing a new audience, which comedy has rarely if ever addressed before.

First, it is a private audience, not a public one. We watch TV alone, in our homes. There is no social audience present. Television producers worry about that a great deal, which is why we have laugh tracks. The laugh track does more than just pretend that things are funny when they clearly are not; it tries to tell us that we are part of the audience that comedy has always required. Laugh tracks, or scream tracks, or cheer tracks are not required for melodramas; melodramas can be accepted in private, like the movies and stories from which they are derived. Only the comedy seems lonely without its audience, and so we turn on the tube and listen to the sound of other people sharing the experience with us. But they are not really doing that, no matter how hard the producers pretend. We are alone with the comedy, just as we are alone with everything else on the screen.

Throughout most of the seventies, most sit-coms completely surrendered their film background, in order to encourage the appearance of a social audience. Most series made a point of being filmed (or taped) in front of a live audience, so that the people at home could feel they were at least looking in on a real comedic performance. But even those attempts are failures. The "live" audiences laugh only at what is on the screen. If someone enters the room wearing a funny suit, the people in the studio do not laugh until he appears on camera and stop laughing as soon as he goes out of the shot. If Bob Newhart's steaks catch fire on his barbecue, no one in the supposedly live audience begins to laugh until the flames are really high and the camera is ready to show them. The live audience is not live, or at least is not responding to a live theatrical comic experience, and is not in fact responding like an audience at all. A live audience at a TV taping simply sits and watches the monitors, each person watching just as privately as if he were at home. And then those of us at home watch our private version with the sound of other people watching their private versions added on.

That we watch this at home far more than in any other place underscores an important part of this new comedy. If there is any sense of audience in the experience at all, it is within the family, but the family watches as a set of separate, private individuals. Watching is a completely passive experience, and a completely private one. Traditional comedy has always been a public and an active experience. Thus, it should come as no surprise that the television medium produces a set of passive heroes and pays little attention to the public social myths of the comedy of the past.

At the same time, more is at work than the television medium itself. The same medium is at work, providing its private passive experience, to the audiences in Great Britain too, but there no passive, defensive, unchanging comedy so completely dominates the attention of the viewers. Some new characteristic has been added to the individual members of the audience outside of the television medium, something that was not shared by past comedy audiences. For the first time, we have a middle-class comedy controlled by an audience that sees itself as middle-class (no matter what its actual status may be). The situation comedy is a precise expression of that situation. It is a defensive comedy rather than an aggressive one, a comedy oriented to the present or the past rather than to the future, a comedy in which property is sacred, the family is eternal, the parents are always right, and authority always wins.

Theatrical audiences, especially those for comedy, have usually been composed of either the very rich or the very poor. In certain times and places, the poor in the audience dominated, as in the *commedia* performances; at other times the wealthy aristocrats provided the dominant taste, as in the English Restoration theatres. Most often, these two groups shared the theatres in an uneasy alliance. But, whoever might be in control, "respectable" people did not go to the comedy and consistently were opposed to its very existence.

Such opposition was not a matter of personal taste but rather a reflection of genuine social conflict, expressed through the generalized attitudes of entire classes. G. Wilson Knight, discussing Restoration comedy, expresses the problem for all comedy throughout history when he says that "moralistic comedy" is a "contradiction in terms." Against comedy,

> morality and convention are impotent; the stuff of life is there whatever we think of it, and it is comedy's business to face it...[as] instinct recognized simultaneously as sin, inevitable and as honourable. For such subtleties the middle classes had neither the inclination nor the language. Clarification could only come through an aristocratic daring.[11]

And that "aristocratic daring" played for the most part to a particular audience that could afford to dare to be simultaneously sinful and honorable, the aristocrats and the poor, and the young of all classes.

Such class distinction in audiences continued even in the supposedly classless society of America. Colonial society for the most part opposed all theatrical entertainments, usually on grounds of protecting the impressionable young, especially the apprentices who were lured from work and wasted time they could more properly have used in working for the merchants. The first plays in this country appeared in the cavalier lands of Virginia and Carolina, and those plays were for the most part comedies from London. In the nineteenth century, the rise of melodrama and spectacle introduced a violent morality to the stage that appealed to the lower middle class and the poor alike, although in different degrees, and the intense humor moved to the music hall and to vaudeville, where the disrespectful and unrespectable masses, especially the incoming horde of immigrants, sought their entertainment, to the continual opposition of the religious and respectable elements. This opposition continued into the silent film era. The middle classes gradually accepted the feature films, especially the spectacle, sin, and redemption films epitomized by Cecil B. De Mille's, but anything that appealed to the young and to the poor was strongly attacked, because they were vulgar and immoral. Rufus's mother in James Agee's A *Death in the Family* speaks for millions when she calls Chaplin "that horrid little man...so *nasty*...so *vulgar!* With his nasty little cane...and that nasty little walk!"[12]

That attitude ultimately resulted in the Hays Code, promulgated in 1930, though not really enforced until 1934, after Hollywood panicked under the violent attacks of the Legion of Decency. Ostensibly concerned with the gangster pictures, the code was a form of industry self-regulation that defined what would be permissible on American film screens and was in fact largely aimed at the traditional subjects of comedy. As Griffith and Mayer point out, it was driven into effect ultimately by the appearance in Hollywood of Mae West.[13] Her comedy was the proverbial straw that broke the camel's back. Despite the code, film comedy continued to function in the same manner as traditional stage comedy. The general level of vulgarity lessened, but the impulses remained the same, and the middle class rarely found anything of interest in the film comedy, except for such consistent winners as the Andy Hardy series.

During the 1920s, large numbers of people had moved to nonmanual occupations, bought homes and cars, and settled down to be middle-class, only to have their position ripped from them by the economic collapse of the 1930s. Whatever class pretensions people might have held during the Depression, there is no doubt that most people thought of themselves as poor. For a while, the old middle class held on, until wages for office help and other white-collar jobs collapsed in response to widespread cheap labor and unemployment.

But after World War II, some important changes began to occur in the social and mental attitudes of Americans that would affect the shape of comedy and the future of television comedy. Two major governmental programs had a major effect. The first was the GI Bill, which allowed veterans to go to school with only minimal economic sacrifice. Men who had not finished high school because they were supporting families before the war and young men starting families who normally would have had to forego further education were given a chance to move up from manual labor, finishing high school or in many cases even moving to professional ranks by using the money for college. Second, the returning veteran found the government willing to guarantee his home loan through the Federal Housing Administration. People who had lost homes in the Depression and millions who would otherwise not have been able to get sufficient credit were suddenly property owners. The suburbs erupted, the automobile appeared in every garage, and social attitudes were revolutionized.

Over the next twenty-five to thirty years, even unionized working men ceased to see themselves as lower-class or working-class. Marxist theory had predicted that the urban capitalist middle class would be squeezed out, gradually degenerating into and being absorbed by the proletariat. In America, this in effect did occur. Even the most powerful business executives now rarely own even a minimal portion of the companies that they administer as wage earners (extremely well paid and rewarded, but wage earners nonetheless). However, when this change occurred, the people themselves refused to accept the proletariat consciousness. The nation as a whole simply decided that the new majority was all middle-class.

This remarkable change in public attitude has no single cause. Rising numbers of white-collar workers have contributed to the idea. Even more important, most laborers possess the traditional signs of the middle class—especially the private home, but also access to higher education for themselves and their children, higher pay scales (although not as high as they appear to be), and access to private transportation through the car and to private entertainment through the television and the stereo. That most people buy poor quality versions of these objects on credit does not affect the essential perception of the status that accompanies their possession. A third factor is the increasing visibility of the genuinely poor since the appearance of welfare payments. The working man, whatever his pay, takes an intense pride, often racial as well as social, in not being on welfare, so that the lower class has come to mean those on welfare rather than those who work for others. The combination of these factors, occurring simultaneously with the spread of television programming, has given America a society in which, as Richard Parker has described it,

> The American middle class is synonymous with the word majority. To be middle class is to stand literally in the middle, to be average. . . . The idea of a minority middle class is about as ludicrous to an American as its antithesis was to a European. [14]

Thus it should come as no surprise that the dominant forms of entertainment express those attitudes that have traditionally been associated with the *bourgeoisie*. The family is inviolable, although the family may be a metaphorical family as well as a biological one. The parent, especially the father, is the ultimate authority. Property is also inviolable and must be protected from those who would destroy it. Change that improves the family's situation is good, but any change that is the least bit questionable or unpredictable must be avoided at all costs. Doctors, lawyers, businessmen, and policemen are the role models and heroes that the children should emulate. Respectable people and their respectable culture and education are to be encouraged and protected. None of these beliefs is at all odd or difficult to conceive within any entertainment supported largely by a group that regards itself as middle-class, and in general these are the tenets of the Victorian popular novel and the problem plays of Arthur Pinero, John Galsworthy, and even Alexandre Dumas *fils*, which were supported by such audiences. It is only when they become a part of what is thought to be comedy that odd things begin to occur.

As we have seen, the comedy has been the only consistently social, active, aggressive form of popular entertainment. If the comedy loses those aspects, through loss of the patterns, heroes, and mythical and metaphorical actions that express them, there are no other generally accepted forms that can represent those impulses. The cultural stimulus for change, for natural impulses, for "progress" if you wish to use that term, disappears if the comedy changes and no new forms that provide such a stimulus arise in their place. It may be an accident, but it is nonetheless a curious coincidence that great ages of comedy in our past have coincided with great periods of cultural change and social growth—the *commedia* with the Renaissance, the world of Shakespeare and Jonson with the Elizabethan expansion, Molière with the change of France from a medieval to a national state and the cultural leader of Europe, the silent films with America's assumption of world economic and cultural leadership, and so on. The periods without comedy have been periods of social and cultural stagnation—the Middle Ages, the decline of Rome, Spain at almost any time since the collapse of the Armada, or the fascist periods of Italy and Germany.

One does not necessarily cause the other, but the myth of change and growth as expressed through the simple traditional comedy and the society open to growth and change have been compatriots in Western history. This is the danger of the television comedy of America; it may simultaneously reflect and encourage our resistance to the future. It may in effect signal that the land of opportunity no longer believes in that opportunity, that the future no longer is a part of our myth. This relationship is circular: the sit-com appeals to bourgeois attitudes, which in turn are encouraged by the sit-com, which in turn demonstrates even stronger attitudes, and so on. It also can be seen in something as apparently far removed as sports. Only after the rise of television, for example, did the defensive unit in football receive any recognition, and only since the dominance of the sit-com has the defensive unit become actually heroic to an audience that is clearly middle-class.

As the nation enters a trying time of change, the mood in the land is no longer one of hope. Even in the worst days of the Depression, there was a persistent feeling that we would somehow come through and things would get better, if not immediately then at least for the children. It was also a golden age of film comedy, following closely upon the silent film golden age of the prosperous and expansive twenties. Comedy spoke to both eras, and spoke in the terms of the ancient, traditional comedy. But recent America has not seemed to have this sense that things will get better. Even in the seventies, when most Americans prospered, there was a pervasive malaise, a sense of desperate protectiveness, of holding on to what we had and of getting everything we could before it was too late. Writing in 1979, Christopher Lasch could summarize the last half of the decade as full of "the despair of a society that cannot face the future"[15] and hardly be challenged.

Now that an economic downturn has become clear, the national mood seems if possible more intense than despair. Joseph Epstein has summarized the mood as well as anyone:

> While Americans as a nation are in fact rich, we feel ourselves to be, somehow, poor. While we have in recent years shown ourselves capable of surmounting bulky problems— pollution for one, extravagant population growth for another— yet we continue to feel ourselves impotent and hopeless. . . . We do not live in a very future-minded epoch.[16]

Epstein says we have lost our sense of ambition; others say we have lost the frontier, the entrepreneurial spirit, the sense of adventure, the creative urge, the willingness to take risks, and so on. It is certainly curious that so many of those things that social critics say we are missing now are a part of the world of the traditional comedy, which we have forsaken.

At least one explanation for this state of affairs must be that as a society we have lost our sense of comedy. Comedy has always expressed cultural hope in Western society. Television's new comedy has no hope for the future; its most visible hope is that things will not get worse, that we can at least protect what we have. In the circle of our daily life, the situation comedy both reveals and encourages our loss of the future. It appeals to that part of our personality that wants to hear that message, and it gives the message daily to those who have not yet succumbed.

174

We are not irrevocably committed to this new comedy. It may change again at any moment. Social upheavals may come, or expected upheavals may not come. The method of financing and organizing television broadcasting may change and thus encourage a revival of longer and more traditional comedic materials. But the signs are not good. Each year the sit-com establishes a stronger hold on our collective imagination and each year the comedies in other media more and more come to resemble the television comedy rather than the traditional comedy of the West. Each year our psychological merging of classes and class attitudes seems more intense, encouraged by the same television programming and political propaganda. If the current economic problems become more desperate, many people may begin to lose their perceptions of themselves as middle-class and look for entertainments that express more traditional viewpoints; they might just as easily roll over and accept their fate, as so many people in past societies have done. Predictions are impossible.

There are some signs that the sit-com is ready to make some major changes itself. Only one of the top 10 sit-coms in the fall 1981 season had premiered since 1977. On the other hand, the same thing happened to the sit-com in the last two or three seasons of the sixties; no one then could have predicted the impact of *All in the Family* and *The Mary Tyler Moore Show*. But the sit-com did not die then and it seems extremely unlikely it will die in the near future, even after all the series of the 1970s wear out their formats and their welcomes. The networks now try out new series for four or six weeks before giving them a "permanent" place in the schedule, but no one has yet suggested that the four to six weeks should be plotted and should end on purpose. For better or worse, the situation comedy gives every appearance of being our comedy. Mork's first year, the surprising film success of *Arthur* and the chaos comedies of John Belushi, Bill Murray, and others—these indicate that the traditional comedy and its myths and impulses are not yet completely dead, though the situation comedy continues to be the overwhelming expression of our national popular will. It may change; one cannot observe the history of comedy and its remarkable survival in its most common form through the vicissitudes and chaos of two thousand years of Western history without a deep respect for its adaptability and strength. But then again, it may not; tragedy never recovered from the rise of a middle class, and comedy may never recover from the combined blow of the television medium and a middle-class majority

175

audience. But if the traditional comedy goes, our world will lose more than a literary type. We will live in a very different world, a world that has lost contact with one of its most important and persistent social myths. We will have changed the way our entire culture thinks, perceives, and expresses itself.

The sit-com is a new comedy. The implications of that simple perception are enormous, and it may very well be no laughing matter at all.

Appendix
Successful Situation Comedies

The following situation comedies have met the basic criteria used in this work for network success, that is, the completion of at least four full seasons in prime time originals and at least one appearance in the top 25 rating averages. Several of these series just barely met the criteria because their fourth season was their final one and apparently existed more because no one had anything better to put in their slots (even though their ratings had collapsed during the third year) than because of continued audience interest. These marginal "successes" are marked with an *. Those series still running at time of writing are marked with (R).

These successful television sit-coms are quite a representative sample of the quality of television work. Whatever value or worth the sit-com may have, those series that have been popular and have stayed on the air have been the "best" by normal critical standards as often or, one might even argue, more often than they have been the "worst." For every *Gomer Pyle* there is also a *M*A*S*H*; for each *Green Acres* there is a *Mary Tyler Moore Show*. Many of the most critically reviled shows are not there—no *My Mother, the Car*, no *Gilligan's Island* despite its strength in the rerun market, no *Flying Nun*. The average American TV audience gets insulted a great deal by TV critics, often for watching shows that, it turns out, large numbers generally do not watch. Almost all of the successful series have something unique, almost classic about them. Within the various subgroups in sit-com history, the successful ones are usually those that were the best, most professional, and most representative examples of their groups.

There are admittedly a number of successful series that have little apparent redeeming social value and that, in retrospect, cannot offer much to any audience but the one they originally spoke to. At the same time, very few of the "quality" situation comedies that the networks have offered in the past thirty years did not find an audience and maintain some success. Perhaps, out of all the failed sit-coms, only *My World and Welcome to It* was a real critical success and an audience failure. Others pleased some critics but not many. The mediocre sit-coms for the most part failed as they deserved to do. The clichés about lowest common denominators may apply in other parts of the network programming, but in situation comedies, success has more often been accorded the good, reasonably intelligent, and critically acceptable shows than it has the dumb, pointless, inane, and unimaginative ones.

This is an important point. The problems of the situation comedy discussed in the text are the problems of the form itself. They will not be affected by a change in network presidents or the hiring of wittier writers. Both "good" and "bad" sit-coms share the same assumptions about form and characterization.

A second point is that there are very few spin-offs on the list. *Rhoda* is discussed in the text; *Gomer Pyle* was spun off from *The Andy Griffith Show*. The other successful spin-offs involved very minor characters in the original series. *Petticoat Junction* developed from the family left behind by the *Beverly Hillbilllies*, and *Green Acres* grew from that; the three of them often shared casts. The characters of *Maude* and *The Jeffersons* made several appearances on *All in the Family* but were not very important on that show. *Laverne & Shirley* claims to be a spin-off from *Happy Days*, but the lines are tenuous; the two principals made one appearance there. Other spin-offs, which used major series characters, such as *Pete & Gladys*, *The Ropers*, and *Phyllis*, did not do nearly as well as expected.

The Adventures of Ozzie and Harriet. ABC, 1952-66.

Alice. CBS, 1976-(R).

All in the Family. CBS, 1971-79. Continued in 1979-(R) as *Archie Bunker's Place.*

The Andy Griffith Show. CBS, 1960-68.

Barney Miller. ABC, 1975-82.

The Beverly Hillbillies. CBS, 1962-71.

Bewitched. ABC, 1964-72.
The Bob Newhart Show. CBS, 1972-78.
The Brady Bunch. ABC, 1969-74.
The Danny Thomas Show. ABC, 1953-57, CBS, 1957-65.
December Bride. CBS, 1954-59.
*Dennis the Menace.** CBS, 1959-63.
The Dick Van Dyke Show. CBS, 1961-66.
The Donna Reed Show. ABC, 1958-66.
The Doris Day Show. CBS, 1968-73.
Family Affair. CBS, 1966-71.
Father Knows Best. CBS, 1954-55, NBC, 1955-58, CBS, 1958-62,
    ABC, 1962-63.
The Flintstones. ABC, 1960-66, animated.
*The Gale Storm Show.** CBS, 1956-59, ABC, 1959-60.
The George Burns and Gracie Allen Show. CBS, 1950-58.
Get Smart. NBC, 1965-69, CBS, 1969-70.
Gomer Pyle, USMC. CBS, 1964-70.
Good Times. CBS, 1974-79.
Green Acres. CBS, 1965-71.
Happy Days. ABC, 1974-(R).
Hazel. NBC, 1961-65, CBS, 1965-66.
Hogan's Heroes. CBS, 1965-71.
I Dream of Jeannie. NBC, 1965-70.
I Love Lucy. CBS, 1951-57.
The Jeffersons. CBS, 1975-(R).
Laverne & Shirley. ABC, 1976-(R).
Leave It to Beaver. CBS, 1957-58, ABC, 1958-63.
The Life of Riley. NBC, 1953-58.
The Lucy Show (Here's Lucy). CBS, 1962-74.
*McHale's Navy.** ABC, 1962-66.
*M*A*S*H.* CBS, 1972-(R).
Mama. CBS, 1949-56.
*The Many Loves of Dobie Gillis.** CBS, 1959-63.
The Mary Tyler Moore Show. CBS, 1970-77.
Maude. CBS, 1972-78.
*Mr. Ed.** CBS, 1961-65.
Mork & Mindy. ABC, 1978-82.*
My Three Sons. ABC, 1960-67, CBS, 1967-72.
The Odd Couple. ABC, 1970-75.

One Day at a Time. CBS, 1975-(R).

*Our Miss Brooks.** CBS, 1952-56.

*The Partridge Family.** ABC, 1970-74.

Petticoat Junction. CBS, 1963-70.

*The Phil Silvers Show.** CBS, 1955-59.

*Private Secretary.** CBS, 1953-57. (This is a questionable entry on the list, since for three of its four years it showed only on alternate weeks, its total episodes adding up to only two full seasons. It is also, I think, unique in that for two years its first runs were on CBS and its summer re-runs were on NBC.)

The Real McCoys. ABC, 1957-62, CBS, 1962-63.

*Rhoda.** CBS, 1974-78.

Sanford and Son. NBC, 1972-77.

Taxi. ABC, 1978-82 (at time of writing, NBC had picked up the show for 1982-83).

That Girl. ABC, 1966-71.

Three's Company. ABC, 1977-(R).

WKRP in Cincinnati. CBS, 1978-82.*

Notes

CHAPTER 1

1. Ratings are from Tim Brooks and Earle Marsh, *The Complete Directory to Prime Time Network TV Shows, 1946-Present*, pp. 802-10; *Variety*, January 13, 1982, September 30, 1981.

2. Cobbett Steinberg, *Reel Facts*, pp. 356-57.

3. Suzanne Langer, *Feeling and Form*, p. 341.

CHAPTER 2

1. Northrop Frye, *Anatomy of Criticism*, p. 163.

2. I. G., "A Refutation of the Apology for Actors," in *Theories of Comedy*, ed. Paul Lauter, pp. 133-36.

3. Jeremy Collier, "Selections from *A Short View of the Immorality and Profaneness of the English Stage* (1698)," in *British Dramatists from Dryden to Sheridan*, ed. George H. Nettleton, Arthur E. Case, and George W. Stone, Jr., p. 389.

4. Steinberg, *Reel Facts*, p. 470.

5. Donatus, "A Fragment on Comedy and Tragedy," in *Theories of Comedy*, ed. Paul Lauter, p. 27.

6. Henri Bergson, "Laughter," in *Comedy*, ed. Wylie Sypher, p. 187.

7. Joseph Stein, *Fiddler on the Roof*, p. 124.

8. Tom Jones, *The Fantasticks*, pp. 39-40.

9. Thornton Wilder. *Our Town*, in *Three Plays*, p. 45.

10. Frye, *Anatomy of Criticism*, p. 163.

11. Saul Bellow, *The Adventures of Augie March*, p. 536.

12. Langer, *Feeling and Form*, p. 342.

13. The Lewis terminology is adapted from Stuart Kaminsky, *American Film Genres*, pp. 208-13.

14. Frye, *Anatomy of Criticism*, p. 170.

15. James K. Feibleman, *In Praise of Comedy*, p. 200.

16. Jacob Bronowski, *The Ascent of Man*, pp. 404-6.

CHAPTER 3

1. *Rhoda* ratings are from Brooks and Marsh, *Complete Directory*, p. 809-10.

2. William Gibson, *Shakespeare's Game*, pp. 6-7.

3. Doris Day ratings are from Brooks and Marsh, *Complete Directory*, p. 807-8.

4. Rose K. Goldsen, *The Show and Tell Machine*, p. 315.

5. Ratings are from *Variety*, January 9, 1980, January 13, 1982.

6. Arthur Berger, *The T-V-Guided American*, p. 73.

7. Bergson, "Laughter," pp. 119-27. Bergson's translator terms the third basic humorous device the "reciprocal interference of series," which is a confusing term at best; for simplicity and clarity I have substituted the term "double meanings."

CHAPTER 4

1. The curious assertions about the Marx Brothers' career problems are from Paul D. Zimmerman and Burt Goldblatt, *The Marx Brothers at the Movies*, p. 101.

2. "Foreword," in *Familiar Faces*, ed. Pat McNees, p. 11.

3. Uno Asplund, *Chaplin's Films*, p. 147.

CHAPTER 5

1. Comparisons of audiences are based on data in *Variety*, January 3, 1979, and United States Bureau of the Census, *Statistical Abstract of the United States, 1978*, pp. 43, 474.

2. George Meredith, "An Essay on Comedy," in *Comedy*, ed. Wylie Sypher, p. 27.

3. Meredith, "An Essay on Comedy," p. 57.

4. Goldsen, *The Show and Tell Machine*, pp. 331-32.

5. This survey was made for and used in William Goldman, *The Season*.

6. Denis Diderot, *The Paradox of Acting*, pp. 14-15.

7. Rooney's box office standing is from John Douglas Eames, *The MGM Story*, p. 166.

8. *Variety*, January 9, 1980.

9. Mork's ratings are from *Variety*, January 3, 1979.

10. The data are compiled from information in *TV Season 1977-78* and Alvin J. Marill, *Movies Made for Television*.

11. G. Wilson Knight, *The Golden Labyrinth*, p. 130.

12. James Agee, *A Death in the Family*, p. 19.

13. Richard Griffith and Arthur Mayer, *The Movies*, pp. 290-97.

14. Richard Parker, *The Myth of the Middle Class*, pp. 15-16.

15. Christopher Lasch, *The Culture of Narcissism*, p. 26.

16. Joseph Epstein, *Ambition: The Secret Passion*, p. 5.

Bibliography

Any work of this kind must depend a great deal on personal memory of movies and episodes seen and digested long before the idea of the book ever surfaced. I have made every effort to verify those memories using available reference materials, many of which are included here. I have also tried to include any works to which I am conscious of a debt in my thinking.

Agee, James. *A Death in the Family*. New York: Bantam, 1969.

"All-Time Film Rental Champs." *Variety*, January 13, 1982.

Andrews, Bart. *Lucy & Ricky & Fred & Ethel*. New York: Dutton, 1976.

Aristotle. *Poetics*. Translated by Gerald F. Else. Ann Arbor: University of Michigan Press, 1970.

Asplund, Uno. *Chaplin's Films*. Translated by Paul Britten Austin. New York: A.S. Barnes, 1976.

Bellow, Saul. *The Adventures of Augie March*. New York: Modern Library, 1965.

Berger, Arthur Asa. *The T-V-Guided American*. New York: Walker, 1976.

Bergson, Henri. "Laughter." In *Comedy*, edited by Wylie Sypher. Garden City, N.J.: Doubleday, Anchor, 1956.

"Big Rental Films of 1978." *Variety*, January 3, 1979.

"Big Rental Films of 1981." *Variety*, January 13, 1982.

Blesh, Rudi. *Keaton*. New York: Macmillan, 1966.

Bronowski, Jacob. *The Ascent of Man*. Boston: Little, Brown, 1973.

Brooks, Tim, and Marsh, Earle. *The Complete Directory to Prime Time Network TV Shows, 1946-Present*. New York: Ballantine, 1979.

Brownlow, Kevin. *The Parade's Gone By*. New York: Knopf, 1968.

Castleman, Harry, and Podrazik, Walter J. *Watching TV: Four Decades of American Television*. New York: McGraw-Hill, 1982.

Collier, Jeremy. "Selections from A *Short View of the Immorality and Profaneness of the English Stage* (1698)." In *British Dramatists from Dryden to Sheridan*, 2d ed., edited by George H. Nettleton, Arthur E. Case, and George W. Stone, Jr. New York: Houghton, Mifflin, 1969.

Deschner, Donald. *The Films of Cary Grant*. Secaucus, N.J.: Citadel, 1973.

————. *The Films of W. C. Fields*. New York: Citadel, 1966.

Diderot, Denis. *The Paradox of Acting*. Translated by Walter H. Pollock. New York: Hill & Wang, 1963.

Donatus. "A Fragment of Comedy and Tragedy," translated by George Miltz. In *Theories of Comedy*, edited by Paul Lauter. New York: Anchor, 1964.

Ducharte, Pierre Louis. *The Italian Comedy*. Translated by Randolph T. Weaver. New York: Dover, 1966.

Eames, John Douglas. *The MGM Story*. New York: Crown, 1976.

Epstein, Joseph. *Ambition: The Secret Passion*. New York: Dutton, 1982.

Everson, William K. *The Films of Laurel and Hardy*. New York: Citadel, 1967.

Feibleman, James K. *In Praise of Comedy*. New York: Horizon, 1970.

Frye, Northrop. *Anatomy of Criticism*. New York: Atheneum, 1966.

Gibson, William. *Shakespeare's Game*. New York: Atheneum, 1978.

Goldman, William. *The Season*. New York: Harcourt, 1969.

Goldsen, Rose K. *The Show and Tell Machine*. New York: Dial, 1977.

Griffith, Richard, and Mayer, Arthur. *The Movies*. Rev. ed. New York: Simon & Schuster, 1970.

Halliwell, Lesley. *The Filmgoer's Companion*. 6th ed. New York: Avon, 1978.

I. G. "A Refutation of the Apology for Actors." In *Theories of Comedy*, edited by Paul Lauter. New York: Anchor, 1964.

Jones, Tom. *The Fantasticks*. New York: Avon, 1968.

Jonson, Ben. *Every Man Out of His Humour*. In *Complete Plays*, vol. 1, edited by Felix Schelling. London: Everyman's Library, n.d.

Kaminsky, Stuart M. *American Film Genres*. New York: Dell, 1977.

Kerr, Walter. *Tragedy and Comedy*. New York: Simon & Schuster, 1968.

Knight, G. Wilson. *The Golden Labyrinth*. New York: Norton, 1962.

Kobal, John. *Gotta Sing, Gotta Dance*. London: Hamlyn, 1970.

Lahue, Kalton. *World of Laughter*. Norman: University of Oklahoma Press, 1966.

Lahue, Kalton, and Gill, Sam. *Clown Princes and Court Jesters*. New York: A. S. Barnes, 1970.

Langer, Suzanne. *Feeling and Form*. New York: Scribners, 1953.

Lasch, Christopher. *The Culture of Narcissism*. New York: Warner, 1979.

McLuhan, Marshall. *Understanding Media: The Extensions of Man*. 2nd ed. New York: Signet, 1964.

McNees, Pat, (ed.) *Familiar Faces*. New York: Fawcett, 1979.

McVay, Douglas. *The Musical Film*. London: Zwemmer, 1967.

Maltin, Leonard. *The Great Movie Shorts*. New York: Crown, 1972.

———. *TV Movies, 1979-80*. New York: Signet, 1978.

Mander, Jerry. *Four Arguments for the Elimination of Television*. New York: Morrow, 1979.

Marill, Alvin J. *Movies Made for Television*. New York: DaCapo, 1981.

Meredith, George. "An Essay on Comedy." In *Comedy*, edited by Wylie Sypher. Garden City, N.J.: Doubleday, Anchor, 1956.

Mitz, Rick. *The Great TV Sitcom Book*. New York: Marek, 1980.

"Network Series Rating Averages." *Variety*, January 3, 1979.

"Network Series Rating Averages." *Variety*, January 9, 1980.

"Network Series Rating Averages." *Variety*, January 13, 1982.

Oreglia, Giacomo. *The Commedia dell'Arte*. Translated by Lovett Edwards. New York: Hill & Wang, 1968.

Ott, Frederick. *The Films of Carole Lombard*. New York: Citadel, 1972.

Parker, Richard. *The Myth of the Middle Class*. New York: Liveright, 1972.

Schickel, Richard. *Harold Lloyd: The Shape of Laughter*. Boston: New York Graphic Society, 1974.

Segal, Erich. *Roman Laughter*. Cambridge: Harvard University Press, 1970.

Sennett, Ted. *Lunatics and Lovers*. New Rochelle, N.Y.: Arlington House, 1973.

Stanislavski, Constantin. *An Actor Prepares*. Translated by Elizabeth Hapgood Reynolds. New York: Theatre Arts, 1977.

Stein, Joseph. *Fiddler on the Roof*. New York: Pocket Books, 1971.

Steinberg, Cobbett. *Reel Facts*. New York: Vintage, 1978.

TV Season, 77-78. Phoenix, Ariz.: Oryx Press, 1979.

Taylor, John Russell, and Jackson, Arthur. *The Hollywood Musical*. New York: McGraw-Hill, 1971.

Thomas, Tony. *The Films of Gene Kelly*. Secaucus, N.J.: Citadel, 1974.

Tuska, Jon. *The Films of Mae West*. Secaucus, N.J.: Citadel, 1973.

United States Bureau of the Census. *Statistical Abstract of the United States: 1978*. Washington, D.C., 1978.

Weinberg, Herman G. *The Lubitsch Touch*. New York: Dutton, 1968.

Wilder, Thornton. *Our Town*. In *Three Plays by Thornton Wilder*. New York: Bantam, 1972.

Wilson, Garff B. *Three Hundred Years of American Drama and Theatre*. Englewood Cliffs, N.J.: Prentice-Hall, 1973.

Zimmerman, Paul D., and Goldblatt, Burt. *The Marx Brothers at the Movies*. New York: Berkley, 1975.

Index

Abbott, Bud. *See* Abbott and
Costello
Abbott and Costello, 10, 42, 45,
112, 116, 122, 142
Abbott and Costello Go to Mars, 116
*Abbott and Costello Meet Captain
Kidd*, 116
*Abbott and Costello Meet
Frankenstein*, 116
*Abbott and Costello Meet the
Invisible Man*, 116
*Abbott and Costello Meet the
Mummy*, 116
Actor: audience perception of,
137–56; in comedy, 14, 52,
139–46, 151-52; in sit-com, 14,
96, 104, 146–53, 155–56. *See
also* Comedian
Adams, Don, 149
Adam's Rib, 136
Adventures of Augie March, The,
25, 37, 111
*Adventures of Ozzie and Harriet,
The. See Ozzie and Harriet*
Advertisers, TV, 126, 129–30, 132,
166. *See also* Commercials

Aesop, 25
After-piece, 24, 63
Agee, James, 170
Aggression in comedy, 37, 51, 55,
98
Albee, Edward, 14, 49
Albert, Eddie, 70
Alchemist, The, 22, 31, 45, 49, 102
Alda, Alan, 96
Alice: format, 60, 65, 75, 79, 97,
152–53; popularity, 81, 178;
woman's role in, 74, 92, 97
All for Love, 49
All in the Family: children's role in,
70, 72, 74, 88; defensive attitude
of, 83, 104; format, 61, 68, 70,
93, 162; hero, 88, 92, 94;
influence, 10, 60, 99, 101, 156,
166, 175; popularity, 136–37, 178
Allen, Fred, 11, 112
Allen, Gracie. *See* Burns and Allen
Allen, Steve, 159
Allen, Woody, 10, 35, 40, 164
All's Well That Ends Well, 20, 34,
38
Ameche, Don, 46, 121

189

Aristophanes; Old Comedy
(Greek); operetta, 22, 55, 120;
opposition to, 28–30, 132,
169–71; Plautine. *See* Plautus;
radio. *See* Radio; reality in,
49–50, 94–95; Restoration. *See*
Restoration; situation. *See*
Situation comedy; sketch. See
Revue; Sketch; society and, 13,
14, 27, 30–34, 50, 98, 129,
173–74; TV movie, 163–64;
variety show. *See* Variety shows;
vaudeville. *See* Vaudeville. *See
also names of individual authors,
movies, plays, and TV series*
Comedy of Errors, The, 28
Comic, The, 148
Comic relief, 113
Comics. *See* Comedian
Comic strip, 112
Comin' Round the Mountain, 116
Commedia dell'arte: actors in, 140;
authority figures in, 27, 31,
91–92; character types, 41, 44,
45, 47; social attitudes, 173
Commercials, 93, 129–30, 138,
161. *See also* Advertisers, TV
Congreve, William, 21, 29, 35, 44,
129
Conway, Tim, 148, 149
Contrast, The, 22, 39, 86
Coogan, Jackie, 115, 119
Cooper, Gary, 40, 143
Corneille, Pierre, 128
Cosby, Bill, 91
Costello, Lou. *See* Abbott and
Costello
Country Wife, The, 29, 44, 49
Courtship of Eddie's Father, The,
74
Coward, Noel, 21, 58, 135
Crane, Bob, 149, 150
Critics: actor and, 139, 144;
audience and, 133, 134–35,
177–78; comedy and, 118, 129,
132–35, 144
Crimson Pirate, The, 116

Crosby, Bing, 45, 47
Cyrano de Bergerac, 71, 141

Daddy Long Legs, 46
Dallas, 147, 167
Danny Thomas Show, The, 72, 73,
74, 87, 104, 179
Day, Dennis, 158
Day, Doris, 70–71
Deacon, Richard, 104
Dead End Kids, 127, 154
Dean Martin Show, The, 159
Death in the Family, A, 170
December Bride, 179
Dekker, Thomas, 29, 49
Demarest, William, 70
DeMille, Cecil B., 170
Demographics, 87, 135–37. *See also*
Ratings, television
Dennis the Menace, 179
Denver, Bob, 146, 150
Depression, the, 114, 122–23, 171,
174
Design for Living, 58, 121
Destry Rides Again, 116, 143
Deus ex machina, 19, 21, 44, 50
De Vries, Peter, 26
Dickens, Charles, 25, 110, 111
Dick Van Dyke Show, The, 93, 146,
147, 150, 178
Diderot, Denis, 138
Diff'rent Strokes, 88
Disguise in comedy, 22, 38
Disney, Walt, 10, 128, 147, 148
Divorce, American Style, 147
Doctor: in sit-com, 76, 91, 96, 97,
172; in traditional comedy, 31,
91, 172
Doctor Faustus, 49
Doll's House, A, 129
Don Juan, 25
Don Quixote, 18, 25, 48
Donna Reed Show, The, 72, 87, 91,
93, 179
Doris Day Show, The, 70–71, 179
Dottore, il, 11, 27, 92
Double Dealer, The, 29

of, 17–25; humor in. *See* Humor;
influence, 14, 18–19, 24, 56;
mythical importance, 37, 49,
53–56, 72, 98; sit-com rejection
of, 63–71, 97–98, 105, 150; use
in movies. *See* Movie, comedy
characteristics
Policeman in comedy, 90, 107, 125,
165, 172–73
Poem, comic, 25
Powell, Dick, 40
Powell, William, 116
Pretension in comedy, 30–32, 78,
123–25
Private Benjamin (movie), 112
Private Benjamin (TV), 91
Private Lives, 21, 135, 180
Private Secretary, 154, 180
Pseudolus, 71
Public Eye, The, 24
Pulchinella, 92
Purviance, Edna, 115, 119
Pygmalion, 22, 35

Quincy, 150
Quiz shows, 10, 147

Rabelais, 25
Radio, 95, 111; comedy, 11, 112,
157; series types, 11
Randall, Tony, 150
Ratings, television, 9–11, 79, 87;
demographics, 87, 135–37; of
movies, 9, 10–11, 136; of
sit-coms, 9–11, 64, 70–71, 81,
87, 101, 104, 131, 147, 175;
success and, 64, 177–78. *See also
names of individual series*
Rattigan, Terence, 24
Raye, Martha, 143
Real McCoys, The, 180
Red Skelton Show, The, 159
Reed, Donna, 147. *See also Donna
Reed Show, The*
Reeves, George, 139
Relapse, The, 29
Remember the Night, 121

Renaissance, 13, 17, 173
Repetition as humorous device, 98
Repertory system, 52, 126, 140
Restoration, 13, 31, 44, 94; comedy,
19, 29, 38, 120, 170; tragedy,
49. *See also names of individual
authors and plays*
Reruns, 67, 68, 95, 146, 150. *See
also* Syndication, television
series
Return of the Native, The, 26
Revenge, 102
Revue, 24, 156, 160
Reynolds, Burt, 47
Rhoda, 63–64, 67, 146, 162, 178,
180
Rich Man, Poor Man, 63
Ride 'Em Cowboy, 116
Rififi, 116
Ring 'Round the Moon, 45
Rip Van Winkle, 40, 41, 141
Rivals, The, 34, 100, 124
Road movies, 45, 47
Robber Bridegroom, The, 41
Rockford Files, The, 86,
165
Rogers, Ginger, 10, 46, 53, 143,
157
Rogers, Wayne, 146
Rogers, Will, 112
Roi s'amuse, Le, 48
Roman comedy. *See* Plautus;
Terence
Romance: in comedy, 17–25, 133;
in novel, 25–26, 37. *See also*
Plot, basic comedy; Lover
Romance, the, 25, 48, 55
Romantic novel, 25–26, 37, 48, 130
Romeo and Juliet, 139
Room for One More, 143
Room 222, 91
Rooney, Mickey, 121, 153–54
Ropers, The, 178
Rostand, Edmund, 141
Route 66, 153
Rowley, William. *See* Middleton
and Rowley